RETHINKING WIDENIN
PARTICIPATION IN
HIGHER EDUCATION

Extending the chance for people from diverse backgrounds to participate in Higher Education (HE) is a priority in the UK and many countries internationally. Previous work on widening participation in HE has focused on why people choose to go to university but this vital new research has focused on looking at why people choose not to go. Moreover, much of the extant literature concentrates on the participation decisions of teenagers and young adults whereas this book foregrounds adult decision-making across the life course. The book is also distinctive because it focuses on interview data generated from across the membership of inter-generational networks rather than on individuals in isolation, in order to explore how decision-making about educational participation is a socially embedded, rather than an individualized, process. It draws on a recent UK-based empirical study to argue that this network approach to exploring educational decision making is very productive and helps create a comprehensive understanding of the historically dependent, personal and collective aspects of participation decisions.

This book examines, therefore, the ways in which (non-) decision-making about HE is embedded within a range of social networks consisting of family, partners and friends, and to what extent future participation in HE is conceived as within the bounds of possibility. It:

- provides a conceptual framework for understanding the value of network-based decision-making about participation in HE, in the light of the changing historical and policy contexts in which it is always located;
- highlights the importance of researching the socially embedded narratives of 'ordinary people' in order to critique the deficit discourse which dominates debates about widening participation in HE;
- discusses the policy and practice implications of the network-based approach for widening participation and educational institutions.

Alison Fuller is Professor of Education and Work in the School of Education, University of Southampton, UK

Sue Heath is Professor of Sociology in the School of Social Sciences, University of Manchester, UK

Brenda Johnston is Senior R   tion, University of Southampton, UK

RETHINKING WIDENING PARTICIPATION IN HIGHER EDUCATION

The role of social networks

Edited by Alison Fuller, Sue Heath and Brenda Johnston

Routledge
Taylor & Francis Group

LONDON AND NEW YORK

First edition published 2011
by Routledge
2 Park Square, Milton Park, Abingdon, Oxon, OX14 4RN

Simultaneously published in the USA and Canada
by Routledge
711 Third Avenue, New York, NY 10017

Routledge is an imprint of the Taylor & Francis Group, an informa business

British Library Cataloguing in Publication Data
A catalogue record for this book is available from the British Library

Library of Congress Cataloging-in-Publication Data
A catalog record has been requested for this book

ISBN13: 978–0–415–57563–8 (hbk)
ISBN13: 978–0–415–57564–5 (pbk)
ISBN13: 978–0–203–81705–6 (ebk)

Typeset in Bembo
by Keystroke, Station Road, Codsall, Wolverhampton

Printed and bound in Great Britain by
CPI Antony Rowe, Chippenham, Wiltshire

CONTENTS

LIST OF TABLES AND FIGURES

ACKNOWLEDGEMENTS

The research reported and discussed in this book would not have been possible without the help and assistance of many people. First and most importantly, we are extremely grateful to our network interviewees for agreeing to participate. They were very generous with their time and in the open way in which they engaged in the interviews. We are very appreciative of the network members' willingness to provide us with detailed narratives about their education and employment trajectories and social relationships. Interviewing members of the same social network was a real privilege and a fantastic learning opportunity for us. We would also like to thank the key informants from a wide range of stakeholder organizations. Their insights, knowledge and experience have played an important role in contextualizing our findings. We hope that in this book and the other papers that have emerged from this research that we have done justice to all research participants' accounts.

Second, we very much appreciate the administrative support we have received. Marie Kenny, our administrator during the research process, held the research process together with exemplary organizational skills and good humour. Alison Williamson has provided invaluable expert assistance in the production of the manuscript and has worked tirelessly to help bring it to completion. Third, we were very fortunate to have the assistance of a team of dedicated researchers involved at various stages of the project, including Laura Staetsky and Patricia Rice, who undertook the quantitative analysis that contextualized the interview study; Karen Paton, the project's research officer; and John Taylor, who was involved from the outset and completed some of the fieldwork. Ros Foskett, Martin Dyke, Felix Maringe and Nick Foskett were involved in all stages of the research and have contributed chapters to the book. Fourth, we benefited enormously from the help and support of an advisory group with whom we met at regular intervals throughout the two years of the research and who contributed much to the development of the ideas discussed in this book. Fifth, we appreciated the opportunity to engage in discussions with colleagues involved in the six other projects focusing on widening participation in higher education that were funded under the Economic and Social Research Council's (ESRC) Teaching and Learning Research Programme (TLRP). We are particularly grateful to Professor Miriam David, the TLRP Director responsible for this strand of work, for organizing meetings and events at which we could present our work and receive formative and constructive feedback from fellow TLRP researchers. Finally, we owe a big debt of gratitude to the ESRC for funding the project (RES–139-25-0232) and to Andrew Pollard, TLRP Director, for being on hand to offer support whenever it was needed.

Alison Fuller, Sue Heath and Brenda Johnston

1

INTRODUCTION

Sue Heath, Alison Fuller and Brenda Johnston

> We must focus not only on how to survive the recession, but on how we
> will thrive in the years ahead. The challenge for the UK employment and
> skills system is formidable. We need to build a system to match the high-skill,
> people-driven economy of the future – a system that responds well to business
> need while opening opportunity for all people. We must increase the ambition
> and aspiration of individuals to gain new skills – *not just once, but throughout
> their working lives.*
>
> *(UK Commission for Employment and Skills 2009: 6 – emphasis added)*

The first decade of the twenty-first century has been characterized by widespread
efforts both to increase and widen participation in UK higher education. Under-
30-year-olds have been the primary target of this activity; yet more recent
government discussions have focused attention on the broader adult population.
The focus here is less on getting under-21-year-olds into university and more on
encouraging those from across the entire working age population to (re)consider the
pursuit of higher level studies in a variety of contexts, even if their full-time
education has been completed many years previously. More recent initiatives to
encourage participation in higher education (HE) beyond 'the usual suspects' have,
of course, occurred in the wake of the 2008 recession, with rising unemployment
acting as a powerful impetus for many adults to consider a return to some form of
study.

This book considers the likely success of this new widening participation agenda
through the lens of recent research which has explored the experiences of adults
who were qualified to enter HE, but who had not done so – or at least had not *yet*
done so – as one of our interests was in exploring whether or not future participation
was regarded as a possibility. Much of the policy rhetoric surrounding widening
participation in HE, and the UK skills agenda more generally, often seems to assume

that the pursuit of ever higher levels of qualification is self-evidently 'a good thing'. Policy makers are consequently left puzzling over the barriers to participation that they assume must exist in order to explain *non*-participation. Yet this is to ignore the complexities of many people's lives and the extent to which decisions concerning potential participation are heavily influenced by a range of factors, including past experiences of formal education, expectations and aspirations linked to an individual's upbringing, and the current educational experiences and aspirations of friends and family members. It is our contention throughout this book that it is, in fact, impossible fully to understand educational decision-making without also seeking to understand the extent to which decision-making is a socially embedded process, rather than an individualized one as well as an historically embedded process.

This introductory chapter starts by providing an overview of the broader policy context within which our own work is situated, before introducing the reader to the specific aims and objectives of our research as well as to some of our theoretical influences. The chapter finishes by providing an overview of the structure of the book.

Widening participation in context

Widening participation in HE has been particularly prominent on the political agenda in recent years, yet a desire to expand access to HE is by no means unique to these years. In the immediate post-war period, HE was very much the preserve of an educational elite, with rates of participation standing at around only 5 per cent of each cohort of school-leaving age. The recommendations of the Robbins Report of 1963 (published under a Conservative government, but subsequently implemented by the incoming Labour government of Harold Wilson) represented an important moment of change, leading to the creation of a new cluster of academically focused universities on the one hand and the rise of vocationally orientated polytechnics on the other (David 2010). By the end of the 1960s, age participation rates amongst those of school-leaving age had, as a consequence, risen to around 10 per cent of each cohort, albeit with large differences in participation rates according to students' social class background (Kelly and Cook 2007). The creation in 1969 of the Open University also provided access into HE for a new group of undergraduate learners, including those without conventional qualifications and academic backgrounds, mature students and those in full-time employment.

The next significant push towards increased participation occurred during the late 1980s, also under a Conservative administration, and this time as a consequence of recommendations contained in the 1987 White Paper *Higher Education: Meeting the Challenge* (DES 1987). This paper called on 'all those with relevant responsibilities to consider carefully the steps to secure increased participation by both young and older people, and to act accordingly' (DES 1987). This led to recognition of a 'third route' into HE via Access courses, which were accorded a key role in securing entry for 'mainly mature' (and, as it transpired, mainly female) entrants, those 'who hold neither traditional sixth form nor vocational qualifications' (DES 1987). The 1987

White Paper was, then, particularly significant in relation to encouraging – and indeed directly facilitating – increased participation amongst mature entrants, largely triggered by the projected downturn in the number of school leavers in the late 1980s and the subsequent need for universities to reach out to new constituencies.

The eagerly anticipated 1997 Dearing Report of the National Committee of Inquiry into Higher Education (NCIHE 1997) provided the backdrop for an ongoing preoccupation with widening participation under successive New Labour governments. Parry notes that the Dearing Report was underpinned by a guiding assumption that 'growth opened higher education to a wider range of students' (Parry 2010: 32), and policies for increased and widened participation were subsequently placed 'at the heart of [New Labour's] policies for creating a learning society' (Parry 2010: 36). Subsequent policies placed a particular emphasis on increasing participation amongst specific disadvantaged and under-represented groups: young people from lower socio-economic backgrounds, those from disadvantaged localities and people with disabilities. The Higher Education Funding Council for England (HEFCE) introduced additional monies for funding places for students from disadvantaged localities via its 'postcode premium', alongside enhanced funding for disabled students. In addition, a wide variety of activities directed at encouraging 'non-traditional' entrants were introduced, the scope of the target group interpreted largely in terms of social class background and principally aimed at 'standard age' entrants. Many of these activities were eventually brought together in 2004 under two complementary initiatives: the AimHigher initiative, *to* which specifically sought to widen access to and participation in HE through raising *increase* aspirations and attainment, and the Lifelong Learning Networks, whose primary *HE* focus was on improving progression opportunities amongst individuals who have pursued vocational pathways. Nonetheless, Chitty (2009: 204) notes that the earlier effect of the introduction of tuition fees, ushered in under the 1998 Teaching and Higher Education Act, was an immediate reduction in applications from under-represented groups, including mature students and those from working-class backgrounds.

Alongside this emphasis on increasing the numbers of (mostly younger) entrants to degree level study, Dearing also emphasized the provision of *sub*-Bachelor degree level education in the form of the new Foundation Degree as a means of engaging, in particular, those with 'non-standard entry qualifications and more diverse aspirations' (NCIHE 1997: 100). Dearing envisaged that a large part of the anticipated expansion in HE would come via widespread take-up of Foundation Degrees, many of which would be provided by the existing network of further education colleges. Dearing noted that such provision could be 'especially important for students regarded as 'non-traditional' to higher education institutions, many of whom need to be able to study near their homes' (NCIHE 1997: 259). Commenting on these specific proposals, Parry notes that:

> Here was a set of proposals intended to respond to future demand from wider parts of society and the economy for local, accessible, flexible, diverse and

distributed forms of higher level education. At the same time, they were counter to, and a rejection of, many of the features that characterized the English transition to mass higher education.

(Parry 2010: 34)

Indeed, much of the expansion that has followed in the wake of Dearing has focused largely on 'standard age' entrants rather than on 'mature' entrants (technically defined as those aged 21 and above), and has occurred within an expanding mainstream university sector rather than outside of it. Perhaps this is unsurprising, given Tony Blair's pledge in his speech to the 1999 Labour Party Conference to 'set a target of 50 per cent of young adults going into higher education in the next century' (BBC 1999). This was subsequently formalized as a target of 50 per cent participation amongst 18- to 30-year-olds by 2010, which did not rule out a focus on 'older' young people. Many doubted that this target was attainable, and indeed the target failed to be met by 2010. Nonetheless, it set an agenda that was taken up further in the 2003 White Paper *The Future of Higher Education* (DfES 2003) and that explored how best to ensure the expansion of places for young people, including through the introduction of capped student fees and the creation of the Office of Fair Access.

It is only in the last few years that the agenda has once again begun to shift towards potential participation amongst older learners, largely as a result of the recommendations of the Leitch Review of Skills published in December 2006. Leitch focused on the expansion of skills and training which would be required in part as a consequence of the projected 15 per cent decline in the number of 18-year-olds between 2010 and 2020 and the consequent need for improved skills across the *whole* working age population. The Review started from a premise that has been claimed repeatedly in political speeches on education and skills throughout the post-war era: that the key to economic growth and global competitiveness lies with the exploitation of individual talent through the development of skills:

> In the 21st century, our natural resource is our people – and their potential is both untapped and vast. Skills will unlock that potential. The prize for our country will be enormous – higher productivity, the creation of wealth and social justice . . .

(HM Treasury 2006: 1)

The Review noted the extent to which the UK lagged behind 'our principal comparators' in relation to the skill levels of the working age population. Critically, it noted that continuing improvements in compulsory schooling would not be sufficient to militate against this weakness, as 'today, over 70 per cent of our 2020 workforce have already completed their compulsory education' (HM Treasury 2006: 1). The report went on to provide a detailed analysis of the distribution of skills amongst the working age population and to outline how this might be improved through meeting a series of ambitious targets by 2020, including the objective of 'exceeding 40 per cent of adults qualified to Level 4[1] and above, up from 29 per cent in 2005, with a commitment to continue progression' (HM Treasury 2006: 3). In order to achieve this growth, Leitch called for a shift away from 'more of the same' (that is, traditional three-year degrees) towards provision based on 'new types of programme offering specific, job-related skills such as Foundation Degrees' (HM Treasury 2006: 67). The challenging agenda set out by Leitch in 2006 has subsequently been monitored and supported by the UK Commission on Employment and Skills (UKCES), a body created following the publication of the Leitch Review. In its most recent report – published in July 2010, following the formation of the Conservative–Liberal Democrat coalition government in May 2010 – the Commission reiterated its ambition that the UK become one of the top eight countries in the world for the skills level of its workforce, yet reported that the 2010 OECD league tables on high level, intermediate and low level skills placed the UK twelfth, twenty-first and nineteenth, respectively. In comparison to the 2009 league tables, these figures represent an unchanged position for the UK in relation to the first of these, and an actual decline in relation to the second and third indicators (UKCES 2010: 41).

At the time of writing, there is evidence that the new coalition government will continue to prioritize adult participation at higher levels and to imply that the UK's failure to boost the skills levels of the adult population is a problem for wider society. The consultation document *Skills for Sustainable Growth* (BIS 2010), also published in July, has reiterated the importance of 'upskilling' for the health of the UK economy, and the need to provide opportunities for progression at all levels, including opportunities for progression from Level 3[2] Apprenticeships to 'higher-level skills'. Importantly, both David Willetts, Minister of State for Universities and Science, and Vince Cable, Secretary of State for Business, Innovation and Skills, have signalled their support for lifelong learning and for vocational pathways into HE. Speaking in July 2010, Vince Cable also noted the 'heavy bias' towards 'traditional, full-time, three year degrees, for 18-year-olds, rather than part-time or adult or FE [further education] learning.' In his view, it was important for the state to correct that bias:

> We need to recognise – even celebrate – the fact that a growing number of our students are going to be adults. Everything we can do to put higher education within the reach of an even wider pool of potential students is good for the economy and good for social mobility.
>
> *(Cable 2010)*

Cable's comments no doubt reflect in part the practical implications of the projected decline in successive cohorts of 18-year-olds over the coming decade, with the consequence that HE institutions will need to reach out to non-traditional constituencies if they are to maintain, let alone expand, current student numbers. However, his comments also reflect evidence from the Universities and Colleges Admission Service (UCAS) of a substantial increase in the number of adults applying for university places in 2010 in comparison with 2009 (UCAS 2010). UCAS reported a 23 per cent increase in the number of applicants aged 25 to 39 over this period, and a similar increase in the number of applicants aged 40 and over, presumably a pragmatic response by individuals to concerns regarding actual or potential job losses rather than as a deliberate contribution to boosting the UK's position in the OECD league tables. Applications were actually up across *all* age groups, albeit most markedly amongst older applicants. Despite his calls for a more diversified student body, Vince Cable has simultaneously signalled the possibility of an overall reduction in the number of places in coming years, rather than an ongoing expansion. In the same speech, Cable questioned the wisdom and value of increased levels of participation, arguing that 'We should not be setting targets, or ceilings for that matter'. Older applicants may well find themselves, then, in increased competition with 'standard age' applicants, despite the projected demographic decline in the number of 18-year-olds in the next few years. This is a cohort which has already attracted the epithet of 'the lost generation' given the restricted employment opportunities available to young people during the current recession (The Prince's Trust 2010). At the time of writing, all the signs point to a sustained period of austerity for the HE sector in the UK, and this is unlikely to result in an expansion of 'home' student numbers for the foreseeable future.

Both the earlier Leitch Report and the 2010 '*Skills for Sustainable Growth*' consultation document uncritically flag up the importance of embedding 'a culture of learning' within wider society, especially (but by no means exclusively) amongst more disadvantaged communities:

> (In)equalities in aspiration by adults drive inequalities in attainment for their children at school. This creates a cycle of disadvantage that locks generations of the same family into persistent poverty. It perpetuates the number of young people unable to read, write and add up and who drop out of school at 16, spending teenage years not in education, employment or training (NEET). This cycle needs to be broken by raising the aspirations of parents and children and standards in all schools.
>
> *(HM Treasury 2006: 22)*

'*Skills for Sustainable Growth*' makes a similar point when it notes that adult learners may, in turn, inspire younger generations to acquire higher level skills. The research findings discussed in this book question the assumptions often made in such statements about the 'problem' of 'low aspirations' and 'non-participation' in learning amongst certain sections of society, and also highlight why these concerns are regarded as more problematic at certain points in time than at others. We choose to highlight this aspect of the policy discourse, though, because it hints at the importance of *networks* in educational decision-making. This chimes with the approach we have adopted in the book, namely an emphasis on how network-based attitudes and dispositions towards learning and educational achievement can have far-reaching effects across generations. It is to these considerations, and our own research, that we now turn.

The need to rethink widening participation in HE

The previous section has highlighted the broader policy context of our research: a context in which policy rhetoric surrounding widening participation has increasingly included references to older learners. In practice, however, most initiatives to actively encourage take-up of HE in recent years – and certainly prior to our own research – have been targeted at younger, standard age entrants. This focus on younger entrants is also reflected in the bulk of research conducted in the area of widening participation that has tended to focus on educational decision-making at 16 and 18. Indeed, the six other projects which were funded, alongside ours, by the Economic and Social Research Council's (ESRC) Teaching and Learning Research Programme's (TLRP) initiative on widening participation in HE were mostly focused on under-21-year-olds (see David 2010). In contrast, we were primarily concerned with exploring the experiences of older learners, who would have experienced their compulsory schooling under very different policy regimes to those experienced by contemporary school leavers, yet now find themselves targeted as potential participants in HE alongside younger cohorts.

Much of the existing literature has also focused on the factors that make participation in HE more or less likely (Ertl *et al.* 2010; Gorard *et al.* 2006; Vignoles and Crawford 2010). Related to this, a strong theme in such research has been the identification of *barriers* to participation, yet much of the literature on this theme has tended to explore these issues not through analyzing the perspectives of those who have never progressed into HE, but through focusing on the perspectives of individuals who have at least some experience of higher education. Whilst this makes sense in terms of investigating the experiences of current or past students, and how certain individuals may have overcome potential barriers, a focus on those who succeed in getting into HE tells us very little, if anything, about the experiences of genuine non-participants. These include not only those who have been deterred from participation for various reasons, but those who have had no desire to participate in HE in the first place. We agree with the point made by Gorard *et al.* (2006) in their review of widening participation literature that this use of participants, in effect as proxies for non-participants, is a major flaw in much contemporary widening participation research. Gorard *et al.* refer to this as the problem of 'missing comparators', possibly arising as a consequence of 'the difficulty of identifying and then including students who choose not to participate in post-compulsory education' (p. 146).

Accessing 'non-participants' is indeed a very real difficulty, but the difficulties of specifically researching the experiences of this group are made all the more challenging by virtue of the 'slipperiness' of the concepts of HE participation and non-participation. Consider, for example, the category of 'HE participant'. At a minimum, this category should presumably include current students and graduates, but should it also include students who subsequently withdraw from their studies? Harrison (2006), for example, has suggested that certain students who drop out of their studies share many of the characteristics of members of groups who are under-represented in HE: in other words, they may be more like non-participants than participants, if we define participants as those who complete their studies. The category of 'HE non-participant' is even more complex, given that a non-participant almost always has the *potential* to become a participant at some future point. Realistically, then, we can only really talk in terms of those who have *not yet* participated, some of whom may well go on to become participants at a later point, but many of whom will not.

For the purposes of our own research, then, we eventually decided to focus our sampling strategy on identifying individuals who were qualified to enter HE but who had not (yet) done so. Our specific focus was on individuals whose current highest qualification was at Level 3 or equivalent. This group includes individuals who will probably never participate in HE and individuals who might well do so in the future; these two sub-groups may well have very different characteristics. This ambiguity of status, however, became integral to our research design as we were interested in the factors which might trigger a shift from non-participation to participation, as well as in the factors which might make future participation extremely unlikely. Something of this ambiguity is captured in the term we eventually came to use to define our sample: 'potentially recruitable'. Our move away from the use of the term 'non-participant' as our research unfolded also reflects our growing unease with the 'ideological baggage' suggested by this term; we were increasingly uncomfortable with the idea of defining people in terms of what they had *not* done, as this seemed to us to be steeped in a deficit model approach to understanding educational decision-making, rather than acknowledging the validity of alternative pathways.

Our research focus was thus distinctive in focusing on older learners in contrast to the more common focus in existing literature on under-21-year-olds, and in seeking to locate the 'missing comparators' whose absence from the widening participation research literature has been lamented by Gorard *et al.* (2006: 146). Our most distinctive contribution to the widening participation literature lies, however, in our focus on HE decision-making as an embedded, rather than an individualized, practice: a practice which can only fully be understood by paying attention to the accounts of broader network members alongside the accounts of the individuals who form the primary focus of our research. We have sought to explore how and in what ways the varying forms of social, cultural and economic capital which are present within different social networks might provide a critical context within which individuals' thinking about HE might be embedded and co-constructed. In one sense, such a starting point was by no means novel, as educational decision-making is often theorized as being inextricably linked to behaviours, attitudes and dispositions which hold sway within individuals' social networks. Much recent research within the sociology of education (e.g. Ball *et al.* 2000; Brooks 2005; Davey 2009; and Reay *et al.* 2005) has been informed by the work of theorists such as Bourdieu, Coleman and Putnam who are renowned for their focus on the transmission of advantage and disadvantage between and within specific networks, including in and through the decisions and actions of network members. However, examples of empirical research which draw on first-hand accounts of wider network members in exploring these themes are few and far between. We wished to address this gap and accordingly developed a research design, informed by qualitative social network analysis (Heath *et al.* 2009; Edwards 2010), that allowed us to situate individuals' decision-making within a nexus of first-hand accounts from those closest to them. This not only highlighted the complexity of educational decision-making, but also the tensions, contradictions and moments of solidarity which occur within networks.

Our two-year project, 'Non-participation in Higher Education: Decision-making as an embedded social practice', began in Spring 2006. The study involved a number of complementary data collection strategies, which are outlined in Chapter 2, but in pursuing network influence we conducted interviews with 107 individuals across 16 case study networks. The type of networks which formed the focus of our research are defined by social network analysts as egocentric or ego networks, consisting of (i) a starting point individual, variously referred to in the literature as an *ego,* a *focal individual* or an *entry point*, this last being the term we mainly use in this book, and (ii) the individuals who are directly linked to the ego, often referred to as *alters* (Trotter 1999), but referred to by us simply as 'network members'. We initially located 16 entry point individuals who were potentially recruitable to HE and conducted preliminary interviews in which we explored their educational and employment trajectories and asked them to tell us about their broader social networks. These 16 individuals then nominated members of their network whom they felt would be prepared to take part in the research, and we subsequently conducted one-off qualitative interviews with an additional 91 network members, before returning to our initial sample for a second interview. The interviews focused primarily on the education and employment experiences of network members alongside an exploration of the implicit and explicit influences of other network members on their decision-making in these spheres, as well as their own influence on others.

The initial 16 interviewees ranged in age from 21 to 63, with a mean age of 46, whilst the broader network sample ranged in age from 13 years to 96 years (both these two individuals coming from one network in which we interviewed four generations of the same family). The initial 16 were all resident in Hampshire and the Isle of Wight, with network members living mostly, but not exclusively, in southern England. The relationships represented within the networks included partners, siblings, parents, grandparents, sons and daughters, aunts and uncles, nephews and nieces, in-laws, best friends, childhood friends, new friends and work-mates. The richness and complexity of our data leads us strongly to concur with Trotter's view that the value of a network approach lies in its ability to allow researchers

> to move beyond the level of the individual and the analysis of individual behaviour into the social context where most people spend the vast majority of their lives, living and interacting with the small groups that make up the world around them.
>
> *(Trotter 1999: 7)*

Such an approach requires a careful engagement with theories and concepts related to researching social change across and within generations, across the life course, and across and within networks. Specifically, the concepts of life course, generation, network ties and social capital have proved to be invaluable to us in conducting our fieldwork and our subsequent analysis. The following section provides a brief introduction to these concepts, with more detailed expositions located within subsequent chapters.

Life course, generation and network-based social capital

The term 'life course' is used to refer to 'a sequence of socially defined events and roles enacted by an individual over time' (Giele and Elder 1998: 22). Unlike the term 'life cycle', it does not assume that these events and roles are biologically determined or that they will necessarily proceed in a pre-defined sequence. Nonetheless there is a powerful normative element to *popular* understandings of the life course, inasmuch as individuals themselves often judge certain events in their lives to have occurred at the right or the wrong time. Merton's concept of 'socially expected durations' (SEDs) captures this well:

> [SEDS] constitute a class of social expectations that significantly affect the current behavior of groups and individuals . . . SEDs affect *anticipatory social behavior:* ongoing behavior that is significantly shaped by socially prescribed and otherwise patterned anticipations.
>
> *(Merton 1984: 266; emphasis in original)*

This suggests that perceptions of the appropriate timings for certain transitions – such as the appropriate age to transfer to HE – have their roots in broader societal expectations as well as in expectations rooted within an individual's immediate social network. As such, members of a network may share very clear ideas about 'the right time' within the life course to pursue certain educational goals, most probably associating participation in HE with the youth stage of the life course, such that participation in HE as an adult learner may be perceived as happening 'too late'.

Perceptions of 'the right and wrong time' will also be strongly linked to *generational* positioning. Miller (2000) distinguishes between family generations, on the one hand, and cohort generations on the other. The former refers to generations in terms of family positioning, that is, grandparent/parent/child, whilst the latter refers to generations in terms of membership of a particular cohort, for example the generation born during the 1930s which experienced the tripartite system of selective secondary education, or those born in the 1960s who mainly experienced comprehensive schooling. By virtue of their common generational positioning, individuals are arguably 'united by similar life experiences and a temporarily coherent cultural background' (Antikainen *et al.* 1996: 34). This enables researchers to look at a particular time period and set of events and see how they have shaped the life chances, understandings and motivations of individuals living through those events.

We have found the work of Giele and Elder (1998) to be particularly useful in considering the link between life course and generation. Their life course approach is based on a consideration of the interaction between four key elements that, in combination, foreground the connections across the life course between and within generations. These elements are: the location of individuals in time and space, which emphasizes the importance of generational positioning; the linking of lives, which emphasizes the socially embedded nature of social and cultural expectations within networks; human agency, which emphasizes active decision-making, despite the influence of network norms; and the timing of lives, which Giele and Elder propose as the means by which the three other elements – historical, social and individual activities – are integrated. Their approach has been useful for considering processes of both continuity and change across networks: it has helped us to understand present day decisions in the broader context of family/network histories, the transmission of network-wide dispositions alongside acts of individual agency, and furthermore has helped us to understand broader reactions to those individual acts of agency. We consider the ideas of Giele and Elder in more detail in Chapter 3.

In researching inter-generational networks we have also sought to grapple with some of the challenges identified by Ahier and Moore (1999) in their work on educational decision-making. Writing specifically in relation to post-16 transitions, but equally applicable to our own research focus on educational decision-making across the life course, they argue that transitions:

> must be located and understood in terms of *networks* of relationships (mainly inter-generational) which provide the resources through which (young) people might actualize whatever options they may aspire to. Hence the key question both theoretically and methodologically is: *where, with whom and how* do these 'negotiations' take place and how might they become the subject of sociological theory and investigation?
>
> *(Ahier and Moore 1999: 517 – emphasis in original)*

Ahier and Moore go on to identify various conceptual and practical issues that, in exploring the transmission of resources and forms of capital within networks, affect people at all different life stages. These include the importance of inter-generational transfers of various kinds, as well as various forms of dependency amongst network members across the life course. They argue that, all too often, explorations of inter-generational transfers have focused narrowly on parents to the neglect of broader kin (and, we would argue, non-familial) networks, and too bluntly on values rather than 'the management of negotiation' through which assets are transferred. They argue that it is necessary to find ways of conceptualizing and mapping the matrix of inter-generational relationships within which the dynamics of transition are embedded; of identifying *what* it is that is being transferred or mobilized within and by these dynamics; and the *principles* and *processes* through which transfers are mobilized (Ahier and Moore 1999: 526). These are some of the challenges with which we have grappled in our own research, and which are played out analytically throughout subsequent chapters.

Granovetter's classic writings on interpersonal network ties and the importance of 'network value' have also informed our work. Prefiguring Putnam's conceptualization of bonding versus bridging capital, Granovetter (1973) famously highlighted 'the strength of weak ties' and, conversely, 'the weakness of strong ties'. He identifies the strength of interpersonal ties as being dependent on factors such as 'emotional intensity', 'mutual confiding' and 'reciprocal services' (1973). He further suggests that a focus on 'strong ties' is associated with analyses of bounded small groups, characterized primarily by the density of relationships (who knows who), and relative lack of weaker ties to other (non-familial) groups and communities. In contrast, 'weak ties provide people with access to information and resources beyond those available in their own social circle' (Granovetter 1983: 209). From Granovetter's perspective, the potential to create bridges beyond one's immediate bounded network is critical to understanding processes of social reproduction and change, suggesting that instability within a network might in itself facilitate the bridging process by causing individuals to reach out beyond their familiar (including familial) associations.

More recent writers have developed these ideas further through focusing on the social capital that a person is able to access within their personal network. As Croll notes, 'the central idea underlying social capital is that social relationships and the personal networks which they create are a resource which can be used to generate outcomes which are valued' (2004: 398). These resources include the provision of information, contacts and sources of advice that, depending on the nature of a network, might either reinforce norms and expectations within that network or open up new opportunities. Bourdieu, Coleman and Putnam are famously regarded as the main exponents of social capital theory. Bourdieu's writings draw a key distinction between cultural capital on the one hand and social capital on the other (Bourdieu 1986), and place greater emphasis on the importance of shared attitudes, dispositions and behaviours within networks in shaping individual outcomes, whilst the work of Coleman and Putnam has a normative dimension to it not evident within Bourdieu's work (Morrow 1999). Yet their ideas remain extremely influential within policy debates on widening participation, to the extent that the language of social capital has entered into common parlance in the pronouncements of politicians, policy makers and practitioners alike. It is for this reason that we tend to focus rather more on developing a critique of Coleman and Putnam's particular take on social capital theory within this book, rather than that of Bourdieu, and their perspectives are considered in more detail in Chapter 5.

The concepts and perspectives briefly introduced in this first chapter are particularly central to the arguments and analyses presented in this book. Perhaps inevitably in a book which has been written by a large, multi-disciplinary team of researchers, other complementary concepts and theoretical perspectives also find their way into some of the subsequent chapters, indicative of the diversity of approaches that now exist within the field of widening participation and educational decision-making.

The structure of the book

In this opening chapter we have sought to outline the policy and research context within which our own work is situated. We have argued that our research project is distinctive in its focus on older learners and on 'genuine' non-participants, and in its exploration of the embedded nature of educational decision-making through the adoption of a research design informed by qualitative social network analysis. This last point is explored further by Brenda Johnston in Chapter 2, who provides a detailed account of our research design and explores some of the methodological challenges that we encountered in researching and analysing educational decision-making within networks. In Chapter 3, Sue Heath provides an introduction to our initial sample of 16 'potentially recruitable' individuals through considering the decisions made about employment, education and training at the point at which they first completed their compulsory schooling, highlighting in particular how and why they came to acquire their Level 3 qualifications in the context of constantly changing opportunity structures. We also consider whether their own concep-tualizations of progression bear much correspondence to those that underpin contemporary policies on education and training. This chapter summarizes the experiences of all 16 of our core sample members, in contrast to subsequent chapters, which focus on specific case study networks.

Chapter 4, written by Felix Maringe and colleagues, focuses on the effects of compulsory schooling on progression decisions across the life course. The chapter highlights the importance of taking into account the specific policy regimes that shaped participants' experiences of their schooling, and focuses in particular on the effects on educational outcomes of gender and social class, including their longer-term legacies within networks. In Chapter 5, Alison Fuller considers the relevance of theories of social capital to understanding decision-making within networks. She argues that applying social capital concepts to our data has enabled us to think in a more nuanced way about the types of social capital available in particular networks and the ways in which these provide resources for particular sorts of decisions and choices (or non-decisions and non-choices). In Chapter 6, Ros Foskett focuses specifically on our sample members' experiences of careers education and guidance. She explores the process of career learning with reference to the individual stories and network histories of the participants in our study, and by such means offers an analysis of career decision-making also based on a social capital perspective. In Chapter 7, Martin Dyke extends our analysis of social capital to locate decision-making and non-decision-making within a framework of power relationships, where circumstances and individual agency combine to provide different capabilities for agency, and he also considers how non-participation in HE has in recent times come to be seen, after C. Wright Mills, as a 'social problem' rather than a 'private trouble'.

Chapter 8, by Nick Foskett, brings us back squarely to the realm of widening participation policies through an exploration of the policy context of widening par-ticipation in recent years and its relationship with the decision-making of individuals who are qualified to enter HE but have chosen not to do so. This chapter focuses on the large-scale components of this process by examining the evolution of national policy in relation to widening participation in HE. In particular it concerns itself with three themes – the origins of widening participation policies in the UK and the issues which have emerged from their implementation; the ways in which those policies appear to have shaped the behaviours and strategies of families and individuals within our research; and the implications of the findings for widening participation policies in the next decade. Finally, in Chapter 9, Alison Fuller, Sue Heath and Brenda Johnston provide an overview of our key findings, arguments and messages from our study, focusing in particular on three themes: the importance of the life course and life stage perspective; the importance of 'knowing the potential student'; and the influence of social capital and other mediating resources. We conclude by considering the implications of these themes for widening participation policy, practice and research.

Notes

1   Level 4 and above is deemed to be higher education in the UK system.
2   Level 3 is deemed to be equivalent to two passes at A level, and is the level normally required for entry to higher education.

2

MAKING SENSE OF COMPLEX SOCIAL NETWORK DATA

Brenda Johnston

The research on which this book is based investigated how educational and employment (non-) decision-making, with particular reference to higher education, might be embedded within social networks consisting of family members, friends and work colleagues. This chapter provides some information about and reflections on the research processes involved in the study in order to provide a resource for other researchers. Scrutiny of research processes yields insights at different levels. First, it clarifies the nature and status of the research findings, enabling the research community, and other interested readers, to make more informed judgements about the value of the research. Second, research processes become more transparent. This enables other researchers to learn from them in the sense of having a concrete research process to critique, extend and improve on. Researching social networks using qualitative approaches is a relatively undeveloped area (Edwards 2010), so such debate is especially useful. Additionally, by reflecting carefully on our research approaches, we aim to enhance both the quality of current and future research that we undertake.

Our study was relatively unusual in exploring the influence exerted on decision-making by a diverse range of personal contacts – whether parents, children, grandparents, siblings, partners, friends or work colleagues – and especially in seeking to foreground the network itself as an important unit of analysis. We wanted to be able to analyse three levels of account: *individual* accounts of decision-making (as is usual within research of this kind), alongside both *relationship*-based accounts (the specific interaction between the decision-making of an individual and that of their mother, for example, or best friend or partner) and *network*-based accounts, which may be embedded across the network as a whole or within specific parts of the network. Our data gathering and data analysis would be shaped accordingly. However, there were no clear models in the literature illustrating how to carry out such an investigation.

The research process involved four overlapping stages. First we accessed and exploitated existing theory and research in the field through a series of literature reviews (Johnston 2007; Maringe and Fuller 2006; Staetsky 2008). Second, we developed a macro-level account of (non-) participation in the general population based on secondary analysis of data from the Labour Force Survey and the Youth Cohort Study. Third, we conducted 32 interviews with key informants working in the widening participation arena largely in Hampshire and the Isle of Wight (the geographical focus of the research, which – perhaps surprisingly – includes high levels of non-participation in HE). Fourth, we collected primary interview data from 16 networks of intimacy focused in each case around one entry point person (embracing 107 individuals in total), these 16 all living in Hampshire and the Isle of Wight. The research processes, therefore, involved analysis of large amounts of complex information, including pre-existing literature as well as primary and secondary data.

This chapter will discuss four aspects of our research methodology: first, the methodological challenges involved in the investigation of educational and employment decision-making in social networks; second, how our study sits in the existing literature and what other studies offered us; third, our methodological positioning; and fourth, how we generated substantive analyses of educational and employment decision-making in social networks, drawing on various sources of information.

The issues mentioned in this chapter are necessarily selective. Further descriptions of the research process, especially its earlier parts, are contained in two project working papers by Heath and Johnston (2006) and Johnston and Heath (2007). Discussion of the data-gathering aspects of the project and their implications can be found in Johnston and Heath (2008). Discussions of the implications of the filtering and selection process in our sampling are discussed in Heath *et al.* (2009).

Methodological challenges

To recap, the research on which this book is based focused on social networks containing at least one individual who had chosen not to enter higher education (HE), despite having the qualifications to do so. The study hypothesized that such networks, linked as they are to varying forms of social, cultural and economic capital, provide a critical context within which individuals' thinking about HE is embedded and co-constructed. The underlying methodological challenges in the study relate to various aspects of investigating (non-) decision-making as a collective process in social networks.

There is a broad swathe of issues relevant to analysis of such network interactions. There are the large questions of how far decision-making and actions result from structural factors, or from individual agency, and how far the two are intermingled and interdependent. The relevant factors operate at different levels. There are macro-level social, political and economic dimensions; meso-level factors such as those of the impact of schools and colleges; and micro-level factors operating at the level of individual families and people and their interactions. Material resources and their allocation and functioning at all these levels need to be considered, as well as cultural factors such as values. In addition, there is a temporal dimension of changing economic, social, political and familial factors. As well as developing an under-standing of the general milieu or habitus in which a person is functioning, it is necessary to explore how micro-level decision-making interactions and processes are actually happening. Both horizontal aspects (various forms of dependency and interaction across the network) and vertical aspects (cohort and family generational aspects) of the networks have to be considered. The social network which is active and influential at the time of the research would not necessarily have been so over the lifetime of the person being interviewed, as family relationships, work situations and friendship patterns change over time. Several of these aspects and levels are dynamically inter-related.

Moreover, we wished to explore various theoretical concepts through the data, perhaps confirming, challenging or expanding on these. As discussed in Chapter 1, some theoretical concepts of interest to us are notions of social capital (Bourdieu 1996; Coleman 1988; Putnam 2000), and notions of the life course (Giele and Elder 1998). We also wished to be able to analyse beyond the concepts offered by those fields in the light of our initial analyses. Different members of the team therefore sometimes brought alternative theoretical perspectives to bear and this is reflected, for example, in Martin Dyke's use of approaches linked to Lukes' work on power in Chapter 7.

Ontological, epistemological, practical, interpersonal and ethical issues underpin these challenges and, indeed, imbue all stages of the investigation. Such issues are especially prominent in an investigation of networks for at least three reasons. First, it is necessary to gather multiple accounts within any single network, accounts which may be potentially conflicting or at least told from different perspectives. Second, researchers need to interview and interact with several members of the same net-work who are likely to be responding to their perceptions of the 'stories' presented by the others to whom the researchers have talked. Third, the theoretical concepts involved are complex, requiring data that are detailed, finely-tuned, robust and sensitive in order to carry out the necessary theoretical explorations.

Given these challenges, investigating how networks functioned as regards educational and employment decision-making was not straightforward. We worked with a number of opportunities and constraints.

How our study sits within existing literature

As noted in Chapter 1, there is a rich tradition of work within the sociology of education that focuses on the ways in which decision-making can be construed as an embedded rather than an individualized process, with the work of Bourdieu standing as a critical benchmark and inspiration in this respect. Often such studies have used quantitative methods, or documentary methods, or both. Many studies on educational decision-making seek to explore the transfer of resources and forms of capital between generations (e.g. Ball *et al.* 2000; Davey 2009; Reay *et al.* 2005) or other issues such as gender roles (e.g. Brooks 2004; Pugsley 1998) or identity, agency and learning (Hodkinson with Hodkinson 2008). However, they rarely focus on more than two generations and even more rarely do they extend beyond the parent–child relationship. Often, even in fields outside education, studies rely on only one interviewee to build up understandings about a broader network/kin-group (e.g. Weston 1991, in her study of gay and lesbian conceptions of kinship). Sometimes researchers use focus groups consisting of unrelated individuals. For example, Archer and Hutchings (2000) used focus groups to investigate the perspectives on HE of working-class individuals who did not themselves have direct experience of HE. However, this is an exploration of (collective) individual points of view, not an investigation of networks.

Methodological texts on biographical approaches (which include life history, auto/biography and biography, the narrative analysis of life and oral history) initially seemed a fruitful source of guidance for us. However, methodological texts on both biographical approaches (e.g. Miller 2000; Roberts 2002; Thompson 1996; Wengraf 2001) and biographical studies (e.g. Antikainen *et al.* 1996; Weeks *et al.* 2001; Weston 1991), while useful in terms of exploring how examination of individual lives can illuminate wider social, psychological, cultural, economic and educational themes, usually advocate interviewing with only one individual from within a network. The aim is to collect the account of the individual and their relationship to the micro-world of the relevant social network as well as to broader society, rather than to conduct interviews with multiple people related to one another in a network.

There are studies where the researchers must have faced similar difficulties to ours. Hodkinson *et al.* (1996), for example, spoke to members of the networks surrounding ten young people making career decisions. Young and Wilmott (1957), in their community study of family and kinship in East London, investigated related people and synthesized their accounts. Watts and Bridges (2006) reported interviewing the peers and family members of their main interviewees, who were young people who did not want to enter HE. Reay *et al.* (2001) investigated the effects of institutional habitus on HE choice for a group of young people and a sub-sample of parents. However, these studies were not systematically inter-generational or focused on extensive networks and there is, from our point of view, frustratingly little information about methodological issues in the published accounts of these studies.

Sociological studies of the family, with greater or lesser discussion of methodology, alerted us to various practical and ethical issues and potential solutions related to data collection. As with our research, they usually involve multiple members of families and are often inter-generational in scope. These studies tend to focus on issues such as: roles within the family; patterns of support; the allocation of resources within a family; how wealth and status are controlled and passed on; issues of patriarchy and matriarchy; how the micro-world of the family relates to the wider society; contradictory descriptions of the same family events; issues of power and resistance within families; the construction and reconstruction of intimate relationships; and gender differences within the family, themes which – to varying degrees – were all of relevance to our own research, too (e.g. Bernard 1972; Brannen 2003; Edwards *et al.* 1999; Finch and Mason 1993; Hockey *et al.* 2002; Perlesz and Lindsay 2003; Ribbens McCarthy *et al.* 2003; Song 1998). Often these studies are based on the assumption that there is not a unified family reality for researchers to find and that in any 'family', however constituted, the important task is to focus on the divergent perspectives on particular family practices (Warin *et al.* 2007: 122). In methodological terms, this entails careful consideration of data collection practices (e.g. Warin *et al.* 2007) and later data analysis (e.g. Ribbens McCarthy *et al.* 2003).

Our substantive interests, however, are far less tightly focused on the details of family practices or interactions and perceptions of common situations, and extend beyond the family to wider network members. They are more focused on broader brush developments over time and life pathways, often of non-family members, that happen to run parallel to one another for at least some time. Our methodological interests are less in reconciling divergent accounts and more with the construction of a complex account of horizontal and vertical aspects of (non-) decision-making within a social network, each network linked to a person who has chosen not to enter HE. Different perspectives, as revealed in interviews within the same network can reveal, for example, generational and gender differences of perspective. We have, then, tried to situate an individual's decision-making within a nexus of *first-hand* accounts from those closest to them, by so doing not only highlighting the complexity of educational decision-making, but also foregrounding the tensions, contradictions and moments of solidarity which occur within networks (Heath *et al.* 2009: 647).

In sum, it felt like a pioneering venture to conduct interviews about educational and employment decision-making processes within networks which were inter-generational and which included friends and work colleagues as well as relatives.

Methodological positioning

It is useful to pause here to reflect on what kind of sense we have been aiming for in the research. What is its status? We share Hodkinson and Macleod's contention that 'no methodology can act as a conceptually neutral lens' and that 'different research methodologies have fairly strong affinities with particular conceptualizations' (2010: 185). In their case, they are discussing learning, but the position transfers easily to decision-making. They further argue that 'decisions about how to research learning [decision-making] are related to decisions about how to conceptualize and theorize learning [decision-making]' and that different research approaches will produce different types of empirical data and different conclusions. Mixing methods 'requires careful and sometimes difficult conceptual work' (Hodkinson and Macleod 2010: 173).

Hodkinson and Macleod suggest that a life history approach uses the subjective perceptions of the participant to 'place the individual at the centre of the investigation' over an extended period of time, placing the participant in an extended macro, meso and micro context (2010: 178–9). This yields findings that illuminate how people make sense of their experiences, that is, the way they construct their understandings. In contrast, a survey approach is more useful in accessing observable, measurable products (Hodkinson and Macleod 2010: 180).

In our case, we hypothesized that educational and employment decision-making is embedded and co-constructed within social networks and chose to investigate this primarily through life history interviews. In addition to interviewing individuals, we interviewed various network members, as well as analysing survey data and interviews with key informant participants. By interviewing multiple network members we sought to extend our understanding beyond an individual at the centre of a rich context, to understand how the network of several individuals functioned within this context, that is, to access the significance and nature of network practices. We recognize that ours is only one of many possible interpretations, although hopefully a 'competent' one, in Guba and Lincoln's (1994: 113) terms, with the reader adding a further layer of interpretive complexity.

Denzin (2001) wrote about the role of individual stories, such as we have in our primary interview data, in the broader societal and temporal picture:

> stories always have a larger cultural and historical locus. Individuals are universal singulars, universalizing in their singularity the unique features of their historical moment. Narratives of the self, as temporal constructions, are anchored in local institutional cultures and their interpretive practices. These practices shape how self-narratives are fashioned. Storytellers have agency and self-reflexivity. Their stories are temporal constructions that create the realities they describe. Stories and lives connect and define one another.
>
> *(Denzin 2001: 59)*

We have sought to use the individual narratives obtained in interviews to reveal such insights.

Our primary data collection processes as well as later stages of interpretation, including relating these data to the secondary data and other knowledge sources, had to be consistent both with our ontological and epistemological positioning and with the need to explore the complexities of network influences as described earlier. Ontologically, we were sceptical of a realist position that would regard interview data as corresponding to some notion of objective truth which we could elicit from our interviewees and later represent. We certainly did not solicit accounts of employment and educational decision-making from our entry point individuals, to then somehow confirm their validity (or otherwise) through the triangulation of accounts across the network as a whole. Instead, we have adopted a constructivist position as proposed by Guba and Lincoln (1994, 2005) whereby:

> Realities are apprehended in the form of multiple, intangible mental constructions, socially and experientially based, local and specific in nature (although elements are often shared among many individuals and even across

cultures), and dependent for their form and content on the individual persons or groups holding the constructions. Constructions are not more or less 'true,' in any absolute sense, but simply more or less informed and/or sophisticated. Constructions are alterable, as are their associated 'realities.'

(Guba and Lincoln 1994: 110–11).

Epistemologically, we view knowledge as being created and mediated by interviewees and researchers as the investigation moves forward, rather than existing in any objectively, knowable sense. The purpose of our enquiry has been: 'Understanding and reconstruction of the constructions that people (including the inquirer) initially hold, aiming towards consensus but still open to new interpretations as information and sophistication improve' (Guba and Lincoln 1994: 113).

Our final aim has been to offer the reader consensus interpretations of the complexities of educational decision-making that are as informed and sophisticated as possible, arrived at through: interaction in the interviews with our research participants; consideration of perspectives and information offered by the secondary data and other knowledge sources as well as the interviews; and reflexivity about our own role in the research process. In the interviews, therefore, we explored the complexities of accounts given to us, probing both their relationships to external events, policies and structures (at macro, meso and micro levels) and the nature of these as experienced and perceived by our interviewees. We sought to be as aware as possible of the complexities of our interactions with our participants.

We would also like to make some comments about the validity of the analytical process in this project. In qualitative research, researchers play, or should play, an acknowledged and integral part in the research outcomes in terms, first, of *influencing* the data by virtue of who they are and what they say and, second, of *interpreting* the data – never a transparent, neutral, value-free process. (In quantitative research in educational settings the same is largely true, but less often acknowledged.)

Qualitative researchers, therefore, have to develop rigorous procedures for validating their findings. Miles and Huberman (1994) suggest a focus on both *internal* and *external* validity. *Internal* validity focuses on the internal credibility and plausibility of the research findings, and rigour and suitability of the research process. *External* validity focuses on the 'transferability' and 'fittingness' (p. 279) of the research conclusions and processes. In qualitative research this transferability may take place through theoretical connections or case-to-case transfer (p. 279). In traditional quantitative research, generalization and validation of findings would most typically occur through generalization from sample to population, but this is usually not appropriate in qualitative research.

To enhance *internal validity*, we have tried to follow a rigorous and appropriate analytical research process. In primary data collection, all team members undertook network interviews apart from the two colleagues involved in the secondary analysis of the quantitative data sets, Patricia Rice and Laura Staetsky. Each network was assigned two researchers who worked together to organize the interviews, discuss practical issues and develop understandings of the emerging data. After each interview, the interviewer wrote a summary of the interview, including factual details about the interviewee as well as short descriptions about aspects such as the interviewee's education, employment, life stage and networks of intimacy. Each interview was transcribed verbatim. There were also numerous informal chats between team members about the various interviews, networks and emerging understandings of each network. Each team member brought a somewhat different perspective to the data, reflecting our varied disciplinary backgrounds and substantive research interests.

We developed various tools to assist with the data analysis. We drew sociograms, that is, diagrammatic representations of networks, and wrote meta-analysis documents. These documents were drawn up by both interviewers of a network and discussed by the rest of the research group at an away day after we had completed the fieldwork. By these means we developed descriptions of entire networks through scrutiny of the individual interviews within that network. We developed continua of network types according to various indicators such as aspirations to be different from now and current attitudes to formal learning of the entry point person. We speculated about the likelihood of different entry point individuals embarking on HE. Through this process we reached consensus understandings about our interpretations of the networks. Our approach provided us with insights into network functioning and required us to refine and reconfigure theoretical conceptualizations. In effect, we sought to build consensus understandings around the interview data in a multi-layered process.

In terms of *external validity*, we have located our research findings within existing explanatory theoretical frameworks, existing quantitative contextual data, and existing widening participation policy and research concerns. Additionally we have opened up our interpretations to external scrutiny in the shape of published accounts. Ultimately, the reader must judge how far we have succeeded in our aim of carrying out a useful, valid and rigorous piece of research.

Generating analyses of educational and employment decision-making within networks

We used a variety of resources to inform our analysis of educational and employment decision-making as an embedded social practice including existing theory and research in the field; secondary analysis of existing relevant quantitative data, leading to the development of a macro-level account of (non-) participation in the general population; interviews with key informants; and collection of primary data.

Contributions from existing theory and research

One of our first activities was to develop a series of literature reviews as a project resource to inform our data analysis. One review (Maringe and Fuller 2006) focused on widening participation policy in the UK in recent decades. The review confirmed and extended our initial assumptions, highlighting a lack of policy interest in widening participation for anyone apart from young adults, as well as a lack of research knowledge about the relevant groups and the importance of our proposed investigation into those who had chosen not to enter HE.

Staetsky (2008) reviewed quantitative empirical research from the fields of economics, sociology or the overlapping fields of economic sociology, on the effects of family background and social networks on educational decision-making. The underlying assumption was usually that participation in HE is a desired social goal. The theories reviewed included those of social capital from the point of view of sociologists (e.g. Coleman 1988) and economists (e.g. Manski 2000); human capital (e.g. Becker and Tomes 1986); psychological theories of needs hierarchies (e.g. Miller 1967), and congruence theory and social participation (e.g. Courtney 1992). The review concluded that these theories potentially provide a coherent theoretical framework for explaining adult participation (and indeed many of the later works emerging from this research project used such sociological theoretical perspectives); however, quantitative empirical work, especially on the participation of adults, is relatively undeveloped. Moreover, exploration of the influence of social networks on educational decision-making of non-participants was particularly problematic for quantitative research in that social networks and social influence are, by nature, complex and dynamic with few types of social influences easily quantifiable. This makes quantitative models of educational participation difficult to construct. As Hodkinson and Macleod (2010: 180) argue, surveys are unsuitable for use when the focus of interest (in our case decision-making processes) 'can neither be observed directly nor quantified very easily as the emphasis [in such cases] is on subjective processes rather than objective products'. The review concluded that family background and social network effects were strong influences on educational outcomes, but much evidence came from research on young people, with findings extrapolated to older people such as those we were investigating.

A methodology review (Johnston 2007) highlighted those challenges entailed in our research, described earlier, as well as the pioneering nature of what we were attempting to investigate.

As well as literature reviews, we drew up timelines of significant educational and employment policy milestones in the UK over several decades in order to contextualize the micro-level interview data we gathered from several generations of network members. The timelines were developed from our existing knowledge as educational and employment researchers, additional reading and aspects thrown up in the interviews themselves which drew our attention to significant macro-level policies as experienced at a micro-level. Chapters 3 and 4 illustrate the importance of an understanding of policies at different times for the school-leaving experiences of different generations.

Contributions from the secondary data

The non-participant adult population with Level 3 qualifications as their highest level of qualification is dispersed throughout the wider population of the UK and is not identified in most existing data sets. However, two data sets offered us some assistance: the Labour Force Survey (Office for National Statistics 2006) and the Youth Cohort Study (Jarvis *et al.* 2006).

The Labour Force Survey has data on adults of all ages in the labour force in the UK. Analysis of the Labour Force Survey 2005/06 (Staetsky and Rice 2010) allowed us to explore the characteristics of those with Level 3 qualifications as their highest level of qualification, and enabled us to compare our sample with this wider population in terms of certain characteristics and patterns such as educational and occupational levels. Our early analysis of the Labour Force data, in late 2006, highlighted gender and age-related differences in educational and employment patterns. In the working population overall, about a fifth held Level 3 qualifications as their highest level of qualification. We included both vocational and academic Level 3 qualifications as well as trade apprenticeships in this group. Trade apprenticeships were far more common among males than females. Older people were far more likely to have lower levels of educational qualification than younger people. Women holding Level 3 qualifications as their highest level had far higher representation than men in administrative, personal services and sales occupations. The analysis also highlighted differences according to very local areas in our region (Fuller 2007a).

Such contextual information was useful when recruiting our entry point sample in that, for example, the apparently high proportion of women respondents in childcare occupations actually reflected the proportion of the general population at that qualification level. The larger proportion of men than women with apprenticeship qualifications in our sample similarly reflected that of the population at large.

Our analysis of the Labour Force Survey provided a broad context for the subsequent qualitative case studies, feeding into many of the papers we have written (e.g. Fuller 2007b, Fuller and Paton 2009, Johnston *et al.* 2008). In terms of Hodkinson and Macleod's (2010) argument, analysis of the Labour Force Survey data worked for us conceptually and empirically in that we used it to provide a quantitative picture that could contextualize our main interview data, not to add to the process-based picture of decision-making offered by our interviews.

The analysis of Youth Cohort Study data (YCS) (Cohorts 10 and 11) (Staetsky 2007) focused on the little-used HE module in that survey and enabled us to compare non-participation and participation in HE amongst 'standard age' students. This information was of only limited assistance to us as it only focused on the factors affecting individual young people's decision-making rather than the influence of network factors. However, as with most surveys, the YCS presupposed answers, rather than eliciting fresh ways of viewing educational decision-making. Our analysis of the YCS fed into our critique of existing literature on 'barriers' to HE (Fuller *et al.* 2008) mentioned in Chapter 1.

Contributions from the key informant interviews

We interviewed 32 key informants from local, regional and national levels, in the widening participation arena. The interviews gave contextual information about the then existing policy and institutional arrangements at local, regional and national policy levels. They enabled an analysis of local institutional and organizational activity to encourage (mainly young) people from deprived backgrounds into HE by raising aspirations and promoting familiarity with HE. As Fuller and Paton (2009) explained, we were able to categorize stakeholders into two groups: the majority who focused on the pre-19s, and the (small) minority who focused on post-19s. Whereas many of the former had been explicitly fostering young people's access to HE, those organizations with an interest in (older) adults had not, at that point, had that remit. From the perspective of our research we noted that there appeared to be no publicly supported agency with primary responsibility for widening participation in HE among this group and little publicly funded advice and guidance available for individuals. In fact, little was known about adults and how they constructed HE and perceived its relevance to their lives.

Contributions from the network interviews

As outlined in Chapter 1, each of the 16 networks in the study included an individual entry point who was 'potentially recruitable' to HE, and their broader network members. We decided to use Level 3 qualifications (A levels or a wide range of vocational or occupational qualifications) recognized as entry level qualifications for HE in the UK, to indicate 'potentially recruitable' status. Subsequent to gaining their Level 3 qualification, our entry point individuals had neither participated in HE, nor were at that time applying to do so. Broader network members had qualifications at different levels.

The sample was purposive. Our interest was in patterns of participation and non-participation across the life course so, in addition to all having a Level 3 qualification as their highest level of qualification, the 16 entry points represented a range of life stages and ages (although all were over age 21). We also sought to generate a relatively diverse sample in relation to the following characteristics: employment status, occupation, geographical location, social class, length of time since Level 3 qualifications gained and ethnic background. The networks ranged in size from three to 12 people, with an average of between six and seven. Some networks consisted of family members, while others consisted largely of friends or work colleagues. Many were a mixture. Heath and Johnston (2006), Johnston and Heath (2007) and Heath *et al.* (2009) provide detailed information on our sampling processes and rationale.

Largely for practical reasons, we opted for a reasonably brief initial interview with potential entry point individuals, when we asked for basic educational, employment and family information as well as a description of network members whom it might be useful and possible for us to interview. Nine potential entry point people were either unsuitable on further investigation (e.g. they were over-qualified) or their network members would not participate.

We then spoke to network members in more detailed interviews. We had initially planned to conduct two interviews with the entry point person before interviewing network members, but decided to interview network members before this second interview in order to enable us go into the second 'entry point' interview with a stronger sense of the values, world view and modes of interaction of network members. This also introduced a longitudinal element into the contact with the entry point individuals, as usually there was a gap of some months between the two interviews. Our interviewing strategy, therefore, responded to circumstances and our experiences. Such flexibility is compatible with a constructivist approach where researchers adapt and develop as understandings, both substantive and method-ological, develop. We had regular discussions about the interviewing process among either the entire research team or a smaller core group at this critical period. The second interviews with the entry points were usually considerably longer than the first.

We did not interview network members as a group (although occasionally our participants preferred to have a family member or friend present). Family or group interviews have been used to advantage by other researchers (e.g. Heath and Cleaver 2003; Pugsley 1998; Rosenthal 1998; Shopes 1996; Weeks *et al.* 2001) in order to probe group dynamics, family psychology and to re-awaken memories. However, a group interview strategy was inappropriate in our study for various reasons. Apart from the practical difficulties of arranging for all relevant persons to be present at one interview, group interviews might also have meant that individuals withheld information that they would have divulged in a 'private' interview. Each individual would have had less time overall to speak. Individual network members may or may not have known one another, given their diverse relationships to the entry point person, which might have made group encounters challenging. Moreover, we wanted to have a strong focus on individual narratives, each with its own internal dynamic, logic and shape, rather than just the points of intersection between the narratives.

We now want to focus in greater detail on the contribution of the network case studies to reflect on how the data helped us access and construct understandings of network influence.

Accessing and constructing understandings of network influence

Investigation of network interactions and the 'influence' of network members on the entry point individual was both central to our study and especially perplexing. It was central to our substantive interests in that it relates to our interest in various forms of social capital (Putnam 2000) and habitus (Bourdieu 1996), as well as issues related to the life course (Giele and Elder 1998). We had to gather data that would give us information on the quality and nature of the relationships and interactions within the network as well as inter-generational transmission of social and cultural capital.

Investigation of these issues of network 'influence' was methodologically challenging in a number of respects. From a principled methodological point of view, we had to consider what we ourselves meant by 'influence' before we could operationalize a means of investigating it. Influence may take a wide range of forms including verbal, emotional, financial or other practical support, or reciprocity and be more or less direct. For example, in some cases husband and wife teams worked to support one another gaining qualifications as adults, offering one another encouragement, sharing childcare responsibilities and working out how to cope financially. Influence could be less concrete – perhaps an example of someone, either within or outside the network, providing a role model for a network member. Influence could include subtle forms of encouragement or praise for particular kinds of achievement. These could be linked to tacit as well as overt norms about good and bad behaviour in particular networks.

In terms of influences which discouraged particular courses of action, these might include verbal discouragement or emotional, financial or other practical sanctions. For example, in some cases, parents would or could not support children financially beyond the end of compulsory schooling. Discouraging influence could be subtle. For example, one participant reported that her parents were happy to let her have what career she wanted, but did not give her any direction or support to do anything especially ambitious. When she mentioned different careers, they said things like, 'Oh but you have to be really clever to do that', giving the message implicitly that she was not clever enough.

The list of micro-level influences above is almost certainly incomplete. These notions of influence clearly relate to notions of bonding capital (the solidarity, emotional and practical support and reciprocation which operate within groups) and bridging capital (more dispersed links and reciprocation between and within groups) (Putnam 2000). They also relate to Bourdieu's (1996) notions of habitus and cultural transmission as well as Giele and Elder's (1998) discussions of life course issues such as generational positioning, and family discourses and traditions.

Micro-level influences operate at different levels: one-to-one interpersonal influences; networks, and perhaps sub-networks, within these. 'Network influence' would not necessarily be uniform across the network, given that our networks were loose groupings of friends, family members and work colleagues, not all of whom knew each another. Values and assumptions might vary within a network, according to factors such as generation and wealth, or whether or not someone is a family member, and so on, as well as individual preferences.

As well as principled methodological matters, we had pragmatic and ethical concerns about how we investigated influence. From a pragmatic point of view, and before the interview stage, we wanted to maximize the likelihood of our potential entry points being prepared to participate in the research: some individuals with whom we piloted materials expressed some anxiety about involving family and friends in our research. We wanted to ask our entry points for two interviews, and access to friends and family for interviews. We decided that if we approached potential recruits saying that we wanted to ask their network members direct questions about the entry point and influences on them, some people might be discouraged from participating. Alternatively, if we were able to say that we wanted to speak to network members largely about each person's own education and employment experiences this would be less threatening and invasive.

The issue of confidentiality also affected our approach. Both from a method-ological and ethical point of view, we wished to offer confidentiality within the research process in order to encourage openness and to minimize the chances that our research would harm participants. Therefore, we did not want to ask direct questions of a network member, based on information that someone else within the network had given us, when the origin of the information might be clear and its revelation cause friction within the network.

Certainly we could, and indeed had to, use our judgement as researchers when deciding how much we should reveal. After all, we might have appeared rather uninterested if we had turned up for an interview apparently knowing very little about the network, when the interviewee knew we had previously spoken to several other members. However, the researchers' understanding of which issues may cause friction is a matter of judgement, and the issues are often of some delicacy. What is commonplace knowledge within a network and what is a secret? What is common-place knowledge within a network, and secret from outsiders (including researchers) in the view of some network members, but not others? For example, the parent of one young network member, Mark, described his severe dyslexia and the serious effects this had had on his school education to the interviewer who assumed that this was well-known in the network. She intended to raise the issue of dyslexia with Mark when discussing his education, but was alerted just before the interview by a parent that although this would probably be acceptable, the 'D word' was rather sensitive. The interviewer therefore, decided to wait for a point in the interview when Mark himself raised the issue. However, he never did and managed to describe his troubled education without ascribing any of his difficulties to his severe dyslexia.

In a few such cases, concerns about confidentiality prevented us from questioning network members about issues mentioned by another network member, but in practice this was not usually the major constraint. Often the second network member would mention the relevant issue of their own volition and if not, we could raise the issue obliquely. Our approach did mean that our focus was on 'my story', as presented by each participant, and this probably encouraged greater openness for the majority of participants.

How far did we want to ask *direct* questions about influence, especially on the entry points, and how far should we have relied on individual accounts in order to probe the general social and cultural environment of the entry point person? Might we have ended up with individual narrative accounts from those within each network that ran side by side, without drawing them together? Additionally, asking direct questions about influence seemed likely to be somewhat problematic, given its multiple aspects and levels, especially since many aspects of influence relate to tacit values and norms. How far could people articulate these influences? Even if people were aware of influences, how far would they be willing to articulate influences on them? What language might we use to ask about influence? How could we explore influence in the interviews, given its complexity and potential sensitivity? These issues remained as sources of a tension and concern throughout the fieldwork, and were revisited on various occasions. These kinds of concern have received little attention in the literature, given the lack of this type of qualitative research on social networks.

In the event, we tried both to achieve individual accounts and to probe to some extent for issues of network influence. We decided to generate a series of individual narratives from network members in relation to their *own* educational and employment decision-making (events, processes, priorities and feelings) and how they made sense of it. The sense-making was a product of the particular experiences of the participants in terms of their own social networks, operating over many years, as well as the individual's historical, social and economic positioning.

In the initial entry point interviews, we did not ask explicitly about influence. In the interviews with network members, we interwove direct questions about influence in a low-key way with a wide range of questions about education and employment. For example, we asked interviewees if they thought they had had an impact on anyone else's educational decisions. The interviewer asked about impact on the entry point person only as a final prompt, after the interviewee had given detailed examples of anyone else they might have influenced. In the second entry point interviews, we probed extensively for more detailed narrative information about educational, employment and network history, as well as issues of influence. We asked explicitly about issues of influence related to the people in the network they had nominated for us to speak to as well as the influence of those we were unable to speak to, for one reason or another. One advantage of our confidentiality policy, and our focus on 'own narratives', was that the potential problem we had been concerned about at the start of the project, that of people reacting to the accounts of others, did not much arise, as far as we are aware.

The interviewees produced valuable information about people who had been strong, direct influences on them. These are the people who had perhaps spoken to them clearly about an educational or employment decision *or* who had exerted specific pressures in the shape of sanctions or threats if a certain decision were made or not made *or* who had provided specific kinds of support *or* people who were aware of specific limitations imposed on them by responsibilities such as childcare. People speaking of such matters were often parents speaking of children, or children speaking of parents, although we also have cases of friends, work colleagues or even more distant connections exerting influence at a key moment. Direct questions about influence accessed some information, especially about significant one-to-one interpersonal influences, but only a small proportion of what we came to understand about influence.

Through eliciting the individual accounts, many aspects of indirect, tacit influence emerged, expressed in the participants' own language and own narratives, through the basic assumptions and values that underlay their stories. By criss-crossing the territory of someone's life, asking direct or indirect questions and perhaps using phatic prompts for each person's narrative of how they had approached various aspects of educational and employment decision-making, as well as family arrangements and attitudes, a complex picture emerged. These narratives, individually elicited, surfaced shared language and experiences within networks and sub-sections of each network.

Our approach did not systematically unveil the nature of network influence. We consider such an unveiling an impossibility, given the multi-faceted, often unconscious and ever-changing nature of such influence. Moreover, understandings of influence are constructed, rather than absolute objective truths that can be uncovered. They are also dependent on memory and shaped by the fluid nature of the networks themselves. However, as we discuss in this book, we have managed to access and construct at least partial understandings of network influence in the 16 networks we investigated, which we have written about elsewhere (*inter alia* Fuller *et al.* 2008; Fuller *et al.* in press; Heath *et al.* 2008, as well as the chapters in this book).

Once we had individual interview data, we were also able to look at patterns of values and assumptions across networks. We were able to make connections to educational and employment policy and macro-level conditions at different stages in time. We were also able to link individual situations to a broader macro-picture, as revealed by the Labour Force Survey and Youth Cohort Surveys. We were able to link the emerging picture from our data with concepts of social capital (Bourdieu 1996; Putnam 2000) and life course (Giele and Elder 1998). In effect, by a some-what fuzzy blend of eliciting participants' accounts of their own educational and employment decision-making, asking low-key questions about influence and build-ing up an understanding of the surrounding macro-context over the generations, we managed to construct understandings of networks and different types of influences functioning within them. Some divergent accounts emerged.

These often related either to a difference in factual knowledge available to the participants or a difference in perception according to position in the network. However, divergence was usually not central to the issues we were investigating, and often the cause of the discrepancy was clear. Differences in perception were helpful to us as they highlighted generational or gender perceptions.

Conclusions

This chapter offers an account of how the complexities involved in investigating educational decision-making as a social practice embedded within networks have played out in the research process. It recognizes the complexity of the investigation, explores its ramifications and is as transparent as possible about our philosophical positioning and related practical decisions. We recognize that our final under-standings of educational and employment decision-making, as embedded in social networks, are constructed and partial.

We also recognize that, as Hodkinson and Macleod (2010) argue, the way we conducted our research influenced our findings. We presupposed a constructed, embedded view of decision-making. If such embedded decision-making processes had not existed, our research approach would not have uncovered them, but our use of appropriate investigative tools enabled them to be at least partially revealed and contextualized. The extended life history interviews with network members plus the contextual use of survey data in conjunction with appropriate conceptual lenses provided a rich picture of educational and employment decision-making as an embedded social practice.

Research on the effects of social networks on decision-making is potentially valuable in other spheres apart from education, although challenging to operationalize. The approach offers understanding of how the decisions of individuals are embedded within their networks and how thinking is co-constructed. Our approach of allowing individuals to tell their own story, prompted by questions about influence, enabled us to develop the individual, relationship-based and network accounts that addressed our study's aims.

3

MOVING ON UP? EXPLORING NARRATIVES OF EDUCATIONAL PROGRESSION

Sue Heath

This chapter provides an introduction to our 16 network entry points through considering their immediate post-compulsory pathways. As will become apparent in this and subsequent chapters, many of our research participants had often been ambivalent about their schooling, and had left with little sense of motivation or any strong desire to continue with their studies. Yet by the time we met them they had all acquired additional qualifications which would be categorized as Level 3 qualifications within the current National Qualifications Framework, hence were potentially recruitable to higher education (HE). So how did they each get to this point? What were their reasons for acquiring these additional qualifications? And had potential progression to HE been part of their reasoning? Such questions form the focus of this chapter, which starts by considering the decisions made about employment, education and training at the point at which our core sample members first completed their compulsory schooling. Individual conceptualizations of progression are explored in relation to these accounts, and we consider whether they bear much correspondence to those which underpin contemporary policies on education and training. In contrast to subsequent chapters, which focus on specific case study networks, this chapter summarizes the experiences of all 16 of our core sample members.

A strong theme emerges in this chapter concerning the powerful influence of family expectations and norms in relation to immediate post-compulsory decision-making. *Non*-decision-making might, in fact, be a better way of conceptualizing this process for many of our participants. Most had an acute awareness of family-related expectations and of what was considered 'normal' for someone from their background. This was often reinforced by the views of teachers and other influential adults, and most had complied with these expectations, albeit not always willingly. Those who did not comply were often fully aware that their actions went against the expectations held by others – and in some cases were rejected precisely *for* this reason. This chapter, then, considers the importance of acknowledging the ways in which sample members' lives are inextricably linked to those of others across generations and how they experienced their early school to work transitions in the context of very specific individual and generational contexts. As such, it illustrates the usefulness of drawing on a life course approach to understanding processes of educational decision-making, an approach which we briefly introduced in Chapter 1. The chapter also draws upon Roberts' (2009) opportunity structures model, which foregrounds the importance of structural factors in affecting post-compulsory pathways, but which also highlights the way in which school leavers' pathways are influenced by expectations and norms firmly situated within their family of origin. As we shall see, the differential impact of social class and gender is particularly relevant to such considerations, particularly as they interact with key changes in the fields of education and the labour market.

Exploring initial post-compulsory pathways: a life course perspective

As noted in Chapter 1, our understanding of post-compulsory pathways is informed by Giele and Elder's life course approach, which is based on a consideration of the interaction between four key elements: the location of individuals in time and space; the linking of lives; human agency; and the timing of lives (Giele and Elder 1998). The first of these refers to the very specific positioning of an individual in relation to individual, generational and historical time, and the ways in which this specific positioning affects their propensity to act (and react) in very specific ways across the duration of their lives. According to Giele and Elder:

> Both the general and unique aspects of individual location affect personal experience and thus can be understood as being socially and individually *patterned* in ways that carry through time.
>
> *(Giele and Elder 1998: 9)*

This is not to suggest that individuals' actions are predetermined by their location in time and space, but that they will certainly be strongly shaped by their unique temporal and spatial positioning. Particularly relevant to our own discussion of post-compulsory pathways is the location of individuals in relation to specific education policy regimes and labour market conditions. In other words, questions of where and when people experienced their schooling and the specific policy contexts of their experiences are vital for making sense of their subsequent pathways, as we shall demonstrate later in this chapter when we consider the changing opportunity structures experienced by individuals within our sample.

The second key element of a life course approach focuses on the linking of lives, both within and across generations. This element emphasizes the embeddedness of individuals within complex inter- and intra-generational networks, which tend to be characterized by shared values, norms, dispositions and expectations (in Bourdieusian terms, a shared habitus), and draws attention to the way in which individuals' actions across the life course are influenced by the social relationships which flow from these connections. This element also fits particularly well with our specific methodological interest in qualitative social network analysis, and our theoretical interest in the diffusion of social capital within networks. Once again, individuals' actions are not predetermined by these connections:

> How well these different expectations, norms or social institutions are integrated or internalised will vary. Some will show discontinuity and disruption, and others will show a smooth interweaving of individual attainments with social and cultural expectations.
>
> *(Giele and Elder 1998: 9)*

That discontinuity and disruption are distinct possibilities highlights the centrality of the third element of a life course approach, which places an emphasis on the importance of human agency and individual goal orientation. In other words, the reproduction of dominant values and dispositions is by no means a given, although in many cases this is precisely what occurs, albeit often in subtle ways. In combination, these two elements – the linking of lives and human agency – point to the usefulness of approaches to inter-generational relationships informed by theories of *sociological ambivalence*. Luscher (1999: 13) has argued that inter-generational relations amongst adults 'can be socio-scientifically interpreted as the expression of ambivalences, and as efforts to manage and negotiate these fundamental ambivalences', whilst Connidis and McMullen use the term 'structured ambivalence' to develop a framework which can provide 'a bridging concept between social structure and individual action, made evident in social interaction' (2002: 559). As we have argued elsewhere (Heath *et al.* 2008), for these reasons the concept of ambivalence provides a useful tool for understanding the bases for social action in the realm of educational decision-making. It is particularly helpful in making sense of the reasons why individuals are on occasions able to step outside of, and act against, the dominant values and dispositions within their network, and yet, on other occasions, act in ways which reinforce those values and dispositions, even when they are acting in ways which are intended as acts of resistance to these dominant values and dispositions.

The final element of the life course perspective as developed by Giele and Elder relates to the timing of lives: how and when a person undertakes actions and engages in events, including both passive and active forms of adaptation. Giele and Elder describe the timing of lives as the medium for the integration of historical, social and individual activities, constituting the critical point at which the other three elements of the life course approach – location in time and space, the linking of lives and human agency – all come together. Various life course transitions play a key role in relation to the timing of lives, including in relation to what Merton (1984) referred to as the power of 'socially expected durations' in shaping ideas surrounding the age appropriateness of certain transitions: 'socially prescribed or collective expectations about temporal durations imbedded in social structures of various kinds'

(Merton 1984: 255–56). As such, individual transitions may at various times be perceived as happening 'too early' or 'too late', and perceptions of the appropriate timings for certain transitions – such as the 'appropriate' age to transfer to HE – are rooted both in broader societal expectations as well as in expectations rooted within an individual's immediate social network.

Changing opportunity structures

We turn now to a consideration of Roberts' model of post-school opportunity structures. This model fits well with the life course approach, as it not only draws attention to the importance of the specific socio-economic contexts of post-compulsory pathways at different points in time, but also highlights the important influence on school leavers' transitional routes of classed and gendered expectations and norms situated within their family of origin. Roberts' approach also complements our emphasis on decision-making as an embedded social practice, through highlighting the way in which dispositions and practices embedded within social networks are fundamentally shaped by the changing nature of the opportunities that are available to network members at any given time – especially at the point of first leaving school.

Roberts has written extensively on the changing opportunity structures which have faced successive cohorts of school leavers over the last fifty years. He argues that:

> Opportunity structures are formed by the inter-relationships between family origins, education, labour market processes and employers' recruitment practices . . . There are push and pull forces. The push is mainly from ascribed statuses (family backgrounds and gender, for example), and the pull is from employers and the labour market. Together they create distinct career routes which govern young people's progress.
>
> *(Roberts 2009: 355)*

Across the period of time covered by the lives of our sample members, distinct post-compulsory career routes have been shaped by several important shifts in relation to the school leaving experiences of young people in England and Wales, shifts which provide the broader context for the location in time and space of our sample members. First, the school leaving age has been raised twice: from 14 to 15 in 1944 and to 16 in 1972. Second, there has also been a steady increase in post-compulsory staying-on rates, notably following the collapse of the youth labour market in the late 1970s and 1980s, but also given a strong impetus by the introduction in 1986 of the General Certificate of Secondary Education (GCSE), sat by school leavers for the first time in 1988. Third, opportunities to enter full-time employment at the minimum school leaving age, particularly via traditional apprenticeship routes, have contracted in parallel. At certain times these opportunities have been replaced by mass-participation government training schemes, such as the Youth Training Scheme and similar programmes which proliferated during the 1980s. Fourth, increased staying-on rates have been accompanied by credential inflation, whereby the worth attributed to qualifications has been systematically devalued, in turn fuelling demand for ever higher qualification levels. These factors are all important in understanding the changing contexts within which our sample members first left school, as well as for understanding the labour market contexts in which they found themselves when we met them.

In considering these changing contexts, Roberts' earlier work on the main school to work trajectories experienced by school leavers prior to the late 1980s, by which time most of our core sample had completed their compulsory schooling, is useful. Roberts (1993) has argued that prior to the rapid rise in youth unemployment from the late 1970s onwards there had been two dominant career routes: a minority of young people – academic high-flyers mainly from middle-class families – would continue in education until at least 18, whilst most started work at 16. These divergent routes are clearly discernible amongst the members of our full sample who left school during this period, with the few who continued beyond compulsory schooling coming from more affluent backgrounds where a tradition of staying on already existed to varying degrees.

Roberts argued that by the late 1980s these two dominant trajectories had been supplanted by a proliferation of options, but it was nonetheless possible to discern three main routes: those based on academic success at 18 or beyond, leading to high-level employment opportunities; those based on transitions into 'good' but not 'top' jobs, which offered average or better pay and conditions, and which increasingly required at least some period of post-compulsory education or participation in higher status government training schemes, or indeed both; and those marked by movement in and out of unemployment, insecure and low paid employment and low status government training schemes. Roberts argued that these different routes were highly stratified:

> [A]ccess was governed by the same predictors that had governed opportunities previously – sex, educational attainment – with social class origins lurking in the background – and places of residence. Beneath all the changes the old predictors remained in excellent working order.
>
> *(Roberts 1993: 237)*

Again, these different routes – and their highly stratified nature – are clearly visible amongst the members of our broader network sample who left school during this later period, with the school to work pathways of our *core* sample members at this same time tending to be characterized by Roberts' second route, into 'good' jobs. This reflects their moderately qualified status: our core sample members might not have been high-flyers on leaving school, but neither were they amongst the group experiencing the most challenging transitional experiences during this period.

Table 3.1 summarizes the post-compulsory pathways of our core sample members, the entry points, the oldest of whom completed compulsory schooling in 1959 and the youngest of whom did so in 2002. Most completed their schooling between

TABLE 3.1 Post-compulsory pathways of the 16 entry points

Male entry point individuals

Adam Vale: left grammar school in 1960, aged 15, to become an articled clerk in an accountancy firm.

John Steers: left technical school in 1970, aged 15, to take up an engineering apprenticeship.

David Upton: left comprehensive school in 1970, aged 15, for a full-time job as a survey cartographer.

Andrew Gregory: left comprehensive school in 1976, aged 16, to take up a shipbuilding apprenticeship.

Adrian Ward: left comprehensive school in 1981, aged 16, to take up a shipbuilding apprenticeship.

John Hanley: transferred from comprehensive school to FE college in 1989, aged 16; started A levels but left during first year to take up a boatbuilding apprenticeship.

Jamil Masuka: transferred from comprehensive school to FE college in 2000, aged 16; started A levels, but left during first year to pursue a full-time job in a maritime company.

Female entry point individuals

Margaret Ash: transferred from secondary modern school to a secretarial college in 1959, aged 15, to take an O level. Left at 16.

Hilary Edwards: transferred from private boarding school to finishing school in Europe in 1959, aged 15. Took an A level and two O levels in one year, followed by a year at a private secretarial college.

Linda Dixon: stayed on in the sixth form of her secondary modern school in 1966, aged 15, to study for secretarial qualifications.

Clare Randall: transferred from secondary modern school to grammar school sixth form in 1969, aged 15. Took A levels, then attended secretarial college for a year at 17.

Liz Drew: left comprehensive school in 1975, aged 16, to take up a full-time job as a bank clerk.

Lorraine Smith: transferred from comprehensive school to secretarial college in 1976, aged 16.

Rosie Armstrong: left comprehensive school in 1988, aged 16, to take up a place on a secretarial Youth Training Scheme.

Joanna Sharpe: transferred from comprehensive school to FE college in 1991, aged 16, to study for diplomas in IT, business and secretarial studies.

Helen John: transferred from comprehensive school to FE college in 2002, aged 16, to take A levels.

the late 1960s and the early 1990s. Overall, seven people left school at the minimum leaving age, whilst nine stayed on for varying periods of time, including two who dropped out before completing their post-compulsory studies. The gendered nature of these pathways is particularly striking. With the exception of Helen John, who is considerably younger than the other female sample members, the early pathways of the women were dominated by secretarial, administrative and clerical occupations and/or training. During the period when most of them left school, such pathways were widely regarded as 'respectable' routes into employment for young women from both upper working-class and more middle-class backgrounds, including those with A levels. In contrast, their male counterparts followed pathways into male-dominated industries, often via apprenticeship routes offering on-the-job training. Again, these were respectable routes for young men – the majority – who left school at the minimum school leaving age (as most did). These highly gender-polarized post-school routes were, then, very typical of their time, as revealed by classic transition studies of this period such as those by Veness (1962), Carter (1966), Corrigan (1979), Griffin (1985), Cockburn (1987) and Hollands (1990).

As we will explore further in subsequent chapters, our respondents' own accounts often suggested that their post-school pathways unfolded with little active decision-making of their own. Instead, they often complied with the expectations of their parents and other family members, as well as those of their teachers, expectations which they largely took for granted as being appropriate to 'someone like me'. Liz Drew, for example, left school with a clutch of CSEs in the mid-1970s. She acquired a clerical position in a high street bank through the intervention of her father, a senior cashier in that same bank, as did her younger sister three years later. Andrew Gregory told a similar story of parental influence. Along with most of his peers, he had been steered towards an apprenticeship on first leaving school in 1976: 'they said, "get a trade and you'll have a job for life".' Two options had been available, both with large local employers: an engineering apprenticeship or a shipbuilding apprenticeship. He chose the latter, largely because his father and two uncles already worked there, and he had remained there ever since.

Others initially followed the expected route before a later self-initiated change of direction. For Clare Randall, for example, the completion of compulsory schooling in 1969 was the point at which her mother – against Clare's own wishes – insisted she transfer from her secondary modern school to the sixth form of the local grammar school. Clare's mother was a teacher, her grandmother a retired head teacher and her older sister had already entered the teaching profession. Clare felt under pressure to apply for teacher training on completing her A levels but had instead transferred to secretarial college and had subsequently gained a secretarial post in a bank, a fairly common route for a young middle-class woman during this period. Clare said that she now had some regrets about having rejected teaching, but at the time it had seemed important to her to assert her independence:

> Because I didn't get on with my mother and I didn't want to be like my mother, I suppose, so I just said 'no I'm not going into teaching, I am going to go and do secretarial'. And the whole idea when I did secretarial was that I would join the Foreign Office and I would travel . . . But then I sort of got married, and . . . it all went out of the window. It all sort of went out of the window then, which was very stupid. Anyway, there we go, another story.
>
> *(Clare)*

In similar defiance of his parents, who had hoped that he would stay on to take A levels, Adam Vale had left grammar school at the earliest opportunity in 1960, moving straight into employment. Despite Adam viewing this as rebellion, it is striking that the options he considered were still firmly in line with his middle-class family background (his father worked in insurance, his mother was a head teacher):

> At that time it was go into a bank, erm, or accountancy, or perhaps become a solicitor or something, and become articled to any of those, and in the end I decided – or *they* (laughs) decided for me to become an articled clerk at a chartered accountants.
>
> *(Adam)*

The position involved a five-year training programme, but after only eighteen months Adam had dismayed his parents even further by joining the Navy, an action which he described in terms of taking control of his own life for the first time. Whilst Adam has never regretted this change of direction, he nonetheless noted that he had 'already apologized to (my mother) many times since that I didn't take the opportunity that was given me'. Like Clare Randall, then, Adam Vale had remained conscious throughout his life that he had acted against the expectations of his family, and that this had come at a cost to his family, if not to himself.

What is interesting to note in relation to both Adam and Clare's experiences is that their actions in refusing to conform to their parents' expectations nonetheless led to the reproduction of strongly gendered and classed trajectories into the labour market. This accords with Connidis and McMullen's approach to 'structured ambivalence' which we introduced earlier in this chapter. According to Connidis and McMullen, individuals experience ambivalence when social structures constrain their ability to exercise individual agency in the negotiation of their interpersonal relationships, with ambivalence then becoming 'a catalyst for social action', either to reproduce the existing social order or to bring about change: 'When framed this way, ambivalence can be a bridging concept between social structure and individual action, made evident in social interaction' (2002: 559). The actions of both Adam and Clare are examples of what Luscher (2005: 106) has described as 'captivation', based on a divergence from the outlook and values of their parents alongside the reluctant reproduction of traditional social forms: 'the guiding maxim here is to "conserve reluctantly"'. In contrast, the actions of Liz and Andrew, above, are examples of 'solidarity', based on a convergence of outlook alongside a desire to reproduce traditional social forms: 'the maxim of action can be characterized as "to preserve consensually"' (Luscher 2005: 106).

Subsequent progression to Level 3

Having considered the initial post-compulsory pathways of core sample members, we now consider their subsequent acquisition of Level 3 qualifications. It is once again critical to understand each person's positioning in relation to the policy regimes which they experienced at key points in their lives and the range of opportunities which were therefore available to them as members of particular cohorts (their location in time and space). These opportunities, and their own motivations for pursuing them, have changed with their increasing age (the timing of lives), demonstrating the interaction of chronological age and cohort membership across the life course. This not only reflects shifting policy regimes and opportunity structures, but also the way in which the more independent they became of their families of origin the more active they felt themselves able to be in taking control of their own lives (human agency), rather than conforming to the expectations of others (linked lives). Their accounts nonetheless continue to reflect strongly gendered and classed norms, as we shall demonstrate.

The 16 core sample members may be categorized into four broad groupings in relation to their experiences of progression: those who gained their Level 3 qualifications through staying on after the end of compulsory schooling; those who gained them through apprenticeship routes pursued straight from school; those who gained them in their early twenties in order to ensure early continued career progression; and those who gained them after the age of thirty, as mature learners. Two of the sample members who obtained a Level 3 qualification in their late teens had also gained a second Level 3 qualification later in their lives. We consider these different groupings in turn.

Qualifications gained through staying on in full-time education

Four women gained their Level 3 qualifications by staying on beyond compulsory schooling for at least a year. Clare Randall and Helen John – who left school thirty years apart – had both stayed on for a further two years in order to take A levels in line with parental expectations, but both with some degree of ambivalence. Clare's unhappiness about having to change school to do this was described above, as was her subsequent transfer to a secretarial college after completing her A levels, a common route at a time when relatively few young people continued on into HE. Helen had also been persuaded by her mother to stay on, despite lacking a clear sense of direction, which she partly attributed to the death of her father – a medical doctor – whilst she was in her mid-teens. For Helen's mother, a nurse, it was unthinkable that Helen might leave full-time education without first gaining A levels at the very least. Such concerns reflect how staying on had become the norm by the time Helen had finished compulsory schooling in 2002, and in particular how very unusual it would have been for a young woman from Helen's social class background to reject this route. Helen had left further education (FE) college in 2004 with two A levels, at a time when most similarly qualified young people were progressing into HE, as indeed her older sister had done before her. Her withdrawal from further full-time study at this point made her relatively unusual amongst her peers, especially those from a similar social class background.

Joanna Sharpe was amongst the first cohort to take the new GCSE examinations in 1988. Despite gaining eight good passes, she had not considered herself sufficiently clever to pursue A levels. Believing that her subsequent employment options would be limited if she left school at 16, and being particularly anxious to avoid following her mother into shop work, she had decided to enrol at the local FE college to study for diplomas in IT, business and secretarial studies. This was achieved without active encouragement from her parents, who lacked first-hand knowledge or experience of post-compulsory education and who, as Joanna described, had relatively low aspirations for her:

> I mean they're good people, but they, they really weren't interested, really. They used to say to me, well, erm, 'as long as you do your best love', that sort of thing. They're not, they weren't like pushy though, which I respect them for. But erm, but also equally I don't think they thought that sometimes if you give people a push they might achieve more . . . You know they never, never discussed the possibility of A levels or university. I'd talk about some careers and they'd say 'well, love, you have to be clever to do that'. Which gives you the impression that you're not. Which I think is a shame.
>
> *Joanna*

This comment highlights the dominant disposition towards education in Joanna's family, which remained unchallenged by Joanna's GCSE success. Despite her achievements, Joanna's parents lacked confidence that a child of their own might be academically able, and had little understanding of how Joanna's achievements might relate to the range of available post-16 opportunities. It was through her own actions alone that Joanna had opened up an 'imaginary future' for herself, even then characterized by relatively modest aspirations in relation to her GCSE success.

Hilary Edwards had been born in the mid-1940s into an upper middle-class naval family. She had attended boarding school throughout her secondary years, with the expectation that she would marry early (which she in fact did) and would therefore not have to worry about a career. Nonetheless, her parents were unhappy for her to leave school at 15, so had sent Hilary to an overseas finishing school where she had obtained one A level and two further O levels, followed by attendance at a prestigious London secretarial college. For Hilary, and unlike Clare and Helen, staying on was not linked to parental ambition; on the contrary, it was a way of occupying her until marriage, although her parents conceded that her additional qualifications gave her 'something to fall back on' should she ever need to support herself. Commenting on the inevitability of her pathway, Hilary noted stoically that 'we did what we did because that's what one did'!

Qualifications linked to apprenticeships and government training schemes pursued straight from school

Four men had gained their Level 3 qualifications via apprenticeships and government training schemes, all four attaining City and Guilds vocational qualifications by day release. Three of the men – Andrew Gregory, Adrian Ward and John Steers – had gained their Level 3 qualifications in their late teens and early twenties as part of the engineering apprenticeships which they had entered on first leaving school in the 1970s. This pathway strongly reflected their shared social positioning; all were from working-class backgrounds where a transition into an apprenticeship with a local employer was the expected post-school route for young men with modest educational achievements, albeit a route which offered possibilities for promotion and career progression. For all three, an apprenticeship had seemed like a reasonable route to pursue, in line with their own expectations as well as those of their parents and teachers. Andrew Gregory, as previously noted, had received little encourage-ment to aim high whilst at school, with the general advice from teachers being to 'get a trade, and you'll have a job for life'; accordingly, he had gained an apprenticeship with a major shipbuilding company. For Adrian Ward, pursuing an apprenticeship had been a means of biding time until old enough to join the police force, but as he had enjoyed the work he had remained with his employer ever since, as had Andrew Gregory. As for John Steers, the oldest of the three men, gaining an apprenticeship had actually exceeded his father's low expectations of him: he had repeatedly told John that he would probably end up as a builder's labourer. John Hanley, the youngest of the four men, left school in 1988, by which time post-16 staying-on rates had increased dramatically due to rising youth unemployment and the collapse of traditional apprenticeships. He had initially started an A level course at FE college, but had felt out of place, believing his fellow students to be far more academically motivated than he was, so had left to pursue a boat-building apprenticeship.

Qualifications gained in the early twenties linked to occupational progression

Two others gained their Level 3 qualifications in their early twenties to satisfy a desire for career progression in their chosen occupational fields. Linda Dixon had left school in the mid-1960s following a year in post-compulsory education when, in accordance with her parents' wishes but with some ambivalence, she had pursued a secretarial qualification. She had subsequently entered the library service as a library assistant, against the advice of her parents and her careers teacher, and had eventually been given the opportunity to study for a City and Guilds qualification in Library Assistantship, which she completed in her early twenties. Jamil Masuka, who left compulsory schooling over thirty years later than Linda, had a few false starts before discovering his vocation. He had dropped out of his A levels, and had then worked for a local company before gaining employment as a bricklayer. It was in this role that Jamil was given the opportunity to pursue an apprenticeship in the building industry. This had allowed him eventually to acquire NVQs at Levels 2 and 3, gaining the latter via an Advanced Apprenticeship in his early twenties. For both Linda and Jamil, the attainment of Level 3 qualifications was linked to a desire to achieve progression within jobs which they already had, on the basis that without additional qualifications they would have been unable to progress further or gain promotions.

Qualifications gained as mature learners

The six remaining core sample members had gained their Level 3 qualifications in their thirties or beyond, as mature learners, some considerable time after first completing their full-time education. Liz Drew and David Upton had pursued these qualifications as part of ongoing progression within their established jobs, whilst Margaret Ash, Lorraine Smith, Rosie Armstrong and Adam Vale had pursued them as a means of making themselves more employable in alternative contexts to the ones in which they found themselves at the time.

We noted above that Liz Drew, who had left school in the early 1970s, had initially gained employment with the same bank which employed her father, before subsequently moving to London to work for an international bank. When we met Liz, she had been working in childcare for ten years, most recently as a lead practitioner in a local pre-school. In her previous job, in a nursery, she had been invited to pursue an NVQ 3 in Early Years Childcare, as part of the general drive to increase the skills level within the childcare workforce. The experience of returning to learning in her mid-forties had been a revelation to her and a great confidence booster. By then her two children were in their early teens, so less demanding of her time than if she had returned to study earlier. This was important, as her partner, who had health problems, was not the most supportive of individuals.

David Upton had been unusual amongst his peers in leaving school at 15, as most had continued into both further and higher education. However, he had not enjoyed school, so had found work with a major local employer as a survey cartographer. Thirty-five years later, David was still with the same company, having gradually progressed through the ranks. As part of his career progression, he had been encouraged to pursue further qualifications by day release, and in his mid-thirties had studied part-time (via block release over a two-year period) for a BTEC National in Surveying and Cartography. Gaining this particular qualification alongside an A level in surveying had been essential for promotion, so he had pursued this route with enthusiasm, but not without a struggle in relation to juggling his time between work, study and his young family.

In contrast to Liz and David, Lorraine Smith, Margaret Ash, Rosie Armstrong and Adam Vale had chosen to return to study independently of their employment status, as a means of making themselves more employable in anticipation of a change of direction. Following several years of ill health and poor attendance, Lorraine had left school at 16 with a clutch of CSEs. She had gained secretarial qualifications and then worked in a succession of secretarial jobs. By her late twenties, she was in an unhappy marriage with two young children, and decided to return to study as both a bid for freedom and independence and an opportunity to prove herself educationally. Gaining a BTEC National Certificate in Business and Finance represented a turning point in Lorraine's life, giving her the confidence 'to believe I was clever and to apply for better jobs . . . it definitely took away that second-class citizen feel and gave me more options'. Lorraine's return to study was, then, primarily motivated by personal transformation rather than a desire for further progression.

Margaret Ash's story is not dissimilar. Margaret had left school in 1959 with one O level, gaining a second O level at college the following year along with shorthand and typing qualifications, and a third in her twenties. By her thirties, she was the mother of a small boy and had a part-time clerical post, having worked in personnel management prior to motherhood. In her mid-thirties Margaret had a kidney transplant, leading to much improved health following a long history of renal problems, and causing her to reconsider her direction in life. She decided that she would like to train as a speech therapist, having gained insight into this occupation through her son's hearing impairment. Margaret had subsequently gained a place on a two-year Access course, studying history of art, sociology, computer science and literature. This was hugely challenging and enjoyable, even though she did not subsequently pursue speech therapy: 'I think it was the fulfilment of something that you know I hadn't done before and the camaraderie with other people of a similar age'. She noted that her husband had been very supportive of her during this period and that she in turn had supported him when, some years later, he had started a degree in his fifties.

Rosie Armstrong had left school in 1988, with eight GCSEs, in line with both her parents' expectations that she would find work and her own desire to earn some money. Reflecting the paucity of options available to school leavers during this period, Rosie had been unable to find full-time employment, so had gained a place on the Youth Training Scheme, where she pursued a clerical route and studied for a Level 2 City and Guilds in Office Work by day release. She later left work to raise five children and in her early thirties, encouraged by staff at the 'Family Learning Centre' attached to her children's school, she had returned to study to 'keep her mind active' and had obtained several qualifications, culminating in a Level 3 qualification, a certificate in teaching adults.

Finally, Adam Vale gained a BTEC National Certificate in his late thirties, following a career in the Navy. Having joined up as a pay clerk, he had subsequently trained as a computer programmer and then as a computer analyst, working in these roles until leaving the Navy at the age of 40. In order to enhance his post-Navy employability, Adam had pursued a part-time BTEC National in Business Administration at a local FE college, and had subsequently gained employment in a post which combined his new knowledge and his established computing skills. Adam had been very pleasantly surprised at how well he had done on the course, to the point that it had made him reconsider what he might have been capable of if he had stayed on at 16:

> I enjoyed doing it, and I did very well with it, I came out with a distinction at the end of it . . . If I had done a bit more at school and stayed on to do A levels, and gone to university – but you know, that was water under the bridge.
>
> (Adam)

Adam also noted that his initial belief that he had got the job because of his BTEC qualification was incorrect; it transpired that he had been employed on the basis of his IT skills and armed forces background and that his employer didn't even know what a BTEC was!

Two other core sample members – John Hanley and Joanna Sharpe – had also obtained a *second* Level 3 qualification in their thirties in addition to those they had acquired earlier in their lives. John, who had gained his initial Level 3 qualification as part of his boat-building apprenticeship, had acquired his second Level 3 qualification, a Diploma in Management, the year before we met him, at the age of 33. He had pursued this route in order to qualify for promotion: as he put it, 'I'm not one to go and get all these qualifications for various things if I don't feel the need'. Lastly, Joanna had acquired a further Level 3 qualification in Office Administration in her early thirties as part of her career development within the NHS, her employer since leaving full-time education.

Level 3 to Level 4?

A key theme running through nearly all of these accounts is a desire to gain additional qualifications at Level 3 primarily in order to improve one's employability, whether in seeking a first job, gaining promotion in an existing job or contemplating a change of career, alongside a desire for personal challenge and self-development (particularly amongst those who had returned to study as older learners). Relatively few of the core sample members had been motivated by a desire for progression to higher level qualifications, whether at the point of applying for their course, during the course of their studies or even subsequently. To some considerable extent this reflects the rather different times in which many of our core sample members had first gained their qualifications: when Level 3 qualifications were more likely to be an end in themselves rather than a means to an end, and when they gave ready access to the sorts of employment opportunities which, in the context of credential infla- tion, are now increasingly only available to those with higher level qualifications.

So what role, if any, had potential progression to HE played in the earlier Level 3 decision-making of our core sample members? Only one individual – Margaret Ash – appeared to have had explicit plans for further progression underpinning her initial motivation for Level 3 study, having opted in the early 1980s to do an Access course quite explicitly as a means of gaining entry qualifications for a speech therapy degree. However, as her studies progressed, her interests had changed, and she had firstly considered studying history of art and then considered a degree in computing. In the event, she had instead used her new knowledge of computing to go into business with her husband, providing computer software training. Commenting on the abandonment of her initial speech therapy plans in favour of this route, she noted that

> Well because *obviously* I had a family and it meant you know, there were only places in Leicester or London and you know with a family I found that it, you know I probably couldn't have coped with it. And the interest came about really that you know having bought a computer during that time and getting

into the software, it just seemed a more logical conclusion and I enjoyed that part of it. [emphasis added]

(Margaret)

Margaret's use of the word 'obviously' is particularly interesting, suggesting a common sense assumption that pursuing HE is probably inappropriate when someone has a young family, even though this had been a central motivation when she had first started her Access course. Margaret did not specifically invoke her status as a mother here, rather she refers to her status as someone 'with a family', but it is striking that similar and frequent comments about the constraining impact of parenthood were made only by the women in our core sample.

Two other women – Lorraine Smith and Liz Drew – stated that transition to HE had not entered into their thinking at all when they had first started their Level 3 courses, yet during the course of their studies they had become increasingly aware of the possibilities available to them. Ultimately, though, they had chosen not to pursue them. As noted earlier, Lorraine Smith had returned to education in her late twenties in large part in order to gain a sense of independence and freedom in the context of a disintegrating marriage. She had been encouraged by her tutors to consider a degree in sociology and economics, which she had 'looked into it very vaguely', but 'the course for that was in Cardiff which was even further away and I was still a mum and a wife and that was about when the divorce started'. Feeling that the timing was really bad, she nonetheless made enquiries about options for studying with the Open University, but noted that:

> [B]y then I'd almost decided that I didn't want to do it . . . Even if I got through a course do I really want the stress and responsibility of a responsible job or do I want to sit back and be told what to do at work and come home and make all the decisions in the rest of my life or not? . . . And that's the way I went and that's what I'm happy with.

(Lorraine)

On completing her NVQ 3 in Early Years Childcare, Liz Drew had similarly given some thought to the possibility of further progression, in this case to an NVQ 4. She had even attended an open day to find out more:

> So we went to an open evening and of course . . . it's almost like, I don't know if it's mini brainwashing or the way they do it, but I came away very inspired and for a week I thought 'yes, this is it, this is it'. And then it just fell away very quickly and I thought 'I really can't be bothered. I really can't be bothered with this'. . . But anyway, that's fallen by the wayside at the moment but I would never say 'never', so . . .

(Liz)

Liz's disenchantment coincided with a series of difficulties at work, which added to her lack of motivation, and by the end of the research Liz had left her job as a pre-school lead practitioner and was hoping to return to her old job – one with fewer responsibilities – at a nursery. To a degree this also reflected her ambivalence about acquiring additional responsibilities: she was very conscious that NVQ 4 was essentially a management qualification, a role which she emphatically did not want. We also noted above that Liz lacks a supportive partner, which has also been an important consideration in her general career deliberations. As her sister, Nichola, told us:

> I think with Liz erm . . . you know, I think she would like to [continue studying], but I think you know, I don't know if she necessarily gets the support from the family, that's the thing . . . And I think that's a real shame because she, you know, she is perfectly, you know, she is an intelligent girl but maybe she's not always had the opportunities . . .
>
> *(Nichola Machin, Liz Drew's sister)*

Amongst our 16 core sample members, then, only three people – all women – had given any thought either prior to or during their Level 3 studies to the possibility of using their Level 3 qualification to facilitate progression to Level 4. That is not to say that other sample members had not *subsequently* considered the possibility of progression, and the stories of these individuals – Rosie Armstrong, Joanna Sharpe, Jamil Masuka and John Steers, all of whom were musing on the possibility of Level 4 participation at the point at which we met them – are considered in later chapters. For the rest of our core sample members, though, the potential pursuit of HE had not been in their minds at the time at which they had acquired their Level 3 qualifications – nor indeed had it been subsequently, with most feeling that potential participation at Level 4 had little relevance to their current lifestyles. Most were by now living relatively comfortable and settled lives and did not see how returning to higher level study might be of value to them, despite being more than happy to pursue courses at lower or equal levels to their Level 3 qualifications.

These perceptions are inevitably shaped by the opportunity structures which had shaped their own earlier school to work transitions. For many of the older members of our core sample, their earlier acquisition of Level 3 qualifications had provided them with the career opportunities and trajectories that, under current labour market conditions, are increasingly perceived to be available only to younger people with Level 4 qualifications. David Upton, for example, who was in his early fifties when we first met him, had entered work straight from school at 15, and through subsequently obtaining a BTEC National qualification had gradually worked his way up to a management position. Such opportunities for internal progression, he argued, were no longer available in his workplace, with the emphasis now being on the recruitment of graduates from outside of the organization. David was aware that any additional promotions would now require a degree but, as subsequent promotion could not be guaranteed, he felt that it would not be a good investment of his time. Critically, he had now achieved everything he wanted to achieve in career terms and wished to focus his energies on his family and other non-work interests:

'doing HE now would take so much time . . . I'd rather spend the time doing something I enjoy, rather than something that would be seen as a chore!'

Conclusion

Official accounts of educational progression are often characterized today by a strong emphasis on linearity and hierarchical forward movement: that students should study for a Level 2 qualification specifically in order to pursue a Level 3 qualification, in order, in turn, to pursue a Level 4 qualification. This might be a reasonable and desirable policy goal for today's school leavers, and we have already noted the ever-increasing staying-on rates at 16, the already very high rates of progression to university amongst students studying for A levels and the increasing rates of progression to Level 4 amongst those with vocational Level 3 qualifications. In addition, the *Skills for Growth* White Paper (BIS 2009a) set a new target that three-quarters of people should participate in HE or complete an Advanced Apprenticeship or equivalent technician level course (at either Level 3 or 4) by the age of 30. This linear model of progression not only provides little acknowledgement that many people take qualifications for reasons not primarily or necessarily linked to future progression, but also provides little support for those who might wish to pursue additional qualifications at *similar or lower* levels to those which they already possess, which would include older learners wishing to retrain. In line with this emphasis, in 2008 the then Labour government controversially withdrew state subsidy for the pursuit of qualifications in England that are equivalent to or lower than a student's existing highest qualification. Instead, it has chosen to focus its funding on those either entering HE for the first time or progressing to higher qualifications.

However, the stories told in this chapter about individuals' motivations for study at different points across their lives often bear little resemblance to these official conceptualizations of progression, instead revealing a very different set of understandings. The Level 3 qualifications of our core sample members had been pursued usually for very specific purposes and very much as ends in themselves, whilst equal or greater value was subsequently placed on the acquisition of both lower and equal qualifications, with little emphasis placed on 'upward' progression. This last point is explored further in Chapter 7, which highlights the generally positive disposition of our core sample members towards learning *per se*, including both formal and informal learning opportunities across the life course.

It is also worth noting that there was a considerable degree of confusion amongst our sample members (and also at times, it has to be admitted, within the research team!) as to how different types of qualification map on to the current National Qualifications Framework. In particular, it was not always very clear whether a particular qualification – especially those which pre-dated the National Qualifications Framework – counted as Level 3 equivalent. Core sample members were not therefore necessarily aware that their highest qualification would in principle allow them access to HE. Yet members of our core sample form part of the key target audience for 'upskilling' the workforce over the next decade or so, in pursuit of the

Leitch Review's goal that 40 per cent of the adult workforce should have at least Level 4 qualifications by 2020. Our evidence suggests that the agencies who will be expected to deliver on this target will face considerable challenges in meeting it, not least because of the disjuncture between the expectations of progression and the specific opportunity structures experienced by many older employees when they were first in formal education, and the culture of progression and opportunity structures which are now dominant within the UK.

4

THE IMPACT OF SCHOOL EXPERIENCE ON PROGRESSION DECISIONS

Felix Maringe, Brenda Johnston,
Alison Fuller and Sue Heath

This chapter examines the 'legacy effects' of compulsory schooling on three members of our sample who had experienced their secondary schooling under contrasting educational policy regimes. It builds on the previous chapter through considering not only the effects of generational positioning on *individual* decision-making about educational progression, but also through exploring the shared experiences of network members located in specific historical moments and how their specific generational perspectives affected the decision-making of those around them. The three case studies – based on the experiences of Linda Dixon, Lorraine Smith and Jamil Masuka, whom we introduced in the previous chapter, and selected members of their networks – also powerfully demonstrate the impact of social class and gender on educational decision-making.

Linda, Lorraine and Jamil experienced their compulsory schooling under contrasting policy regimes in England: respectively, the later years of the post-1944 selective tripartite system; the early years of the comprehensive system which followed; and the diversified system which emerged in the wake of the 1988 Education Reform Act. Each regime was characterized by distinct opportunity structures and expectations of progression, strongly shaped not only by specific education policies but also by structural inequalities within society. In this introductory section we provide a brief overview of some of the key characteristics of the contrasting policy regimes experienced by Linda, Lorraine and Jamil, before moving on to consider their first-hand experiences in more detail.

Linda Dixon completed her secondary schooling in the late 1960s. This was a period when many Local Education Authorities (LEAs) had already moved over to the comprehensive system of secondary schooling (see below), but secondary provision in Linda's locality was still based on the tripartite system which had been ushered in by the landmark 1944 Education Act. The Act had established the principle of free, compulsory secondary schooling, with provision based on a selective three-tier system consisting largely of grammar schools and secondary modern schools, alongside a smaller number of technical schools. Grammar schools provided an academic curriculum, preparing pupils for 'professional and good white-collar jobs' while secondary modern schools provided a more practical curriculum targeted at children 'whose future employment will not demand any measure of technical skills or knowledge' (Ministry of Education 1945: 13, cited in Tomlinson 2005: 16). Grammar schools were attended by approximately a fifth of children in the 1950s and early to mid 1960s, with most other children attending secondary moderns. Allocation to these different types of school depended on a child's performance in the much criticized 11-Plus examination, upon which depended not just their secondary schooling but their likely employment pathways. Linda Dixon sat, and failed, the 11-Plus; her secondary school years were accordingly spent at her local secondary modern school.

Despite supposed 'parity of esteem' between the different sectors, secondary modern schools were poorly resourced in comparison with grammar schools and tended to employ less well qualified teachers. There were also stark differences in terms of the credentials available to pupils in the different types of schools, which affected their opportunities for future progression. From 1951, grammar school pupils were allowed to sit General Certificate of Education (GCE) Ordinary level (O levels) examinations, and by 1962 16 per cent of children obtained five GCE O levels or equivalent at the end of their compulsory schooling. The GCE was the passport for entry to Advanced level (A levels) examinations and, in turn, potential entry to university, although only around 5 per cent of young people progressed into higher education (HE) during the 1950s, rising to around 8 per cent in the early 1960s (Tomlinson 2005: 217). In contrast, secondary modern pupils were issued with a school leaving certificate, essentially proof of attendance rather than of accomplishment. In protest at this inequity, many secondary modern head teachers began to enter pupils for GCE examinations, resulting in the introduction of the relatively undemanding Certificate of Secondary Education (CSE) in 1962. By the time Linda came to leave school later in the decade, some pupils were officially permitted to sit GCE examinations as well, although Linda was not amongst them.

Post-compulsory progression throughout this period was largely based on gender-demarcated pathways (Bynner *et al.* 1997). These gendered demarcations reflected a secondary curriculum which was based on the assumption that, whilst boys should be actively prepared for a lifetime of paid employment, girls' primary vocational concerns – probably following a short period of immediate post-school employment – related to marriage and domesticity (Ministry of Education 1963). As we shall see, these assumptions very much shaped the expectations of Linda's teachers and parents, causing great frustration not only to Linda, but also to her grammar school-educated older sister.

In addition to ongoing gender inequalities, educational opportunities in the post-war era also remained profoundly shaped by social class (Furlong 2009). Far from promoting equality and social mobility, critics argued that the tripartite system had failed to deliver on its promise of a meritocratic transformation of opportunities for all. Grammar schools were disproportionately populated by pupils from middle-class family backgrounds, whilst the relatively small numbers of working-class pupils who entered the grammar schools often found the experience to be extremely alienating (Jackson and Marsden 1962; Lacey 1970). Tomlinson (2005: 218) has also highlighted the deference of many working-class families who perceived education to be 'not for the likes of us', an attitude which declined only gradually over the course of the twentieth century.

Criticism of the tripartite system grew in the decades after 1944. The 11-Plus examination was widely criticized for being culturally biased towards middle-class children, and for favouring boys (who performed less well than girls at 11) through differentiated pass marks to ensure broadly equal numbers of boys and girls in the grammar school sector. Numerous studies also demonstrated problems with assessing academic capability at the age of 11, making it difficult to argue that intelligence was genetically inherited and stable throughout life (Chitty 2009; Tomlinson 2005). Rather, environment was increasingly accepted as playing a significant role in the development of intelligence (e.g. Newsom Report, Ministry of Education 1963; Pedley 1978). The differentiated system of public examinations also reinforced class inequalities through directing pupils towards substantially different opportunities. By the 1960s, further pressures had mounted, as it became clear that higher levels of education were necessary to support economic growth. There was also a growing middle-class backlash led by parents whose children had failed to get into grammar schools and who were increasingly discontented with the secondary modern sector.

In 1965, the Labour government instructed LEAs to draw up plans for comprehensivization, whereby children of all abilities would be educated in the same local school, and by the mid-1970s the majority of LEAs had introduced comprehensive schools. Lorraine Smith, whose experiences of secondary education in the 1970s form the focus of the second case study in this chapter, was part of the last cohort in her LEA to sit the 11-Plus examination. Like Linda Dixon she failed, but at the end of her first year of secondary schooling her secondary modern school merged with the local grammar school to form a new comprehensive school. Mergers of this kind and the subsequent end to academic selection led to a situation where it became more usual for children of different social classes to attend the same school. Nonetheless, pupils from different backgrounds were often segregated *within* comprehensive schools through the practices of streaming and setting by ability, especially in the later years of secondary schooling (Furlong 2009: 345; Sukhnandan and Lee 1998). In Lorraine's school, for example, former grammar school pupils automatically entered Band One (the GCE route) while former secondary modern pupils automatically entered Band Two (the CSE route). Those in Band Two could move to Band One and take GCEs if they were good at maths, English and French.

In 1970, 47 per cent of pupils still left school without qualifications (Tomlinson 2005: 217). In 1972, the school leaving age was raised to 16 to give all pupils the opportunity to sit public examinations. By 1976 boys and girls were achieving equally in terms of attaining five or more A to C grades at O level or the equivalent at CSE (Tomlinson 2005: 196). Yet girls remained under-represented in mathematics, science and technical subjects and over-represented in arts and domestic subjects (Pratt *et al.*1984). Although it was frequently argued that this reflected girls' own 'choices', timetabling practices, careers advice and teacher direction invariably reinforced this trend (Pratt 1984). As a consequence, school leavers of the 1970s continued to follow highly gender-differentiated post-compulsory pathways (Griffin 1985; Sharpe 1976). As we shall see, Lorraine was no exception to this pattern.

As noted in Chapter 3, most of our 16 entry point individuals experienced their secondary schooling under either the tripartite system of the 1950s and 1960s or the comprehensive system of the 1970s and 1980s. Only three had experienced some or all of their secondary schooling in the years following the Conservative government's 1988 Education Reform Act (ERA), including Jamil Masuka, whose experiences form the basis of the third case study included in this chapter. The 1988 Act ushered in reforms which included the marketization of education through the mechanism of parental choice and the establishment of central government control over curriculum and assessment. The introduction of this market-led education system, increasingly played out against a backdrop of secondary school diversification (for example the introduction of specialist schools and academies), arguably shifted interest away from equality issues back to concerns over 'standards' and a preoccupation with league table performance. The post-1988 emphasis on 'choice and diversity' has therefore perpetuated a situation where parents do not compete on a level playing field for the most coveted school places, and where pupils from working-class and ethnic minority families are often concentrated in the most poorly resourced and poorly performing schools.

1988 was also the first year in which school leavers sat the new General Certificate of Secondary Education (GCSE) examinations, which replaced the two tier system of GCEs and CSEs. Immediately prior to the introduction of the GCSE, attainment levels had risen to the point where over 80 per cent of school leavers achieved passes in public examinations (Tomlinson 2005: 13). Under the new GCSE regime, virtually all school leavers eventually came to leave school with at least one GCSE pass, with passes graded from A–G. Nonetheless, the 'gold standard' has remained the attainment of at least five A* to C grades, equivalent to the old A to C grades at GCE, and typically it has only been students with these grades who can take A levels. Staying on rates in the post-compulsory sector also increased over the course of the 1980s resulting in higher rates of progression into university. By the late 1980s, around a third of young people continued on into HE; by 2002, more than 40 per cent of the population had participated in HE by the age of 30 (Tomlinson 2005: 13; 217).

The other big story linked to the introduction of GCSEs has been the comparative success of girls relative to boys in attaining five or more A* to C grades. It is important to note that boys' pass rates have also improved since GCSEs were first introduced, but the media has tended to focus on girls' overall higher achievements. The media has also tended to overlook the fact that it is mostly students from white middle-class backgrounds who attain these higher grades, with working-class pupils of both genders and from certain non-white ethnic groups continuing to underperform. By the mid-1990s, 48 per cent of girls were achieving five or more A to C passes compared with 39 per cent of boys (Tomlinson 2005: 196). In 2000, the year that Jamil gained his GCSEs (all at Grade C and above), 55 per cent of all girls and 44 per cent of all boys achieved those higher grades (DfEE 2001). This period also saw the introduction of National Vocational Qualifications (NVQs) based on the accreditation of workplace competence against national occupational standards (Raggat and Williams 1999). After a false start at A level and a period of employment without any formal training, Jamil went on to achieve NVQs at Levels 1, 2 and 3 in bricklaying.

Legacy effects: three case studies

Having briefly outlined some of the key features of the respective policy regimes experienced by Linda, Lorraine and Jamil, we now focus in more detail on their own specific experiences of secondary education in order to explore how these shaped subsequent transitions and educational decision-making, as well as those of their network members. The discussion also explores how themes of gender and social class pervade their accounts.

School selectivity: the experience of Linda Dixon

Linda Dixon's network included 3 family generations and 11 network members (see Figure 4.1). The focus here is on Linda and those of her relatives and friends who had experienced their compulsory schooling during the 1950s and 1960s, when the type of secondary school attended depended on performance in the 11-Plus examination. All the network members described themselves as White British. Some

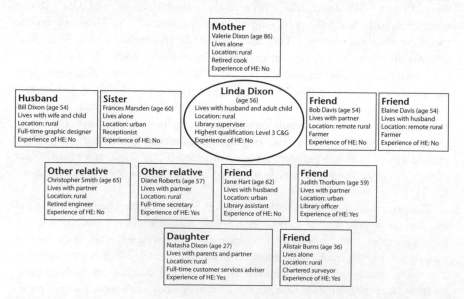

FIGURE 4.1 Linda Dixon's network

described themselves as working class, some as middle class and others said that class was not something they could relate to. Linda described herself as 'sort of upper working class I suppose, if you've got to label it. My parents had their own house'.

Linda attended primary school during the late 1950s and early 1960s. Although in the top stream at primary school, she failed the 11-Plus and remembered that only 'about half' of this 'top stream' passed. Linda suggested that success in the exam was related to children's social background rather than their superior academic ability:

> It really was a class thing . . . very often you would know people that weren't particularly bright at school, but came from the right background, that would end up at the grammar school . . . I presume, you know, it was the parents or . . . People would think 'Well how did they get there?'
>
> *(Linda)*

At secondary school in the mid to late 1960s, Linda was again in the top stream and passed several CSEs at Grade 1 (deemed to be equivalent to an O level pass). She suggested that the level of work had been well within her capabilities:

> I never found the work particularly difficult at secondary school . . . I was always in the higher stream . . . I guess that was better than going to grammar school, where I would have been at the bottom and struggling all the time. Because obviously, it was very academic at the grammar school.
>
> *(Linda)*

Linda perceived that she had no choice in her post-school pathway as decisions were made for her. She recounted a pivotal event when her parents met with the school careers advisor while she waited outside the interview room. Afterwards 'they came out and said . . . "Oh we've decided you're going to . . . do the secretarial course"'. This pathway was undertaken by most of Linda's female peers, yet 'I never wanted to be a secretary . . . you were just channelled into certain areas'. Despite her reluctance, she stayed on[1] to take this one-year course and gained the relevant RSA certificates.

An opportunity arose for Linda to take A levels at this point, as they had been newly introduced at her school, but her parents wanted her to start work. Despite the curtailment of her education, Linda explained that her father had tried to be supportive and had acted in what he believed were her best interests:

> He always encouraged me . . . he was always much more interested in my education than my mother was. And always really chatted to me about school and encouraged me to do my best and really . . . he never made me feel inadequate in any way. He really liked the idea of me doing this secretarial course, he saw me going out and being personal secretary to someone. That's what he thought would be really good.
>
> *(Linda)*

However, Linda's father had different views on his son's education: 'He would have liked my brother to go to university . . . he always used to talk about my brother going, but unfortunately he never went either. He sort of dropped out.'

The youth labour market was still buoyant in the late 1960s and Linda had quickly found work as a library assistant, an occupation in which she had been interested for some time, despite her careers teacher having told her that she would need A levels to secure such a post. Five years later, Linda studied for a City and Guilds qualification in Library Assistantship by day release and, when we first met Linda, she still worked in the library service as a supervisor. Working as a librarian had fitted in with family life, and had provided her with maternity leave and employment conditions which allowed her to fulfil what she saw as her primary roles as wife and mother at the same time as keeping her job: 'Being a wife, mum . . . you cannot be too ambitious, stick to your job and ensure stability in the financial flows . . . let the husband do the ambitious thing, it's not for us, at least not during our time.'

Two themes dominated the accounts of Linda and her peers: the legacy of the 11-Plus and the role of gender in shaping their educational and career expectations. For example, despite failing the 11-Plus, Linda's friend Elaine had achieved four or five CSEs and wanted to go to art college, but had not been given the opportunity. She was expected to get a 'female' job and commented: 'I got a job in the dockyard as a typist . . . and that's what I did . . . because my parents, well my dad at that time influenced you so much that that was what you had to do.'

Another friend of Linda's, Jane Hart, failed her 11-Plus. She nonetheless did well at secondary modern school, sitting and passing six O levels:

> I was a pretty average student at junior school, but once I got to secondary school I seemed to be a late starter. I sort of then went galloping ahead and was in the top group, the top class for O levels . . . so it was probably a good job I hadn't gone to grammar school. I might have floundered a bit there.
>
> (Jane Hart, Linda's friend)

Jane received no encouragement to build on her academic success at 16 and was only expected to consider and pursue standard female occupational choices, such as secretarial work. Like other women of her generation in the network, she has prioritized her family and children; despite a lengthy employment record, she has always worked part-time and has not sought career advancement.

Another network member, Christopher Smith, also failed the 11-Plus, noting that 'you were deemed a failure if you did not pass'. Christopher's experience indicated that post-school trajectories were heavily influenced by expectations that 'secondary modern boys' would enter traditional male apprenticeships in engineering: 'the career advisor I asked was pretty limited . . . [name of town] was an engineering town which was just sort of, if you weren't at grammar school, you know you came out of secondary modern schools, where are you doing your apprenticeship?'

The overwhelming message from these accounts is that during this period young people were channelled into a narrow range of classed and gendered pathways by societal and family norms. Neither were grammar school pupils exempt from these pressures, as illustrated by the case of Linda's sister Frances, who passed the 11-Plus. Frances achieved five O levels and wanted to progress to art college. However, both her father and the art teacher opposed this option and thought it more appropriate for her to obtain office work. According to Frances, the art teacher said: 'I wouldn't advise going to art college; not for girls'. . . 'Not for girls, no'. He said, 'Really, just a career in the Civil Service for a couple of years until they get married probably is the best thing'.

In Linda's view, Frances 'really bears a life-grudge because she was very, very artistic. She really is clever, and she dearly wanted to go to art college'. Instead, Frances had worked as a clerk, in retail and as a doctor's receptionist, providing a secondary income in support of her husband who also had traditional views about maternal and paternal roles and his position as the family 'breadwinner'.

Members of this cohort generation experienced their compulsory education before the school leaving age was raised to 16 in 1972 and when only a minority of young people stayed on. The accounts provided by Linda and her contemporaries represent a group who attained relatively good educational qualifications (broadly equivalent to Level 2 in contemporary terminology), but who were not expected to obtain A levels and progress to university even if they had passed the 11-Plus and attended grammar school. Their trajectories reflect the opportunity structures that were available. Their narratives reveal the limited educational aspirations of the time, particularly for young women, which stand in stark contrast to current patterns of participation whereby female entrants to HE now outnumber males.

Comprehensivization: the experience of Lorraine Smith

Lorraine Smith's network included five family members from three generations who described themselves as White British and as somewhere between middle and working class (see Figure 4.2). Lorraine described herself as having a working-class background (from a council estate, with parents who voted Labour), but now having more middle-class values, which extended to owning her own home. Lorraine had worked mostly in secretarial roles and had achieved a BTEC National Certificate in Business and Finance (equivalent to two A levels) in her early thirties.

Lorraine attended secondary school during her local education authority's transition to comprehensivization in the early 1970s, a process which was completed the year after she had sat – and failed – the 11-Plus. According to Lorraine, because so many children had done well in the examination that year the LEA chose to base their decision in part on prior performance in primary school, not just on the examination results. Lorraine had lost out through this process due to a poor attendance record owing to illness and her grandmother's death, the latter a key and traumatic event in her childhood. Lorraine entered the secondary modern school, only for it to merge a year later with a local grammar school to become a

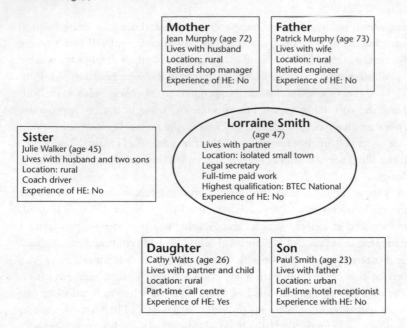

FIGURE 4.2 Lorraine Smith's network

comprehensive. We noted earlier that former pupils of these two schools were placed in separate 'bands' (Bands One and Two, respectively), although those in the lower ability band could move up if they were good at maths, English and French. Despite being competent at maths and English, Lorraine's French was 'appalling', so she remained in the lower band.

Lorraine was a middle-ability pupil who 'just sailed through. I mean I was never brilliant but I was never backward . . . I managed to find a place in the middle of the class and just sit there really'. However, she perceived that the school's primary focus was on Band One pupils and this contributed to a sense of inadequacy. She noted that this focus 'leaves a lot of people feeling like it did me, like a second–class citizen because you can't get jobs without O levels'. This feeling of inferiority was mentioned by Lorraine when she described her delight at gaining further qualifications as an adult, as it had helped dispel her self-perception of being 'second class'.

At 13, Lorraine's schooling was disrupted by curvature of the spine, which meant that she had to wear a traction brace in her teenage years, which she described as 'a torture chamber really'. Lorraine could not wear her uniform as the brace made her two sizes larger, and the school's insistence that she buy a new uniform had led to disputes between the head teacher and her mother. Lorraine had hated secondary school because of the stigma of having to sit CSEs rather than O levels, not having her physical needs recognized and because of her general anger at life. She described how after the mock CSE examinations, a friend was told that she was not permitted to sit CSE Mathematics:

The teacher was one of these that had his six favourite boys in the front of the class sort of attitude and couldn't be bothered to teach the rest of us, so I must admit I took her in hand and she got a Grade 2 and I got a Grade 1 CSE, and we didn't spend a lot of time at school getting it because I suppose it was a way of fighting back, 'We will do this and sod them', that sort of attitude. And very much my teenage years were like that.

(Lorraine)

Lorraine perceived her post-compulsory occupational choices to be constrained by a combination of her low educational attainment and her gender, as well as by family traditions and expectations:

I mean girls that did CSEs were taught to be nurses or secretaries. There weren't career choices really, unless you had a flair and you wanted to be a hairdresser or a beautician, you know . . . there was no going on in education really.

Because really, I mean their generation, Mum was a secretary and an accounts person who grew up, got married and had children, and I think they sort of expected that that's probably what I'd end up doing. And I think the way I was raised that's probably what I thought I'd do as well . . . And actually it's exactly what I did. Yes, so you weren't given great expectations . . . but you made that decision, you never even considered it.

(Lorraine)

Lorraine said that the feelings of inadequacy that stemmed from her schooling had led her to return to study later in life:

It's a confidence issue, isn't it, because a lot of people say you're a second-class citizen. You weren't given any choices or options, there was no way you were taking A levels, going to uni, doing anything. You were sub-standard somehow. It was never said, don't get me wrong . . . but the way life treats you afterwards and the choices you get and the wage packets [make it clear] . . . It's why I went on and did the BTEC. Because when I was 30 I thought 'could I ever have done it?' It's equivalent to a couple of A levels isn't it?

(Lorraine)

Her choice, of course, was influenced by her liking for mathematics and the availability of a part-time college course which she could fit in around child care. Later, Lorraine had an opportunity to enter university but chose not to because of the distance involved, her role and responsibilities as a mother, her unfolding divorce and her ambiguous feelings about formal education (which still remain).

Lorraine's younger sister, Julie, had transferred to the same secondary school as Lorraine, by then a comprehensive. Julie had struggled with reading and writing in primary school and had been in a remedial class. However, she perceived herself to have been of average ability at secondary school, noting that she was part of a peer group that was:

> all sort of average CSE students, so nobody was going to be a high flyer of the people that I was socialising with . . . I wasn't with the ones that were real strugglers that were inclined to rebel and I wasn't with the really clever ones that were gonna get on, we were just this little bunch in the middle somehow.
>
> *(Julie, Lorraine's sister)*

In addition to academic subjects, Julie was also encouraged by her parents to study typing and commerce. They felt that office skills would provide a 'back-up for what I really wanted to do, which was to work with horses'. After completing her CSEs and gaining several at Grade 2, Julie left school to pursue this long-time ambition. Julie echoed comments about post-16 options made by Lorraine – and, indeed, by the earlier cohort generation of Linda Dixon's network:

> I think unless you were clever and you were gonna do A levels, then you pretty much did and in those days the school seemed to just say, well, the boys were expected to either go into engineering, because there was a big engineering company in [her home town], and the girls were expected to do secretarial, or hairdressing or nursing, um, and that was sort of the choice.
>
> *(Julie, Lorraine's sister)*

Julie had later gained employment as a coach driver, an occupation more commonly done by males including her husband, who had trained her, despite this earlier channelling. By the time we met Julie, she had done this job for many years. Nonetheless, she always prioritized her responsibilities as a wife and mother and, despite sometimes working 40-hour weeks, still described her job as casual and as 'fitting in' with her other commitments. These had included returning to study to obtain a GCSE in English when her two sons were young. She was delighted to gain a Grade B, but had not considered pursuing further academic qualifications as an adult.

Despite the changing policy context, it is striking that Lorraine and Julie's schooling during the early years of comprehensivization shared many of the features experienced by Linda Dixon and her peers in the selective system over a decade earlier. Whilst their comprehensive school catered for children of all abilities at the point of entry, pupils were immediately allocated to streams or bands which dictated the nature of the curriculum and the opportunities for credentialism to which they had access. The distinction between O levels and CSEs remained and was perceived by Lorraine and Julie to be a highly significant factor in how they thought about their own ability as well as the post-compulsory and career options that were available to them as females.

So far our focus has been on the two sisters. Lorraine's children, Paul and Cathy, were in their early to mid-twenties at the time of the research, and their experiences highlighted the markedly different policy regime of the post-1998 era. They too had attended comprehensive school, but they had both taken the new GCSE examinations and, like the majority of their generation, had stayed on in post-16 education. Cathy had also been the first in her family to gain a degree, providing a good example of how recent policies relating to increased and widened participation in HE have influenced the trajectories of young people, especially females, from modest socio-economic backgrounds and from families without any prior experience of HE (Heath *et al.* 2010). Jamil Masuka's experiences are also relevant to a consideration of this changing policy context and we now turn to his experiences and those of his network.

Contemporary education: the experience of Jamil Masuka

Jamil Masuka was in his early twenties at the time of the research. Born in the mid-1980s, he had completed his compulsory education after Labour came to power in 1997. Jamil, then, was at secondary school at a time when widening participation in HE was a government priority. He lived with his parents in a small town and had two brothers and one sister. Jamil had a mixed ethnic background, with a Black African father and a White British mother. His nominated network included various relatives alongside friends who were all White British (see Figure 4.3). Some members of Jamil's network described themselves as middle class (including Jamil's father) and some as working class (including Jamil's mother). Jamil viewed himself as 'middle or lower I would have thought. Because the upper is people, the white collar jobs.'

Jamil had experienced some racism at school, but claimed that it had not affected his studies. He noted, too, that he had not worked particularly hard at school, as he had preferred the social to the academic aspects of schooling: 'I really enjoyed school.

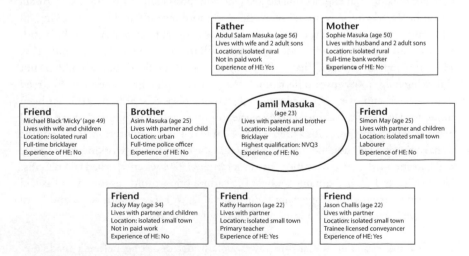

FIGURE 4.3 Jamil Masuka's network

It was just lessons that I had a problem with because the social side of school was brilliant. You see all your friends in one place. But lessons I think were the downside.'

Nonetheless, as we noted earlier, Jamil had left school with good GCSEs (all Grade C and above) and, in line with contemporary institutional expectations for young people with this level of attainment, he had gone on to start A levels, even though most of his friends, including his girlfriend, had progressed straight into employment. His ambition at this point had been to join the Royal Air Force but, despite expectations that college would be easy, he had left during the first year due to difficulties in managing the workload. He had felt isolated, and the efforts of his teachers and his parents to persuade him to stay were unsuccessful: 'I don't think my dad was too pleased. I think, well most of the family are quite, not education-orientated, but parents always like their children to do better than them, don't they?'

Jamil's father Abdul Salam had been educated in Africa prior to taking A levels and a degree in the UK. He was strongly committed to education and had attended an elite school founded by his grandfather. Describing how family values superseded individual aspirations, Abdul Salam recalled how he had had to abandon his own ambition to become a pilot in order to fulfil his father's wish that he acquire a university education:

> So we had this impasse where I didn't want to go to university and they wouldn't support me to go to become a pilot . . . in Africa: it's more what your family wants you to do rather than what you want to do . . . I come from a family where education is paramount . . . and the higher qualifications you have the better it is.
>
> *(Abdul Salam, Jamil's father)*

After obtaining an engineering degree (and later postgraduate qualifications) Abdul Salam had worked for aviation companies and more recently had been working on a freelance basis. Living in the UK and with a network of British friends and a British wife, Abdul Salam had had to adjust his approach to education and family authority. His wife, Sophie, reported that he 'found that very difficult to see his children not following in his footsteps and his family's traditions'. Sophie has sometimes disagreed with her husband over their children's educational decisions, although she has been influenced by her husband to recognize the importance of education: 'Where Abdul Salam was brought up . . . it's a privilege to be able to have an education, it's cherished to have the opportunity.' Sophie explained that she came from a working-class family and had attended a secondary modern school in the 1970s where she had taken CSEs. Most of her friends had obtained jobs at the earliest opportunity, as their families had expected their children, especially their daughters, to leave school at 16 and 'earn your own keep and not be a burden financially to your parents':

> I think my educational career was already decided long before I made any decisions. I did not have any real choice in the matter . . . if you were a daughter;

it was not encouraged to progress beyond 16 . . . because for a girl it was a waste
. . . you're just going to end up getting married and having children.

(Sophie, Jamil's mother)

On leaving college, Jamil had obtained a job in a transport company, but soon
realized that his prospects for progression were limited. Through a friend, he
acquired an apprenticeship in the construction sector and went on to achieve NVQs
at Levels 1, 2 and 3 in bricklaying. At the time of the research, and still employed
as a bricklayer, Jamil was working towards a Level 3 BTEC National Certificate in
Building Studies by day release at the local FE college and was considering going to
university to take a construction-related degree such as quantity surveying:

As I got older, you get a little bit more perspective don't you and I realised
that maybe I do need qualifications to get on and all the rest of it. So I've been
going back through college and gradually I'm in my fifth year now and so I've
sort of slightly been getting on with my education.

(Jamil)

Jamil liked to make his own decisions, but recognized the role of his family and
friends as well as chance:

A lot of what I've done since that first bricklaying thing has been done
through my own choice. I expect a lot of them have hoped that I'd make the
choices that I did eventually end up making . . . they know I don't like being
told what to do, they've sort of put the advice there to take, sort of dangled
the carrot and I've gone that way. I think chance and luck has played quite a
big part in the way things have turned out.

(Jamil)

Jamil's friends, then, and not just his family, had played an important role in his
educational and career decision-making. This was equally true for his older sister,
Michelle, but in her case progression to university had been an important shared
goal within her friendship group. In contrast, Jamil's friendship group was not
oriented towards progression to HE. They were sceptical about the value of
university, referring to concerns about personal debt and whether it would lead to
graduate-level employment. Gaining skills valued in the labour market was
perceived to be preferable to obtaining higher level qualifications, particularly if they
were not vocationally or professionally oriented. This was a position which was even
shared by Jamil's friend Jason, who had progressed into HE: 'I suppose looking back
I wouldn't have done the politics degree . . . I didn't enjoy university you know
. . . I wouldn't go back and do it again. I wouldn't be 100 per cent convinced it's
worth a) the time investment, and b) the debt.'

Jamil had access, then, through part of his social network, to a strong discourse
countering the push to widen participation in HE, and this contributed to his

decision to leave college to learn a skilled trade. Nonetheless, his network also included positive family attitudes to HE and an older friend, Micky, who thought Jamil should go on to university. Micky recognized that the employment market had changed since he was young, when 'it was either into a factory, or into light tool-making, or into the building game or . . . weren't really much else'. Micky had an instrumental orientation to HE, privileging degrees which were likely to lead to jobs:

> You know, you go to university and people come out with a degree in something and you think well, what use are you gonna put it to? Oh, I don't know yet – well, what's the point of three years of your life getting it, you know? If you've actually got something to go to at the end of it, Christ, yeah, go for it.
>
> *(Micky, Jamil's friend)*

The varied experiences of Jamil's network reflected a range of competing educational and employment discourses underpinned by intersecting (and sometimes conflicting) classed and gendered standpoints. They help explain his post-compulsory trajectory, and the sense of negotiating risks and opportunities that pervades his narrative. This interplay between normative decisions and individual(ized) choice, positions Jamil and his friends as exemplars of the changes and continuities under-pinning recent sociological understandings of young people's extended transitions (e.g. Brooks 2009; Furlong and Cartmel 1997).

Discussion

This chapter has explored the effects of specific educational policy regimes on the progression decisions of three entry points and their social networks. The three entry points were selected because they each experienced their compulsory schooling during very different educational periods. Linda Dixon had first-hand experience of the post-war selective tripartite system based on the 11-Plus examination. Lorraine Smith was an early product of the comprehensive system which was introduced to counteract the harmful effects of an overly selective tripartite system. Jamil Masuka experienced his schooling in the wake of the 1988 reforms and the introduction of the relatively inclusive GCSE examination system. The chapter has outlined the key features of the three educational policy regimes and the changing social and economic conditions which underpinned them. The discussion of the three networks enabled the lived reality of these contexts to be illustrated through the accounts of the entry points and members of their networks. Through this evidence, we were able to perceive macro-level effects at the level of educational policy, institutional structures and labour market factors; meso-effects at the level of schools, colleges and employers; and micro-effects at the level of families and friends. These diverse influences are experienced through social and economic structures and processes, and cultural and familial traditions and norms. The individual, situated in his or her network, mediates these influences within a greater or lesser range of potential options or opportunity structures (Roberts 1993, 2009).

As argued in Chapter 3, Giele and Elder's life course perspective (1998) offers a powerful lens for making sense of decision-making about education and employment. The relevance of *locating individuals in time and space* is clear as the network accounts have signalled the strong relationship between policy regimes and interviewees' experiences and opportunities. The school leaving age, the 11-Plus and available examinations had very real consequences for young people during the years of their compulsory education and beyond. The nature of the labour market also had an important backwash effect on compulsory education experiences. Employment prospects changed dramatically for school leavers in the mid-1970s and 1980s as the decline of primary and manufacturing industries created historically high levels of unemployment and it became much harder for school leavers, particularly those with no or low levels of educational attainment, to find jobs. Geographical location affected both the organization of the educational system experienced and also the prevailing employment market for families who were often not geographically mobile. Comparative analysis of the 1958 National Child Development Study and the 1970 British Cohort Study (BCS70) sheds light on the changing role of qualifications in this context, highlighting that 'most young people born in 1958 who left school in 1974 [the minimum leaving age point] could expect to obtain employment regardless of their educational attainment, whereas for young people born in 1970 who left school in 1986, school attainment became a key prerequisite' (Schoon *et al.* 2001: 5). In the BCS70 cohort, family background was an important factor in post-16 transition decisions, with those from higher social classes more likely to stay on in education (Bynner and Parsons 1997).

By the 1990s young people were much more likely to remain in education post-16 and to acquire the educational qualifications that were growing in importance for accessing jobs with career prospects. These trends can be seen in the educational trajectories of the younger members of the networks discussed in this chapter, such as Jamil and his siblings and the Smith and Dixon children and grandchildren, as well as across the network sample as a whole.

As well as confirming the relevance of individuals' temporal and spatial positionings, the accounts provided in this chapter also highlight the relevance of 'linked lives' in terms of shared values, dispositions and expectations and the powerful influence of families on paths taken through compulsory schooling. Parents' normative expectations usually led to standardized and conformist patterns of participation, either because the values and expectations were expressed in the family environment and subsequently internalized, or because they were enforced by sanctions and financial considerations. Gendered expectations featured strongly, particularly in the account of the Dixon and Smith networks where interviewees recounted examples of where they were explicitly directed towards specific course and career destinations on the basis of their sex. For the older cohort generations, boys were prepared for such options as traditional trade apprenticeships and girls for office work. Girls were also prepared for family life and their roles as wives and mothers. Even girls who passed the 11-Plus had limited options and aspirations available to them. Their teachers (including careers teachers) often reinforced gendered occupational stereotypes, and their parents even when supportive had horizons limited by their own experiences and knowledge of opportunities. Younger boys and girls apparently had more choices, but were still bound by traditional gender roles. Despite having obtained a degree, Cathy, like her mother Lorraine Smith, had married young and had a baby and was working in a part-time administrative role. Although there are more options open to young men and women than were available to their parents, stereotypical gender expectations still played an important role. Jamil chose to be a bricklayer, a traditional male occupation.

Interestingly, the evidence relating to the effect of social class, although strong, is more implicit and indirect in nature. It is an underlying theme throughout the accounts. Many identified themselves as working class, especially in their origins, and had educational and employment trajectories traditionally associated with this class background. Jamil's generation had more decisions to make, more routes to navigate, yet social class remained a strong underlying influence. A key 'choice' was whether or not to prioritize academic achievement at school. Jamil's own experiences co-existed with an eclectic array of educational experiences and aspirations in his family and friendship group but, at the end of his schooling, the limited educational and employment aspirations of many around him outweighed those represented by his father's ethnic and cultural background. In contrast, his sister Michelle had taken a different pathway and after A levels had progressed to university as part of a female friendship group reflecting the contemporary gender gap in educational performance and aspiration between many boys and girls. As Furlong (2009) has suggested, then, although the paths young people choose today may appear to be individualized, the outcomes are strongly influenced by what they perceive to be the options and opportunities open to them – and these remain strongly class- (as well as gender-) related. In the case of those from lower socio-economic backgrounds and with limited experience of HE, these are usually associated with a preference for vocational pathways and local study.

Giele and Elder (1998) were careful to include the notion of 'the timing of lives' as well as individual agency in their conceptual framework. This element invites analysis of how and when people make particular transitions and engage in particular forms of participation within the context of their time–space location, social relations and individual agency. The life course perspective allows timing to emerge as an important feature of decision-making: Jamil may go on to participate in HE, but at a time more appropriate for him than at age 18. Lorraine studied for her Level 3 qualifications at 30. Others across the networks were similarly making decisions about participation in education in line with their perceptions of what was appropriate for them as their lives moved dynamically into and through different stages (see also Fuller *et al.*, in press), even though the timings they chose were often at odds with more generally anticipated 'socially expected durations' (Merton 1984). Researching educational participation across the life course reveals that divergence from system norms may be more commonplace than a linear view of academic achievement recognizes (Ecclestone *et al.* 2009).

The push of family and gender and the pull of employment opportunities (or otherwise), as well as the changes in the nature of these push-pull factors in the three different periods discussed, is clear in the accounts. Older members of the networks started work at the earliest opportunity, whilst younger members tended to move into 'good' but not 'top' jobs (cf Roberts 1993). Most people discussed in this chapter were neither extraordinarily successful nor unsuccessful at school. They were 'average' pupils who reported that they did not attract much attention or particular care at school, often passing under the radar of teacher attention. Even those who went to grammar school fitted in with the basic opportunity structures recognized by their families, either because of family sanctions against further education, a lack of confidence to pursue other options or preconceptions of what was a desirable route.

Overall, this chapter has shown that locating network accounts within their relevant educational policy era(s) is important to understanding the legacy effects of compulsory schooling experiences on subsequent decision-making about participation. The experiences of the three entry points and their peers, each representing different cohort generations, are also illustrative of the changing availability of educational and employment opportunities over the last fifty years. The introduction of the GCSE and the expansion of HE over the life course of our participants are crucial factors. When Linda Dixon and Lorraine Smith were at school only a small minority of even academically successful young people took this route. In contrast, members of the younger cohort were far more likely to achieve 'good' qualifications at 16, stay on in full-time education and progress to HE. Jamil is an interesting case in point. His narrative included justifications of why he had decided to leave college before sitting his examinations in order to get a job. He also articulated a rationale for why a few years after leaving full-time education he is currently developing his qualifications with the intention of gaining a degree as part of an overall career plan. As Roberts (2009: 365) pointed out, 'well-qualified 16 to 18 year-olds have alternatives' to university. This contrasts with the accounts of the earlier generations represented by Linda and Lorraine, and where reasonable qualifications at 16 were not closely linked with post-compulsory participation, educational progression and broad career options. As Jamil's mother Sophie reflected, there was no 'real choice in the matter.'

Note

1   It is likely that Linda's secondary modern school 'went comprehensive' while she was attending during the mid-to late 1960s, opening up more opportunities for post-16 study in a school sixth form.

5

THE RELEVANCE OF SOCIAL CAPITAL TO UNDERSTANDING DECISION-MAKING IN NETWORKS

Alison Fuller

In a competitive labour market situation, people who choose to pursue further and higher levels of education are seen to be making rational decisions to invest in their human capital in the expectation that this behaviour will be rewarded through higher wages and 'better' jobs. However, as John Field (2005) has pointed out, there are limitations in the extent to which the decision to participate in lifelong learning can be explained solely in economic terms. Led by the work of social theorists such as Bourdieu (1986), Coleman (1988) and Putnam (2000), the role of social and cultural factors is increasingly seen as integral to an understanding of the education and career trajectories of diverse social groups. The route to success is not always, and for all groups, framed in terms of progression ever higher up the educational and qualification ladder. Other destinations may be equally or more valued within certain communities, neighbourhoods or families who have different status-seeking traditions and criteria for judging the success of their members or offspring.

With regard to young people but also older adults, policy makers keen to create a more highly qualified workforce and to improve social mobility draw both on economic and social discourses to raise educational aspirations amongst groups, particularly from lower social classes, that are under-represented in HE. However, their approach can easily be viewed as constructing those who do not participate in HE as being 'in deficit' (see *inter alia* Reay *et al.* 2005; Thomas and Quinn 2007) whilst simultaneously undervaluing alternative biographies that do not involve the acquisition of higher level qualifications. One longstanding manifestation of this relates to the persistence of an academic–vocational divide, where those who pursue and attain technical and craft skills, for example through work-based pathways such as apprenticeship that do not require degrees, are routinely perceived as being less able and as having lower status than their graduate peers. Highly skilled work, for example as carried out by qualified plumbers, electricians, hairdressers and chefs (who have achieved Level 3 qualifications), are assigned a lower social class (manual skilled) than those who acquire jobs categorized as managerial or professional or whose work is classed as non-manual skilled. Recent research by Vernon Gayle *et al.* (2009) has analysed survey data from the Youth Cohort Study (YCS) of England and Wales that reveal the substantial increase in the proportion of the cohort staying on in education after completion of their compulsory education. However, they noted that the likelihood of young people with similarly good attainment at GCSE (five or more GCSEs at A* to C grades) staying on differed according to the occupational background of their parents: the higher the family's social class (defined by occupational status), the more likely the young person was to stay on. Not all 16-year-olds with good GCSE results progress directly to A levels. Some may pursue vocational qualifications including via apprenticeships, some may get jobs, while others may have a spell not in education, employment or training (NEET).

As highlighted in the introductory chapter, one of the key conceptual frameworks that we have drawn on to help us analyse and reveal the relevance of the network in influencing our entry points' choices has been 'social capital'. Our research has focused on the social network rather than the individual, as a way of exploring the social dimensions of decision-making about education and employment and shedding new light on the embedded and tacit nature of the decision-making process. Social capital may be viewed as a resource accrued through the interpersonal relationships that exist within a group of (connected) individuals and the other networks to which members have ties. This resource may be drawn on by members (often implicitly) to help sustain the network and support the achievement of collective goals. The notion of social capital is founded on the insight that social relationships have value that can be mobilized to facilitate particular courses of action and activities and that help create 'horizons of possibility'. Like economic capital, social capital can flow between and within generations. According to an important early article on the role of social capital in explaining children's educational attainment, James Coleman (1988) argued that the availability of social capital and crucially its transmission from parents to offspring via their ability to spend time helping and encouraging their children made a significant contribution to the younger generation's educational success. This chapter first outlines some of the key concepts relating to social capital before drawing on two of our networks to illustrate how the conceptual framework can help explain participation decisions.

Social capital

In a comprehensive review of the social capital literature, David Halpern (2005) discusses how the concept has been applied at micro-, meso- and national levels and reviews debates about the elasticity of the concept and how effectively it can be applied to both small-scale and intimate networks such as the family as well as large-scale populations such as nations where most people do not/cannot know each other. Halpern's discussion starts from the well-known definition of social capital developed by Robert Putnam: 'Features of social life – networks, norms, and trust – that enable participants to act together more effectively to pursue shared objectives

. . . Social capital, in short, refers to social connections and the attendant norms and trust' (Putnam 1995: 664–5, in Halpern 2005: 1).

Halpern goes on to argue that social capital has three core dimensions or components – 'networks', 'norms' and 'sanctions' – that can be identified within groupings varying from micro to macro in scale (2005: 27). These are shown diagrammatically in Figure 5.1. For the purposes of our research into the influence of social networks on education and employment decision-making, the focus is on the micro- and, to some extent also the meso-level, and on identifying the role of social capital generated and flowing between people who, in the main, are known to each other.

We have analysed the flows of influence in our study primarily through focusing on the social relations between members of the achieved sample (network interviewees) in each case study, and the ways in which these relations (often tacitly) influence the entry point's decisions. Our approach recognizes that social capital not only inheres in the relations between members of the achieved sample, but also with others. These 'absent relationships' include what we have called the 'shadow network' of individuals whom the entry point named as being important to them but whom we were unable to include for diverse reasons (see Heath *et al.* 2009 for

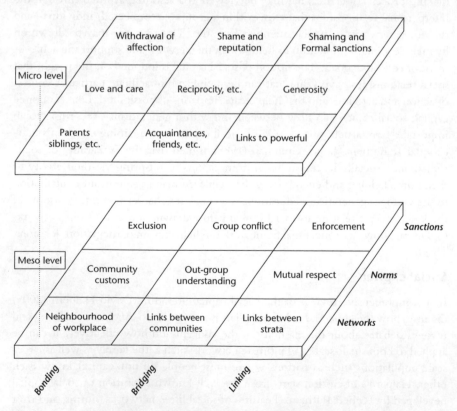

FIGURE 5.1 The dimensions of social capital (after Halpern 2005)

a detailed discussion of this issue). Social capital resources are also available through the network's links with other groups, for example through employment, or institutions such as education and training providers, and formal sources of information and advice. In this regard, it was the name of the institution (e.g. Learndirect, Family Learning Centre, workplace learning centre) rather than particular individuals within them which were identified as having been relevant by our interviewees, and that we suggest, therefore, can also be seen as part of the value generated by the network's openings onto wider sets of social relations.

'Norms', the second component of social capital identified by Halpern, relates to group values and expectations. These provide a critical aspect of the underlying and usually tacit framework for decision-making that guides individuals' choices and behaviour and that, for example, can help explain patterns of male and female participation. Group norms are associated with the trust relations and expectations about reciprocity that help constitute the context within which decision-making is embedded. Networks (such as many of ours), characterized by high levels of trust, emotional support and taken-for-granted assumptions that members have each others' best interests at heart, are likely to generate collective perceptions of what 'the right decision' is for a particular individual. As we illustrate throughout the book, the evidence from our research suggests that network norms are a relevant factor in explaining decision-making about educational participation for our entry points and other network members.

From a contrasting, more voluntaristic, perspective Giddens (1990, 1991a) discusses the changing role of tradition as a guide for individual action. He suggests that, under what he calls the conditions of 'late modernity', the role of tradition is decreasing as risks, threats and opportunities are experienced and negotiated at a personal rather than collective level. A hypothesis based on this thesis would suggest growing numbers of people are making the sorts of educational and employment decisions that break with the norms and expectations that characterize their social group or network. Processes of de-traditionalization and individualization in decision-making have been associated with what some sociologists conceive as the rise of the 'choice biography', particularly amongst younger adults, and the corresponding decline of standardized biographies (e.g. Beck and Beck-Gernsheim 2002; du Bois-Reymond 1998, 2004). Given our focus on the social network as the unit of analysis, our evidence can make a useful contribution to methodological and substantive debates about the relative explanatory power of such trends, as opposed to the ongoing influence of group norms and expectations in explaining adults' decisions about whether or not to participate.

The third component of social capital that Halpern invokes is the notion of 'sanctions'. As he outlines, sanctions can be used to monitor the network and its norms, and to 'punish' members whose behaviour may threaten its continuity (2005: 10). Schuller et al. (2000) suggest that Putnam's more recent work has developed a critical and 'darker' conceptualization of social capital that recognizes the potential for disruption within networks and the associated threat to their sustainability (perhaps arising at least in part from de-traditionalization). It is helpful to recognize the relevance of power and conflict as well as trust and reciprocity to the making, doing, fracturing and remaking of social relations. For example, it may be that there are differences between the norms shared by sub-groups within a network (e.g. about the gendered employment and caring roles of parents with young children), or between the norms that exist between the family members of the entry point's social network, but which are not shared by the friendship members of his or her network. It is important to bear in mind that evidence of the norms and sanctions at play is likely to be implicit, often revealed indirectly by the comments and views of members about the behaviour of other members rather than, for example, as in the case of a social or sports club where members agree to abide by a list of published rules and regulations.

As our evidence indicates, the power of unwritten guides for action should not be underestimated when it comes to making sense of decision-making about educational participation. In particular, our historical and life course perspectives signal the importance of exploring the transmission of social capital across the generations in order to help understand where tradition has been a guide for action (Giddens 1991a, 1994) in terms of people's participation decisions. This recalls an earlier point that the status of particular destinations and trajectories may be viewed differently by social groups with diverse standards and values.

The use of the term 'capital' is, of course, significant as it captures important connotations of power and resources. However, social capital researchers have noted that the concept has different dimensions and effects and have, therefore, found it helpful to distinguish between different types or varieties of social capital. In this regard, Robert Putnam is responsible for developing the now well-known distinction between bridging and bonding social capital, and in his book *Bowling Alone*, Putnam (2000) draws attention to this distinction. The former refers to the values of solidarity, mutual reinforcement, support and specific forms of reciprocation associated with homogeneous groups. The latter refers to more diffuse and indirect forms of linkage and reciprocation between and within groups: 'bonding social capital constitutes a kind of sociological superglue, whereas bridging social capital provides a sociological WD-40' (2000: 23). For Xavier de Souza Briggs (1998), bonding social capital facilitates 'getting by' while 'getting ahead' requires bridging social capital (cited in Putnam 2000: 23). The suggestion here, then, is that those networks characterized by strong group norms and sanctions on member behaviour are also likely to have high levels of bonding social capital. In Granovetter's (1973) terms, the interpersonal ties are strong, the network is 'dense' (most members know each other and communicate very regularly); and, as Bott (1957) would suggest, the group is 'close-knit'. It follows that it will be hard a) for an outsider to become a network member, and b) for an insider to break with traditional behaviour. The boundaries of a network viewed as high in bonding social capital are likely to be conceived as relatively impermeable.

By contrast, those networks whose social relations contain abundant bridging social capital are likely to be more accessible to newcomers. Members are more likely to have diverse social relations, giving them access to other networks and the social capital that may be mobilized through having extended and multiple sets of social relations. As the quotation from de Souza Briggs suggests, bridging social capital can be drawn on to identify and take advantage of new opportunities. Granovetter (1973), writing before the language of social capital gained momentum, found that the 'strength' of what he called 'weak ties' was evidenced in research that showed that those with more extensive social contacts were more likely to hear quickly about the availability of jobs and so be in a position to apply early or have someone put in 'a good word for them' with the prospective employer.

The notion of bridging capital is useful in characterizing the nature of inter-group ties. However, it is not so clear how helpful it is for capturing the ways in which social capital might facilitate vertical movement between groups with differential levels and types of power such as, for example, from a weaker socio-economic class position to a stronger one. This sort of 'upward mobility' is more likely to occur if more weakly positioned networks have the ability to access the resources available to more powerful social groups. The question arises then: in what ways could social capital increase mobility to the benefit of disadvantaged groups? It was to address this issue (in relation to people in developing nations) that Woolcock (1998) invoked the notion of 'linkage' (linking social capital) to capture how connections between social networks positioned in different hierarchical locations could be facilitated. He makes the distinction between the sources of social capital available through different sorts of social relations and the benefits that might accrue (what he has called 'the consequences' of social capital (1998: 185)). The nature of the benefits depends on the combinations of and the extent to which social relations can be mobilized to engage in the relevant social practice (e.g. decision-making about whether or not to participate in HE).

Halpern (2005) finds it helpful to think of 'linking capital' as a third variety of social capital that enables vertical connections to be made between social groups occupying different power positions, in contrast to bridging capital that facilitates horizontal inter-group connections. In their discussion of 'linking social capital', Thomas and Quinn (2007: 60) refer to it 'as the ability to access institutional resources', such as the HE sector as well as other educational and employment organizations, and careers advice and guidance services. The point here is that social networks may accrue diverse types of social capital. The extent to which people can draw on the network's resources to make choices and pursue (shared) goals will be influenced by the norms and sanctions that characterize the nature of those social relations.

More recently, Quinn (2005; Thomas and Quinn 2007) has developed the concept of 'imagined social capital' to capture the idea that individuals may draw on symbolic resources such as characters from literature or role models whom they do not actually know to shape their 'horizons for action' (Hodkinson et al. 1996). The availability of this type of social capital helped explain the accounts of the members of the Sharpe network we have written about elsewhere (Fuller et al. in press). As we shall see from the network evidence presented below, having access to different types of social capital is relevant to understanding our entry points' ongoing educational and career decision-making.

Network evidence

The rest of this chapter will draw on the data generated by two networks to provide illustrations of how various forms of social capital reside in social relations and how they provide different resources on which members can draw to achieve mutual objectives (evidenced by the norms and sanctions also in operation across the network or sub-network). The constraints of space mean that the illustrations are inevitably brief and selective. Each of the following vignettes includes a summary account of the network, its members and key features as well as an indication of how the varieties of social capital shed light on participation decisions. Given that most of the networks involved in our research are populated by individuals nominated by our initial interviewees as people they feel close to and whom they feel are influential in their educational and career decision-making, we can also expect the groups, in general, to be close-knit.

The Gregory network (see Figure 5.2) is one of our smallest cases with an achieved sample of just three members of the same family; our entry point Andrew Gregory, his wife Mary and their married daughter Sarah Richards. The most obvious absent member of the achieved network was the Gregory's son whom we were not able to interview. This is an extremely close family, with strong inter-personal ties between members of the immediate as well as extended family, particularly on Mary's side. Andrew and Mary are both in their mid- to late forties, Sarah is 23 and Robert is 21. Sarah lives with her husband locally and Robert lives at home with his parents. This network 'scores highly' on all the indicators normally invoked to characterize interpersonal strength. The members see each other frequently and spend time together, including going on holidays. Sarah phones her parents every day and visits at least twice a week, often having her evening meal with them. They confide in each other and reciprocate services such as cooking and do-it-yourself household tasks, and they appear to be emotionally intimate. During the network interviews, there was discussion about when Sarah and her husband

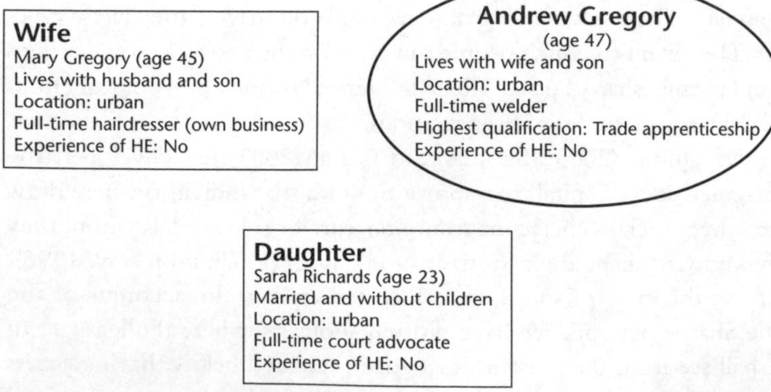

Wife
Mary Gregory (age 45)
Lives with husband and son
Location: urban
Full-time hairdresser (own business)
Experience of HE: No

Andrew Gregory
(age 47)
Lives with wife and son
Location: urban
Full-time welder
Highest qualification: Trade apprenticeship
Experience of HE: No

Daughter
Sarah Richards (age 23)
Married and without children
Location: urban
Full-time court advocate
Experience of HE: No

FIGURE 5.2 Andrew Gregory's network

would start a family and how the grandparents would be (and were looking forward to being) involved in babysitting and helping. By the time of Andrew's second interview, Sarah was pregnant and discussions about support arrangements had intensified. In speaking about her brother, Sarah said: 'Oh, me and my brother are best friends, there's only about two years and a half between us, he's 21 April the first and he, he's done very similar to me really.'

Andrew and Mary both came from working-class occupational backgrounds. Andrew's father was a 'storesman', whilst Mary's mother had a small catering business and her father was a docker. Both Andrew and Mary left school at the end of the compulsory phase and saw themselves as average at school. They were both accepting of their respective family expectations that they (like their siblings and cousins) would leave school to get apprenticeships in occupations typical for males and females respectively. Andrew was offered two engineering apprenticeships, and accepted one at the large company where his father worked. He served a full five-year craft apprenticeship, becoming a highly skilled and specialized welder with some supervisory responsibilities, and is still working at the same firm. Andrew commented:

> Well, at the time, as I say, when I left school you was encouraged to get an apprenticeship because they'd say once you're a tradesman you've got a job for life, that's what people in them days were saying. And it's been a very comfortable way of working, you know, I've always been employed here and um, you probably get in your little comfort zone if you know what I mean . . .
>
> *(Andrew)*

In recent years, Andrew has had the opportunity to take courses through his employer's workplace learning centre. The centre is supported by the employer and the Union Learning Fund.[1] Although he was resistant to the idea of participating in provision at a formal educational institution, the availability of courses at work was appealing. At the time of the interview, he expressed interest in taking advanced IT courses at the centre, but this level of study was not currently being funded.

Mary completed a three-year hairdressing apprenticeship and after working as a qualified hairdresser started her own salon. The theme of apprenticeship is central to illustrating the nature of the bonding social capital that has developed in this family and how it has contributed to, and is evidence of, the integrated character of the network. Apprenticeship is viewed as the preferred post-compulsory destination and is perceived as providing strength in the labour market, material success, status, job satisfaction and a platform for long-term employment prospects and opportunities. The tradition of participating in apprenticeships (as the route to perceived success in the network) has been transmitted down the generations and has acted as a 'guide for action'. In the case of Andrew and Mary, it has produced standardized biographies for males and females from their social class. Apprenticeship in occupations structured along gender-stereotypical lines was seen, at the time (mid-1970s), as the appropriate and desirable destination for children from their sort of family backgrounds and with their level of educational attainment. What is interesting, though, is that Andrew and Mary's children, Robert and Sarah, also chose to leave school (in the early 2000s) at the earliest opportunity. Despite gaining a string of very good GCSE grades and attending schools where it had become the institutional norm to stay on and pursue A levels with a view to progressing to HE, they both chose to pursue apprenticeships. Speaking about his son, Andrew acknowledges Robert's educational success: 'He went to the same school I went to [name of school] but then again, he was in the top, top class. Um, he come out, he had virtually straight As, I think he had one B.'

In commenting on Robert's decision to leave school at 16 to take up an engineering apprenticeship, Andrew indicates that he saw this as the preferred option: 'Er, he was at the right place at the right time, um, he got offered an apprenticeship with the firm he's with now.' The training programme has enabled Robert to attend college on a day-release basis to gain further qualifications.

Apprenticeship was also seen as a highly positive pathway for Sarah. She had experienced a quite extended period of bullying at school and, although she had come through this towards the end of her secondary education and had made friends who were staying on, the positive connotations of the apprenticeship option in the family were persuasive. It is interesting to note that Sarah recognizes that in opting to pursue an apprenticeship rather than do A levels she was going against the norms of the school and experienced some disapproval as a consequence:

> I think they were quite surprised that I wasn't going to college because in my particular school all the talks we had about career was going to college, there was nothing about doing a Modern Apprenticeship whatsoever, and my careers teacher gave me, she basically said if you don't go to college and university then I'm not going to make anything of my life, erm, but I still ignored her advice and went for it.
>
> *(Sarah)*

Sarah has completed an apprenticeship in business administration with the county constabulary after being alerted to the opening by one of her aunts who worked there as a human resources manager. As Andrew observed, 'Well, she [the aunt] gave her the nod there's a job coming up, go for it'. This provides a clear example of the bridging social capital available in the wider social relations of the network and how it was mobilized to connect Sarah with a career option, compliant with network norms in terms of education–work transitions. There is also an element of 'linkage' in this instance, as the social relations accrued within the family were connected *up* to the institutional resources available through gaining an apprenticeship with a large and well-resourced employer such as the police. Sarah made the point that: 'I knew I wanted a career, I knew that much, I knew in my own mind that a way of doing that was to start in the bottom of a good organization and try and work your way up, erm . . . that's what I wanted to do . . .' The apprenticeship enabled Sarah to attend college on a day-release basis to gain further qualifications.

The chance to 'earn and learn' is highly valued in the family: 'That's it, the work-route, yeah, the work paid for her education, so they paid for all, you know, she did her day-release and work paid for it'. In addition, apprenticeship has provided family members with the opportunity to do jobs which they enjoy and to be successful. As Mary observed about her own experience as a trainee, then a qualified hairdresser, in an upmarket salon: 'I had quite a high-powered job, it was quite good, we were high-flyers, we were doing all the colours and the trendy hair.' In relation to the decision-making of their children, the parental generation's experiences of apprenticeship were sufficiently positive to overcome the current institutional norms that expect those with very good performance at GCSE to pursue the conventional full-time academic route to university. In this case tradition, including gendered occupational choices, remains a very powerful guide to action.

At the time of her interview, Sarah was working as a court advocate in the Crown Prosecution Service, having taken the opportunity to pursue this through an employer-sponsored training programme that would also provide her with the opportunity to train as a lawyer at a later date. Sarah, then, might well participate in HE for career reasons and as a means to build on her existing employment success.

The point that has been illustrated through the example of the Gregory network is the strength of the norms, values and expectations that have shaped post-compulsory participation in education and training behaviour within and across the generations. The strength of the social relations and the associated bonding social capital that has accrued, and been transmitted and mobilized, helps explain the continuity of apprenticeship take-up even when, in the case of the younger generation, Sarah and Robert were expected by their schools to stay on. The apprenticeship and work-based options in this case (and the extended family network within which they are located) are viewed as the trusted route to status acquisition, characterized by employment, job satisfaction and material success. This route is clearly privileged and represents the normative education to work biography in this network, further standardized in terms of entry into occupations normally associated with males or females. Apprenticeship is preferred to the uncertainty, unclear benefits and risks this family perceived in the HE route. Sarah outlined her perceptions of university in the following way:

> I've got two views of university, I've got people that are at university that are there to be a professional like a doctor or someone like that and I've got lots of people that I know that have gone to university because they don't know what they want to do, so they've just gone there to get a degree to work out what they want to do erm . . . if you asked my granddad about somebody at university he would just call them a tax dodger . . .
>
> *(Sarah)*

In the case of our entry point, Andrew, his general wariness about the education system means that he is unlikely to participate in HE if it involves attendance at college and university. On the other hand, if further courses were available and funded through the workplace learning centre that gave him access to higher level knowledge, skills and qualifications, and that were work and career related, then there is a much greater likelihood that he would participate. Andrew has access to an extended social network through his employment which has generated bridging and linking social capital. He has been able to mobilize this through his participation in courses at the company learning centre. However, the availability of linking social capital was restricted, in the sense that the higher level courses that could support his promotion at work were not on offer.

The potential, then, for Andrew to achieve higher level qualifications has remained unmet because of the nature of the social capital resources to which he has access. Drawing on Edwards and Foley's (1998) work, Halpern observes: 'Their point is that it is not sufficient simply to describe the size and density of a person's network. We must look at the resources that the network connects the individuals to.' In Andrew's case, his standardized post-school biographical choices were mobilized through his social network and its associated norms, values and expectations around employment and educational decisions and tacit awareness of the threat of sanctions for any break in traditional behaviour. The legacy of this trajectory has continued to influence his (non-) decision-making as an older adult, and the dominance of downward and sideways transmission of social capital in this network. For Andrew, the linking social capital available through the learning centre at work was insufficient substantially to reshape his educational trajectory and interrupt the network's norms.

The summary of the Gregory network above has highlighted the importance of exploring the nature of the resources available through the social relations within the network and those to which it has linkages. As suggested above, social capital scholars have argued (Edwards and Foley 1998; Halpern 2005; Woolcock 1998) that having openings onto powerful resources may facilitate vertical, not just horizontal, connections, with consequences for social mobility. The second case that I am going to discuss provides a good example of how this may occur. In so doing it will also draw attention to the combination of capitals that are available in a network and how they can combine within and interact across levels (Woolcock 1998: 170) – in this instance between the micro-level of the social network and the meso-, institutional level of a Family Learning Centre (FLC) and the opportunities it provided for people to pursue a wide range of courses and qualifications alongside and with the support of peers.

The Armstrong network (see Figure 5.3) represented the most materially disadvantaged of all our 16 networks. The entry point, Rosie (aged 35), has five children. At the time of the first interview she was living with her partner (the father of her youngest three children), but the couple had separated by the time of the second interview. Rosie had not been in paid employment for some years. She nominated an all-female network consisting of three generations, five friends of a similar age to her, a younger generation represented by her daughter, Laura (aged 13), and an older generation represented by her (ex-) partner's mother, Liz, who was also an old friend. Three of the friends were in full-time employment, one was

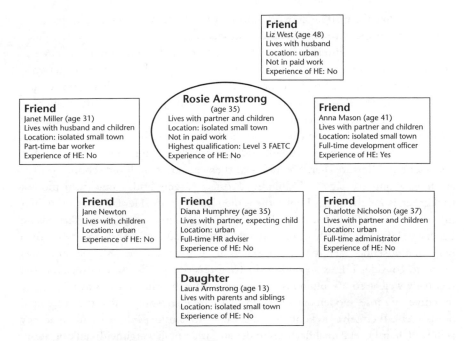

FIGURE 5.3 Rosie Armstrong's network

in part-time work and the employment status of the fifth was unclear. Liz was not in paid employment. Rosie's (ex-) partner worked in a pub. Rosie's friend Anna is a 'family development learning officer' with the local FLC. She is the only member of the network to have experience of HE, and this is being gained as a part-time mature student in an area of study related to her employment. Rosie has also been highly involved with the FLC on a voluntary basis.

The entry point and most of the members of this network live in a relatively isolated small urban community, with no easily accessible local HE institution or university. Several interviewees and the other people they discuss have somewhat chaotic and disturbed lives, where they struggle to achieve emotional and financial stability. In addition, disability has had a major impact. Liz and Janet, friends of Rosie's, suffer from physical disabilities which either prevent them from being able to obtain paid work or mean that their capacity for paid employment is highly limited. Mental illness of family members and partners, or abuse, or both, has had a serious impact on the lives of Jane, Janet and Charlotte.

The norms and values of this all-female network are seen clearly through the women's shared experiences, particularly in terms of their children, and often unstable and relatively short-lived 'partner relationships'. Early family formation is also a feature of the women's lives, often as a result of unplanned pregnancies. Ongoing childcare responsibilities are seen as a factor limiting women's ability to participate in post-compulsory education and training, and to develop careers, but these women do not express this as 'a problem' – rather it is 'just the way things are for women like them'. The network norm is that children come first and that child rearing is the primary responsibility of mothers.

Rosie has a difficult relationship with her parents and is not particularly close to her two sisters. She did not nominate either of her parents or sisters as network members, but their ongoing influence is an important element in her narrative and 'shadow network'. Rosie presents her parents as being judgemental and disapproving, particularly about her choice of partners, early pregnancy and the number of children she has had. Rosie claims that she has distanced herself from her parents in the sense that she expects them, and particularly her mother, to criticize her behaviour and 'lecture' her. She refers to them as 'strict' and 'old school' in their attitudes about marriage and children. Rosie's parents both came from modest backgrounds and they left school at the earliest opportunity. Her father went straight into the Army and her mother took a job in a sewing machine factory. There is no history of HE in the family or of academic success. Although Rosie did better than her sisters at school, her good exam results at 16 were not seen as a reason to stay on or to consider HE as an option. In Chapters 3 and 4 we saw how achieving relatively well at 16 was often insufficient to ensure that individuals stayed on. The narratives of those 'moderately qualified' at 16 are interesting in that they often did not perceive themselves as being 'good enough' to consider HE, particularly if they achieved their Level 2 qualifications under an earlier policy regime. In talking about the attitude to education that her parents had from their own experience and when she and her sisters were at school, she said: 'you like done your time [at] school and then it was [a] job you get into' (Rosie).

Rosie recognizes that the context underpinning decisions about educational participation has changed significantly since her parents were at school and also since she left school in around 1990. This is evidenced by her own and her parents' support for the idea of Laura going to university (and in contrast to the lack of inter-generational change in attitudes discussed in the Gregory case study). Laura has expressed a strong interest in becoming a secondary school teacher and is expected on the basis of her existing results and predictions to achieve the necessary entry level qualifications. Rosie commented that her parents were: 'absolutely over the moon that Laura wants to go to university'. They have also offered to help support her financially while she studies. Rosie attributed the change in their perspective to wider social change as well as the contemporary demands of the labour market: 'I think they've changed with the world in general I think basically and you know you've got to get education now to get a job basically . . . and to get anywhere in life' (Rosie).

Rosie is conscious (through the 'sanction' of disapproval) that she has transgressed the family norms and values through her 'lifestyle choices', particularly having her first child before getting married, leaving her then husband and then having other children with a partner of whom they did not approve. They find it hard to understand why someone in her circumstances should have had five children:

> But they were like you don't need any more now, that's enough. And then
> I went on to have one more and they were like well you definitely don't need

any more now, four is more than enough. And then I went on to have one more and it was like, oh, you know you get the disapproval sort of thing . . . They're good at disapproval.

(Rosie)

In contrast to her parents, Rosie's friends are empathetic, share similar life experiences to her and are not judgemental. Most of Rosie's friendship relationships are stable: some have been long lasting (Charlotte and Diana), others are newer but are very supportive (Anna and Jane). One of the friendships (Janet) broke down completely between the first and second interviews with Rosie and after our interview with Janet. Three of the women have become Rosie's friends through their involvement with the FLC. As we shall see below, the bridging and linking social capital accruing to Rosie through her network's opening to the resources of the FLC has been particularly influential on her decision-making about educational participation and future aspiration to enter HE. Men exist in the shadow of the achieved network sample: their direct voices are absent. They appear in the inter-viewees' accounts but often as abusers, sometimes violent, sometimes with mental health problems and usually as unreliable or inadequate 'providers'.

After leaving school at 16 with around eight GCSEs at A*–C, Rosie participated in a Youth Training Scheme (YTS) programme which involved her working in an office for four days a week and attending college on day-release to follow secretarial and administrative courses. As mentioned above, in the context of her family norms and expectations, staying on was not considered, whereas pursuing secretarial and office skills was seen as an attractive and high-status option for someone from her background and in comparison with working in supermarkets or warehouses like her sister. Since then she has worked in a variety of part-time jobs, including in the retailing and hospitality sectors, and as a nanny. In recent years she has mainly not been in paid employment and with five children has had substantial childcare responsibilities.

Nine years ago, Rosie first participated in a course run by 'Family Learning', a publicly funded initiative made available in local schools. The aim of Family Learning is to improve the literacy, numeracy and general education levels of parents, and in so doing to raise their confidence and ability to help their own children. Mothers often attend the classes while their children are in school. The initiative also provides free childcare and the courses themselves are free. 'Family learning' can be seen as an intervention designed to increase the value of family social capital and its inter-generational transmission from parents to children. Anna, Jane and Rosie have all been active participants and stress the important and trans-formative role that it has played in their lives. Rosie spoke at length about how she was first approached and got involved:

[I] got collared by her [daughter's] teacher at the time, Mrs [AAA], and she said 'oh', she said 'you'll come and do it'. I said 'do what?' and she's like 'we've got a course starting at school' and she said 'it's to do with the [Brown]

College' . . . She said, 'and it's English, maths, basic English, basic maths, computers, IT, basic IT' and we get to work with the children in school, well our own children in school. She said, 'you'll do it won't you, it's like an all day thing'. So I was like 'OK'. So that was every Thursday . . .

(Rosie)

Rosie went on to make the link between her own involvement and the participation of other women with whom she could identify. The effectiveness of word of mouth recruitment between peers was also stressed by Anna:

They'll say oh I did Family Learning; it was brilliant, you want to come along. And that is, it's probably about the, you know the best way. And people that have been through Family Learning are the best people to encourage you to do Family Learning . . . because they can answer the questions quite honestly and openly.

(Anna)

Providing evidence of how social capital can flow down the generations, Rosie observed that her participation in the course had had benefits for her daughter as well as herself:

Rosie: but yes, I'd take Laura, my eldest one, into school and then I would go straight into school myself, and we had our own little classroom and there must have been about eight of us. I'm sure there were eight mums and we had [tutor's name], she worked for the college then but she's now head of Family Learning . . . that [participation] really done my daughter well that did, because she's sailing through school. She's doing really well.

Interviewer: So sorry, what did her good?

Rosie: Me doing the course with her . . . And that basically just led on to another course coming up and another course coming up and so over like the nine years . . .

The eight mothers continued taking courses together and also became involved in helping out in the school's classrooms and at school break times too. A couple of years after this, one of the Family Learning development officers introduced them to another tutor who offered a course leading to the Level 3 Further and Adult Education Teacher's Certificate (FAETC). Rosie explained:

we started doing the FAETC. I had, I had only done a few months of the course and I had so much family-wise going on that I just couldn't keep up, so I dropped out, but the other girls went on to finish it and they started working for the Family Learning, so I missed an opportunity there, I know I did, but I can't look back. And then I done other courses through them but the FAETC . . . she repeated it a year or so later, maybe two years later and I redone it, I restarted it again from the beginning and sailed through it . . .

(Rosie)

Since then, Rosie has progressed to the second stage of the qualification which has involved her in teaching practice with adults in the centre. Her existing qualification allows her to teach adults, but her experience has convinced her that she would like to train to be a school teacher and she plans eventually when her childcare commitments ease to enrol in the Open University to take a degree and become a teacher. Rosie stated: 'I have looked into it that far.' For Rosie, then, the opportunity to access Family Learning was perceived as what she called 'a real, real turning point.' This was because:

It was the fact that, in the playground you say hello to mums and what have you anyway but the fact that you were actually working back in a classroom environment really with other women and so you wasn't just doing the course, you was chatting about home life as well and you had someone to sound off to, and they were going through the same thing that you were going through. If they were having trouble with one of their kids or you were having trouble with one of your kids you'd get different suggestions from different people and you'd be 'oh, well I haven't tried that, I'll give it a go' and it really was a turning point for me.

(Rosie)

She went on: 'it's brilliant, it [Family Learning] just opens so many doors and different opportunities for different people. I mean one of the girls that was on one of my courses years ago is now an accountant.'

Anna also provides a highly positive account of the impact of Family Learning on her education and career. Anna is an enthusiastic learner and has pursued numerous courses as an adult and, among other achievements, has become a qualified aromatherapist and reflexologist. She started at the FLC after her second daughter began school. She explained: 'I decided to come and do the course as a parent to support her learning.' Since then Anna has gained her FAETC and, at the time of the interview, was part way through an Open University degree and also another Level 3 qualification in Parenting and Family Learning.

Prior to their involvement in the FLC, Anna and Rosie knew each other as acquaintances and this was relevant to Anna's participation: 'Well the relationship with me and Rosie is actually quite interesting. Because Rosie did Family Learning the year before I did Family Learning' (Anna). Subsequently, they have become close friends and their relationship provides a useful illustration of how social capital can operate as a 'collective good', when various forms of social capital combine to create rich resources that can be drawn on in pursuit of shared values and objectives. The relevance of bonding social capital is illustrated through relational features such as reciprocity and mutual support. As Anna said:

it's like when we've had things like the childcare course, we've said oh [Rosie] you've got do it and you've got do your FAETC 'cause you're so good at it you know . . . So then again it's been, so it's kind of equal.

(Anna)

The power of linkages

In addition to the bridging and bonding social capital that develops through friendship relations, it is clear from Rosie's and Anna's accounts that they have benefited from their participation in Family Learning and the effects of the linkages that it has enabled. The following extract from Anna's narrative provides strong evidence of the power of linking social capital as she provides examples of where participation in the FLC's provision has directly contributed to participants' ability to access more advantaged socio–economic positions. Anna was asked by her line manager at the FLC to record her perceptions of how participation can affect people. She recounted her explanation during our interview, using vivid metaphor to refer first to how participation can transform people's aspirations and confidence:

The only way I could explain it . . . was saying about it's like doors and keys. That you know, to be able to support people in learning, is like being able to give them a key to unlock a door. And once they've unlocked that door you know, it's, what's beyond it is so exciting that they really enjoy that for a while, but then they want that next door and you know and it's all about unlocking doors and making your way through things . . . But it doesn't just unlock, it doesn't just get them a qualification, it doesn't just do that. It, it gives them a chance to, their self-esteem you know, that they, when you see people that have never had a qualification in their life and have been told they're stupid, or they'll never achieve, and then we work with them and so much is on the self-esteem before you ever get to anything else.

(Anna)

Second, Anna outlines the effect on parent–child relations by indicating how participation can change the way parents relate to their children. The following quotation illustrates how social capital resources can be introduced into a family network through parental participation in Family Learning and how those new resources can flow on to the next generation:

They're actually, and they become different and then you see how they interact with their children differently . . . it's kind of like . . . that, that's changed now, so that child will not go through what that adult went through, because that adult is different . . . That adult's not treating their children the same way their parents treated them towards learning.

(Anna)

Finally, Anna spoke about individuals whom she knows have been helped into work, further training or higher education following their participation:

> And we've had people that have gone on to university . . . we've had, I've had learners who have gone on to do midwifery, I've had learners who've gone on to do their teaching, I've had learners who've gone into the Police Force, from being unemployed some of these are . . . I've had unemployed people going to work. I've had people come off disability that have gone in and done further training.
>
> *(Anna)*

Evidence about social capital from the Armstrong network has been helpful in illustrating both how varieties of social capital can be accrued in dynamic combination and the powerful potential to influence social mobility that access to linking social capital brings. It does this by creating real examples of people who have been enabled to behave in non-standard ways and by generating a narrative about the achievements of 'similar others' and, in so doing, starts to normalize such trajectories. In Rosie's case, the emotional and practical support that the friends provide each other has helped her to access a combination of bonding and bridging social capitals that have facilitated her move away from the norms of her family network (represented indirectly by her account of her parents' expectations). She has drawn on these resources to help develop a biography that differs from the standardized model both in terms of her domestic lifestyle and household formation, and in terms of her engagement with Family Learning and the access this has given her to institutional resources that, in time, are likely to see her participate in HE in her journey towards becoming a qualified teacher. The strength of the tie with the FLC lies not only in the nature of the institutional resources it offers, but in the way these are bound into and flow through the interpersonal relations in the community, producing a collective good and a repository of accounts that nourish the creation of the group's and its individual members' 'imagined social capital' (Quinn 2005).

Conclusion

This chapter has utilized evidence from two of our social networks to illustrate how the lens of social capital(s) helps makes sense of decision-making about educational participation. Applying social capital concepts to our data has enabled us to think in a more nuanced way about the types of social capital available in particular networks and the ways in which these provide resources for particular sorts of decisions and choices (or non-decisions and non-choices). More directly, as the examples indicate, the framework of social capital can provide an important contribution to our development of explanations for why some entry points would appear more likely to participate in HE in comparison with others.

Halpern (2005) is right that the varieties of social capital (bonding, bridging and linking) are helpful heuristics. From the perspective of our research, they provide a framework for approaching the network data analysis and illuminating the complex relational nature of decision-making about educational participation. However, it is not easy to operationalize the varieties as neatly separate concepts. The evidence presented in this chapter and throughout the book suggests that the networks are not readily categorizable in terms of one or other form of social capital; rather, they appear to incubate and produce a range of interwoven resources. In different networks one form of capital may appear as particularly relevant to explaining patterns of educational participation. The benefit of the network (as opposed to the solely individual) account is that other types are likely to be revealed during the process of mapping and unpacking the web of social relations and how they are practised.

Importantly, the evidence from both the Gregory and Armstrong cases has highlighted how forms of social capital are in dynamic relation with the norms and sanctions also at play in the social network and, in addition, how 'the capitals' can be mobilized in combination when objectives are shared. Nonetheless, the evidence presented in this chapter suggests that the consequences in terms of our two entry points' decisions about future participation in HE are likely to be strongest when bonding, bridging and linking resources are available and can be mobilized. This notion is nicely captured by Woolcock's observation:

> Top-down resources and bottom-up capacity building need to be in a dynamic and cooperative relationship in order to assemble the range of people and materials capable of overcoming problems or to take advantage of opportunities.
>
> *(Woolcock 1998: 185)*

To Woolcock's point we could also add the need for the sort of narrative and symbolic resources which Quinn refers to as imagined social capital. It appears that this type of capital can also help extend horizons of action, as we encountered in the Armstrong network. On the other hand, as we saw in the Gregory network and in other cases in this book, such narrative and symbolic resources are just as likely to be drawn on to reinforce normative behaviour and decision-making within networks. There is a danger, then, in reading across accounts of personal transformation and the availability of imagined social capital. Not only can this type of social capital be invoked in relation to examples of behaviour which are seen as progressive, mould-breaking and inspirational, but it should also be seen as part of the dialogic and symbolic processes that underpin explanations of standardized education and employment decision-making and trajectories. The value of the conceptual framework proposed by Halpern to help explain participation decisions is precisely its conceptualization of social capital as constituted by inter-related and dynamic components (involving notions of network, norms and sanctions as well as varieties of social capital). This approach helps account for the processes of continuity, change and difference we have found in our networks and produces insights which go beyond those that can be generated from human capital perspectives on decision-making about educational participation.

Note

1 The government created the Union Learning Fund in 1998 to support union-led projects designed to encourage union members to take up lifelong learning opportunities. Details can be accessed at http://www.unionlearningfund.org.uk

6

CAREER AND EDUCATION DECISION-MAKING OF NON-PARTICIPANTS AND THEIR NETWORKS

Ros Foskett

A strong theme in the life stories of the people who took part in the research reported in this book was a description of the decision-making processes that they use to help them navigate their compulsory and non-compulsory education and their career pathways. This chapter will examine what we mean by career and careers education and how research on decision-making about careers and education has informed our understanding of the processes involved. The process of career learning will be explored and it will be illustrated with reference to the individual stories and network histories of the participants in our study. An analysis of the social networks has enabled us to identify the sources of information, advice and guidance that people use in their decision-making and from this we offer an analysis of career decision-making based on a social capital perspective.

A central part of the evidence base for the research was the set of interviews undertaken with the entry point participants, and friends and family members nominated by them as being significant in their decision-making about education and career. Several sub-themes were developed in the narratives. First, individuals spoke about *experiences* gained from being part of their social network which had influenced them, either positively or negatively, in their decisions about education and employment. Second, they described the sources and types of *information* they used to find out about the different options open to them. Third, the decisions of the participants were coloured by the perceptions they had of their own *abilities*, the value and relevance of their qualifications and the educational skill sets they had acquired through both formal and informal education and work. Fourth, each individual also expressed *preferences* towards education and employment which, in part, reflected their background and history. These four themes provided considerable insight into where people look for information about education and employment, how they make sense of it and how they use it when formulating plans about the next stage in their career journey and the opportunities available to them. Each of these themes will be unpicked in more detail later in the chapter.

Some definitions

'Career' is something of a slippery concept. The etymology of the word comes from the Latin *carrus* (wheeled vehicle) and therefore it has commonality with other words, such as car and chariot, suggesting movement or travel (Oxford English Dictionary online 2009). Indeed we use the word 'career' to describe rapid motion, albeit with a lack of control or care. The heart of the concept of career is dynamic indicating a change in an individual's activity as time passes. In the higher education Careers Education Benchmark Statement, a career is defined as 'an individual's pathway or progress through life' (Stanbury 2005: 2) and as such includes periods of time when a person is in formal education and paid employment, as well as pursuing other activities such as voluntary work or informal learning. Importantly it also includes times of unemployment, family duties or time out such as a gap year between school and university.

The decisions people make about their career and the role that education might play in those decisions are happening all the time. The focus is often on the processes that individuals engage in to help them make better decisions and in particular the formal interventions and curriculum provided in schools and colleges. Terms in use are many and varied (e.g. career education, career management, career development learning, careers information, advice and guidance) and there is considerable overlap in their definition. Career education is often at the heart of the provision in schools and colleges. It encompasses:

> those formal processes that empower individuals to identify, develop and articulate the skills, qualifications, experiences, attributes and knowledge that will enable them to make an effective transition into their chosen futures, and manage their careers as lifelong learners, with a realistic and positive attitude.
>
> *(Stanbury 2005: 2)*

In most cases, career education consists of a range of teaching and learning processes delivered by an institution either face-to-face, through learning materials or electronically, designed to help an individual reflect on their previous experiences and prepare and plan for the next stage or stages.

An important element of the formal provision is careers guidance (sometimes called careers information, advice and guidance). The Organization for Economic Co-operation and Development (OECD) definition states:

> Career guidance refers to services and activities intended to assist individuals of any age and at any point throughout their lives, to make educational, training and occupational choices and to manage their careers. Such services may be found in schools, universities and colleges, in training institutions, in public employment services, in the workplace, in the voluntary or community sector and in the private sector. The activities may take place on an individual or group basis and may be face-to-face or at a distance (including help lines and web based services). They include career information provision (in print,

ICT-based and other forms), assessment and self-assessment tools, counselling interviews, career education programmes (to help individuals develop their self awareness, opportunity awareness, and career management skills), taster programmes (to sample options before choosing them), work search programmes, and transition services.

(OECD 2004)

The definitions of careers education and of careers guidance both demonstrate the breadth of activities associated with current practices informing careers provision. There are a number of important elements in the definitions. It is clear that the word 'career' needs to be defined broadly to include an individual's progression through learning and work. Therefore it encompasses the decisions people make about educational opportunities as well as preparing people for employment. It is not just fitting people to a job or to fulfil a single occupational role, yet in the interviews we conducted this was exactly how careers services were seen. Good careers education will provide individuals with information about a range of opportunities in the education and labour markets and provide them with the skills to choose, plan and make good decisions. The best provision today also includes information, advice and guidance for individuals on a wider range of issues that they face that may produce barriers to continuing with learning or finding and developing their experience of work such as finance, family matters and disability.

A historical perspective

A facet of the research that provided an interesting challenge in analyzing the data was that the participants (entry point individuals and network members) had experience of making career and education decisions against different models of provision through time. One of the important conceptual lenses we used in the research to examine the evidence has been a consideration of life course and the generational perspective which places individuals within their historical context (Giele and Elder 1998). Careers education in England and Wales has changed significantly over the last fifty years or so and the type of service prevailing when an individual attends school can affect their experience of careers provision and their view of its importance. People's experience will reflect government policy on providing careers education and information, advice and guidance, the objectives of the service at the time and what level of resource was made available.

The policy context for career education is dynamic (Foskett and Hemsley-Brown 2001). As part of its review of Education and Training provision for 14–19-year-olds in England and Wales, the Nuffield Review (2008) published a paper on guidance and careers education which provides a useful summary of the changing pattern of provision from the 1960s when careers education lessons were first introduced through to the present day. It shows how ideas have fluctuated over time. They have swung between blanket provision for all students (e.g. entitlement interviews in the 1990s) to being targeted at students identified as having particular needs (e.g.

a focus on the 'Not in Employment, Education or Training' (NEET) group in the early 2000s).

The nature of careers provision has reflected both the views of the political party in power and the prevailing economic context. For example, in the 1980s the Conservative government under Prime Minister Margaret Thatcher focused resources through the curriculum development associated with the Technical and Vocational Training Initiative (TVEI) as part of its policy framework to tackle youth unemployment. Careers interventions became more targeted, because of reduced public spending, on the groups most in need of support. This contrasts with a system of careers provision which developed in the latter part of the 2000s which devolved responsibility for information, advice and guidance (IAG) from the Connexions service to local authorities which received funding to commission IAG for young people under the Labour government. During periods of targeted provision (the TVEI initiative in the 1980s, focus on Years 9–11 at the end of the 1990s and the provision for the NEET group in the 2000s) some individuals received formal careers provision and others did not. Such changing practices over time have therefore resulted in an adult population with widely varying experiences of formal careers education and a sizable proportion with no experience of it at all. The decisions of these adults need to be understood in the context of the changing availability of education and employment opportunities that are a feature of the past forty years or so.

A matter of choice

In recent years there has been a strong trend to put the learner at the centre of decision-making, especially at each of the transitions as students move from primary school, through the secondary and tertiary phases, and beyond into HE and employment (Levin 2003). In particular, students navigating the 14–19 curriculum are faced with a multitude of choices about institution type, qualifications, vocational versus academic routes, and decisions about whether or not to enter HE. Such choices are framed by the governments which have introduced the underlying policies on education and Lumby and Foskett argue that even this landscape of 'choice-based market systems is itself the choice of government!' (2005: 103).

As people make their choices in education, and as they pass from education into the labour market or enter the NEET group, schools and colleges have a direct responsibility to help students make choices by offering them careers IAG. This is usually offered nowadays through some separate service such as an internally operated careers service or external provision such as the Connexions service. Students may also experience embedded provision which is designed to comple-ment the IAG offer such as careers education or work experience which is part of the curriculum. This formal provision is designed by the education system and is delivered to the students at a point where they may be overwhelmed by the available choices (Lumby and Foskett 2005). They need to decide whether to stay in edu-cation or leave; to apply for vocational training or academic studies; or to enter employment or to delay entry. These choices, among many others, are made in the context of the complex social networks of friends, peers and family to which the students belong (Hodkinson *et al.* 1996).

Our understanding of how people make choices has developed considerably in recent years from a traditional view that people make linear and rational decisions on the basis of complete, or at least very full, information (e.g. Janis and Mann 1977). In this case the model of support needed is very simple: if a person is given enough, good quality information they will ultimately make the right choice based on logic and rationality, and will want to optimize the outcome on some measure such as salary return or job satisfaction. However, more recent work on choice does not presume in the same way that the choices we make are rational and logical, and does not shy away from the ambiguity of decision-making. A number of different models have been put forward from the research. Lumby and Foskett (2005) argue that such models largely fall into three categories:

1   Structuralist models (e.g. Gambetta 1996) which argue that people have little actual choice as their paths are determined by the institutional, cultural or economic constraints prevailing at the time.
2   Human capital models (e.g. Becker 1975) which argue that people make rational choices on the basis of the estimated economic return that they will receive from making one choice over another.
3   Models based on subjective choices influenced by personality (e.g. Hemsley-Brown 1999) where rational choices are overlain by preconceptions, prejudices, family influences, etc.

Foskett and Hemsley-Brown (2001) developed an integrated model, drawing on elements of all of the above, which sets decision-making in the context of the environment (society, economy, culture and policy), the influencers (e.g. teachers, friends and parents), and the characteristics of the choosers themselves. The model shows a complex set of factors which influence those making choices and it shows that, 'while choice is not strictly rational, it is also not irrational or random' (Lumby and Foskett 2005: 107).

Career and education decision-making by individuals is affected by a range of internal and external factors. Any decision is going to be made within an environment which is multi-factorial and dynamic and researchers have investigated how far any decision is freely made (e.g. Lazarick *et al.* 1988). Internal influences such as self-efficacy, confidence and expectation are important in helping explain decision-making behaviour. However, external influences, defined as being 'perceived by the individual to have originated beyond the self' also have an impact (Duffy and Dik 2009: 32). Such factors are of particular relevance to the outcomes of this research as they pay particular attention to the influence of family expectations and needs, and life circumstances.

By looking at the decision-making of individuals in relation to their social network, we have been able to consider the impact of such external factors. In some cases such factors may have a direct impact on the path an individual takes. For instance, there are examples in our networks where school choice has been completely determined by family expectation. One example of this is where school choice follows family norms. In the case of the Edwards network independent education was a tradition and the older members of the network had experienced no element of choice in the schools they attended. This traditional view prevailed even for the younger generations with independent education being seen as the only answer to poor school experiences. Another example of the impact of family expectation is where a person's career choice has been greatly influenced by family. For example, in the Upton network, David chose his career direction after having been taken to see his uncle's place of work. The narratives of the individuals in this network stressed the importance of security of employment: 'getting a good job', that is, a secure job, was given priority over continuing in education.

Life circumstances also feature in the narratives of our participants when describing the choices they made in relation to education and career. Duffy and Dik refer to life's circumstances as being 'all of the uncontrollable situations, events and conditions that occur at an individual and societal level that may constrain career decision-making' (2009: 33). Once again there are many examples of such external events happening in the accounts of our participants. In some cases, they are things which individuals reported as having a positive impact on the trajectory of their career such as the chance conversation that Peter Sharpe had in a pub which led him to leave his unfulfilling manual job and to train to be a surveyor. On the other hand, there were many examples of specific life circumstances which people reported as having a more negative or limiting impact on their choices. Examples include Helen John (the John network) who decided not to attend university after her father died and Gill Henson (from the Sharpe network) whose career in speech therapy was curtailed through illness. Factors such as these must not be underestimated in trying to make sense of the way people make decisions about their education and careers. It is impossible to build a model of career learning which encompasses all life's twists and turns. However, supporting people to become independent decision-makers who can flex according to the situations they find themselves in, and who can spot opportunities and act upon them, is central to good provision (Hodkinson and Bloomer 2002).

One model of career learning which is commonly used as a framework in schools, colleges and HE is DOTS (Law and Watts 1977). This is the model which underpins the Careers Benchmark Statement used in HE in the UK (Stanbury 2005). The acronym stands for: Decision-making; Opportunity awareness; Transition learning; and Self-awareness. Decision-making is the process involved in enabling an individual to weigh up personal factors, which may include the external factors described above, and to make a sound plan for future career direction. Opportunity awareness includes helping people to increase their knowledge of options by employing sound research techniques. Transition learning involves promoting understanding of how to seek and secure opportunities especially at important transition points such as leaving school or changing job. Finally, self-awareness includes developing the ability to identify and articulate motivations, skills and personality traits as they affect education decision-making and career planning.

The four aspects of decisions, opportunities, transitions and self are articulated and dynamic and an individual will visit each part multiple times during a career. These processes may occur in the formal or informal environment. The model can either be used to understand a single decision at a particular point in time or it can be used as a framework to understand multiple decisions over time. Often career decision-making only focuses on the 'next step' – which is about making a change which may be into full- or part-time employment, full- or part-time education, or into other activities (such as undertaking a gap year or embarking on child rearing) which may have an impact on a longer-term career plan. The thinking underpinning this model informed this analysis of the interviews undertaken in our research. In analysing the transcripts we explored what influenced the decisions taken, the opportunities considered, the transitions made and the aspects of self which emerged from the interviews.

Career decision-making and widening participation

At the start of this chapter four themes were identified which emerged from the analysis of the network interviews. The qualitative analysis of the networks allowed us to examine in detail what people reported about the education and career decisions they made and the factors that they perceived to be important in their career planning processes. Four themes emerged focused on experience, information, abilities and preferences. We will illustrate these themes with reference to David Upton's network. The Upton network is used here as an example to illustrate how the 16 networks informed our thinking more generally. This network has been chosen because it is multi-generational and it demonstrates the importance of both geographical place and time in the range of choices available to people as they make their decisions about careers and education.

The Upton network is illustrated in Figure 6.1. When we interviewed him, David was a 52-year-old cartographer who was married to Christine (aged 48). Christine worked as a learning assistant in a local infant school in a medium-sized city in the south of England. David and Christine had two daughters who both lived in the parental home. Jenny, the elder daughter (aged 23), was qualified to go to university but had chosen not to participate, and she was working full-time as a team administrator in a marine service organization. The younger daughter, Michelle (aged 19), was at university studying design. We also interviewed David's mother and father (Kathleen and Michael) and his sister, Janice Bentley. The network, therefore, consisted of three generations. David and Christine Upton had always lived and worked in the same city and the family was limited in the range of their geographical action space. Apart from Janice, who lived about forty minutes away, the whole family lived in adjoining roads. Overall the family expressed relatively low career aspirations and there was not a strong push for people to continue in education. Elements of the four themes, experiences,

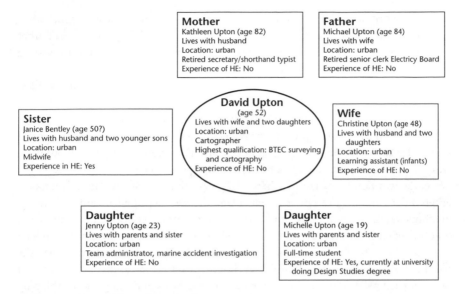

Mother
Kathleen Upton (age 82)
Lives with husband
Location: urban
Retired secretary/shorthand typist
Experience of HE: No

Father
Michael Upton (age 84)
Lives with wife
Location: urban
Retired senior clerk Electricy Board
Experience of HE: No

David Upton
(age 52)
Lives with wife and two daughters
Location: urban
Cartographer
Highest qualification: BTEC surveying
and cartography
Experience of HE: No

Sister
Janice Bentley (age 50?)
Lives with husband and two younger sons
Location: urban
Midwife
Experience in HE: Yes

Wife
Christine Upton (age 48)
Lives with husband and two
daughters
Location: urban
Learning assistant (infants)
Experience of HE: No

Daughter
Jenny Upton (age 23)
Lives with parents and sister
Location: urban
Team administrator, marine accident investigation
Experience of HE: No

Daughter
Michelle Upton (age 19)
Lives with parents and sister
Location: urban
Full-time student
Experience of HE: Yes, currently at university
doing Design Studies degree

FIGURE 6.1 David Upton's network

information, abilities and preferences, can be identified in this network, as in each
of the other networks.

Experience

This first theme relates to the key experiences an individual has through their
membership of a social network of friends and family which have influenced the
decisions they have made about education and employment. Such experiences
include the impact of family expectations, life circumstances and generational position, that is, the impact of the historical economic and social conditions prevailing
at the time. As a child, David had not enjoyed school and had tried to 'just get
through it'. He was keen to leave and there was no push from his parents, or from
the school or careers service, to encourage him to stay on.

University was seen as valuable only in terms of getting a good job and not
valuable in its own right. In fact, Michael Upton was critical of his granddaughter
going on to HE and questioned the value of her getting a higher level qualification
in design, which he saw as limited in its employment potential. His grandson was
going to university to read law, which he saw as much more relevant to the
employment market and therefore more valuable. Overall his view was that too
many people went to university:

> I'm not altogether sure . . . that I feel that every child should go to university,
> I think some should go to university, but perhaps at the back of my mind I
> have the feeling that too many children go to university, who ought to be out

. . . working. I think, you know, if . . . it seems to me that sometimes, they chop and change, they do one course at university and they change to another course and they don't seem to know what they're doing . . . and it's wasting their time and the university time.

(Michael, David's father)

The family desire for individuals to enter the labour force at an early stage into what was seen as a secure job that provided an income was very strong and this superseded any thoughts of staying on in education. Early entry into the labour force was a factor we found in many of the networks. Another common theme in the networks was family dynasties where a high proportion of the family members entered the same area of employment. Dynasties we identified included banking, boatbuilding, military careers and health. In the Upton network, the family has a tradition of entering employment connected to the sea (a marine dynasty). Kathleen had a naval tradition in her own family: her father had been in the Royal Navy, she had been in the Women's Royal Naval Service (WRNS) and on a number of occasions had worked in administrative roles for the Navy and a large ocean shipping line. Janice Bentley, David's sister, had trained as a nurse in the Navy, and his daughter worked in marine accident investigation. David himself had worked as a cartographer and the family had a long history of interest in the Sea Cadets.

In the network, there was also a strongly gendered view that the traditional nuclear family model was best, and that mothers should be at home to look after the children and the husband. Any paid work for women should fit around this expectation and this was so in the case of the three married women in the Upton network. The two older generations voiced the view that choice was limited and that you did what was expected of you. There was no expectation that work would provide satisfaction and satisfying experiences had to be sought through leisure activities.

Information

Another of our themes is the *information* an individual uses in education and employment decision-making. In this theme we explored the main sources and types of information, where individuals looked for information, the value they placed on it and how they used it. Almost all the information on careers and education that the Upton family mentioned came from the family. Although a number of people in the network have Level 3 qualifications which could provide entry into university, these were not seen as stepping stones allowing progression, but as end points. The interviews revealed that there was no real sense of career planning within the network even among the younger members and despite the fact that Janice's husband was a qualified careers adviser.

The Upton network members spoke about both formal and informal careers advice and guidance. All members of the network were critical of the provision they were offered throughout their education and this was a very strong feature of all the networks. David's experience of formal careers provision was a visit to the local colleges with his dad to attend open evenings and a reactive careers service which only supported those who asked:

> I don't remember ever having any . . . I know . . . in the last year of school . . . I went to a couple of colleges with my dad, just to see what the college was like you know, they have an open evening . . . to see what courses were available and I can remember going down to the old . . . technical college and also to [college name] just to see what courses were on offer . . . but I don't remember ever having any careers advice at school as such, no . . . I think it's one of those things . . . if you wanted it, you asked for it, if you didn't ask, you didn't get.
>
> *(David)*

Janice's experience was of a more proactive service and she spoke of her experience of having a careers interview while at school. However, she saw it as narrowing her choices rather than providing her with the information and guidance she needed:

> We all had an opportunity to see the careers advisor. I more or less told him what I'd decided . . . what I wanted to do though . . . I wouldn't say it was a negative experience that I had from the careers advisor, I did say that I wasn't absolutely sure that I wanted to do nursing and that obviously I felt that I wanted to fall back on something, so I was gonna do A levels . . . and it was then that he suggested that perhaps instead of doing A levels, I do a secretarial course or something like that . . . and I'm not sure quite where that came from . . . from his perspective, whether I'd mentioned that my . . . mum was a secretary, I don't know, but I . . . I just, I said 'I don't . . . I can't imagine anything more boring for me than to sit in an office . . . all day.'
>
> *(Janice, sister)*

Abilities

The third theme which emerged from the data analysis centred around the perceptions and particular features of the *ability* level of individuals, their qualifications, and their educational skills sets. This theme was particularly influenced by the individuals' perceptions of themselves and their ability to access educational and career opportunities. In many of the networks it manifested itself around the attitude people had to gaining qualifications and their views on the value of education. David and Janice had both internalized their parents' view that university 'wasn't for the likes of them'. Kathleen and Michael perceived that their children were not clever enough to carry on in education and should find a good job as soon as possible, despite the fact that David and Janice had been the academic equals of many of their friends who had gone on to university:

> *Interviewer: So, you said a lot of your friends were going on to university at that stage.*
> *Janice*: Yeah . . . and although I love my parents to bits, I don't think they would have even thought that I would be capable of going to university . . . which is a shame, isn't it? But, I think that's the way it is . . . so not that I felt suppressed or anything . . . but some of my best friends went to university, so it wasn't as if I wasn't up there with them, in intellectual . . . you know conversations and things . . .
> *Interviewer: Just wasn't expected of you? . . .*
> *Janice*: No

David also expressed the view that qualifications were only of limited value and that experience should be valued more highly than qualification, an attitude that mirrored that of his parents. He had taken vocational qualifications through his employment but had not enjoyed doing this and had not gone on to undertake higher level qualifications. However, despite the family's low value on qualifications David, Janice and their parents expressed the view that it was 'unfair' that more highly qualified people get promoted before those with experience and spoke of the 'threat' posed by younger, more highly qualified entrants.

One of the most dominant features of the Upton network was the emphasis placed on informal learning and experiences, which was mirrored in many of the networks we studied. Many people were engaged in numerous activities in their leisure time which featured significant learning which was highly valued. In this network, Janice's husband and David had both written books, and the whole network was into community engagement through Scouting, Sea Cadets, church and the Duke of Edinburgh Award scheme. Jenny spoke very passionately about the opportunities she had been given through this scheme and felt that this had been the pinnacle of her achievement:

> That picture over there probably . . . is, I think, is probably one of the best pictures ever. That's on the day that I got my Gold Duke of Edinburgh's award and I went up to the Palace. Mum even cried a little bit and I think yeah, they're very proud of me for that, and certain other things you know. But that day was kind of like; it was kind of my graduation day, because I didn't go to university. So it was kind of a special day for me . . . And that was my kind of graduation . . .
>
> *(Jenny)*

Preference

The final theme we identified was the *preferences* of individuals, that is, the way that individuals express preferences towards education and employment and act on decisions within their network. In this theme we explored the extent to which individuals were able to act on their own preferences rather than being constrained within the tramlines of 'normal' behaviour within their network. The interviews in the Upton family provided evidence of gendered and standardized biographies. All members, except Michelle, were early entrants into the labour market and followed gendered employment paths. Information about careers was highly influenced by the knowledge held within the family. For example, David's career path as a draughtsman had been introduced to him through an open day visit to see where his uncle worked.

The Upton family saw education mainly in instrumental terms as a means of getting secure employment and choice was very limited by the family. An example of this was the options that Christine had been given by her father. She followed a two-year Pitman's secretarial course as he had said she could either be a secretary or a hairdresser. The choices people made also reflected their network norms. In the case of the Upton family this reflected classed and gendered expectations, and the low aspirations of the population in the geographical area in which they live. Again this was a common factor in a number of the networks. In the case of the Uptons there was a tension between the narrowing of choices by family and the complete lack of guidance given in selecting from this range and developing a plan for the future. The following quotation from Michael, David's father, illustrates this ambivalence about choice when asked about advising children:

> I don't think I'd want to [influence them] . . . to help them to choose for themselves maybe, but . . . I wouldn't want to have told David or Janice that that's what they've got to go for . . . we know that David was lucky where he went . . . we had an open day . . . and he came along and said, 'That is the job I want to do.'. . . He'd chosen for himself, but maybe we had, by taking him along to the open day . . . I was always interested in straight-line drawing, never freehand . . . so it may have been that he watched me when he was younger and taken it on board, I don't know. But, I wouldn't purposely want to influence them too much.
>
> *(Michael, David's father)*

The four themes discussed in this chapter are present in all the networks in terms of the choices people have made about education and careers. We have shown here how these manifested themselves in one of the networks, but the themes existed across the networks we researched. One of the important conceptual lenses used to examine the evidence has been a consideration of the generational perspective which places individuals within their historical context (Giele and Elder 1998). The generations represented in the social networks have experienced career and education decision-making in different ways. For example, the duties of women in the home and their participation in the workplace have changed during the lifetimes of our participants, yet the Upton network demonstrates how many attitudes are slow to change. The evidence from our study still shows many participants with standardized biographies in terms of their gender, social class and age. In career terms, we have also identified that certain families reflect career 'dynasties' where members enter the same or similar jobs, and the Upton family is no exception with its strong tradition of entering careers linked to the sea.

Career decisions and whether to participate further in education are often made early on and individuals become set on career tramlines from which they find it difficult to escape. One of the dominant messages that came through our data was the inadequacy of the support provided in terms of education and careers advice and guidance. In the next section, we will look specifically at the sources of information and guidance that individuals use in more detail and offer a perspective using a social capital framework.

Careers guidance from the social capital perspective

The analysis of the individual networks was followed up with a meta-analysis to examine the theme of careers information, advice and guidance (CIAG) in detail across the networks. Social capital has provided an important conceptual lens to examine this evidence (Foskett and Johnston 2010). Network members described different types and sources of CIAG in their interviews. From this evidence we have developed a typology of the characteristics of the sources of information that people use in their decision-making. In each network it was possible to identify the main influencers and types of influence which had been instrumental in providing guidance to the entry point people (Figure 6.2). Some of these come from within the network (intra-network influencers e.g. parents and friends) and some have come from outside (extra-network influencers e.g. work or the media). In addition, some information had come from formal sources (e.g. school) and some from informal sources (e.g. chance chat in a bar). Figure 6.2 summarizes these influencers and Figure 6.3 shows the characteristics of the sources of influence.

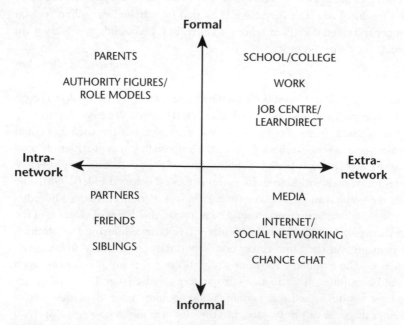

FIGURE 6.2 Decision-making influencers

The four quadrants have quite different characteristics in terms of the CIAG influences (Figure 6.3). In Quadrant A, the CIAG that individuals receive is based on family traditions in terms of employment and the education and career pathways that people follow are influenced by family status, class and history. As we saw in the case of the Upton network, many of the networks demonstrated elements of family work dynasties where generations followed similar career paths in, for example, the armed services, health professions or marine industries. This type of influence provides strong steer, but with information that is partial and incomplete. We can look at this in terms of the social capital available to individuals by drawing on Putnam's definition of social capital as 'connections among individuals – social networks and the norms of reciprocity and trustworthiness that arises from them' (2000: 19). In this quadrant, therefore, the individual's choices will be affected by bonding capital, the strong ties which link individuals with others in the network. This is likely to constrain the breadth of choice available to individuals although it may provide great support in the choices individuals make.

In Quadrant B, information about education and career choices is informal and is dominated by partners, friends and siblings, that is, the individual's peer group norms. The information is partial and incomplete, and is again a form of social capital likely to tie the individual to the group. However, by inclusion of members from other families (partners and friends), there may be an element of 'bridging capital' which brings a wider range of possibilities into the experience of the individual and, therefore, may act to broaden horizons and allow the individual to move into career and education areas beyond the guide of tradition. In the case of the Upton network,

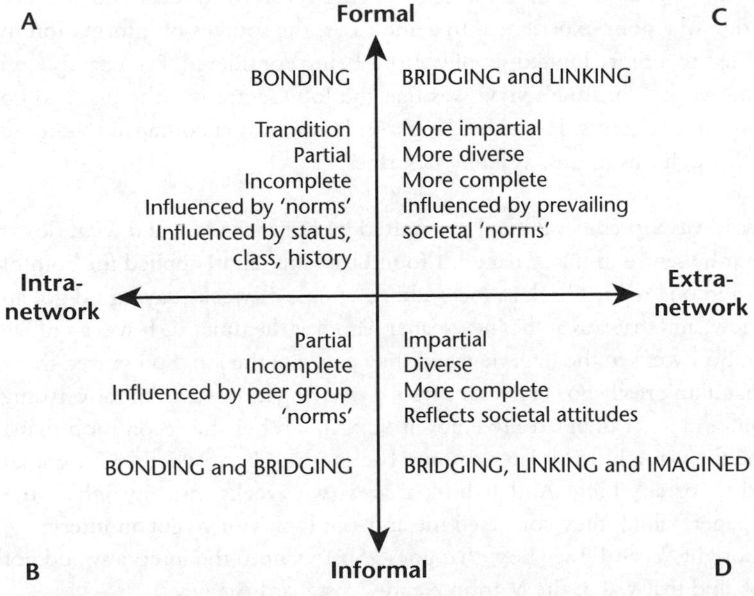

FIGURE 6.3 Sources of influence

there was very little talk in the interviews of this type of bridging activity leading to a broadening of horizons.

In Quadrants C and D, the individual is getting CIAG from outside the network of intimacy. In C, the main influences are from school, work or some other formal institutionalized source such as the Job Centre. The messages and information provided by these sources will be influenced by societal norms, but may be more impartial, more complete and more diverse. The network interviews show that people's experiences of the formal services provided, now and in the past, do not always provide evidence of this. As we saw in the Upton network, there were many personal stories of poorly delivered, partial and inadequate advice. In some cases, people were so disillusioned with their experiences that the formal CIAG was bypassed, ignored or discounted, as illustrated by this quotation from Michelle Upton:

> I sort of find the careers people a bit depressing. Well it was, in school at [school name], she was a bit hopeless. I went to see her a couple of times because like you know you don't have a clue . . . and then when I went to [college name] I realized that it was the same lady and I was like, 'Oh no, okay I'm not going to go and see you then'.
>
> *(Michelle Upton)*

The influences in this quadrant can provide bridging and linking capital (Woolcock 1998). Linking capital is the ability to access resources from formal institutions including universities, schools, colleges and careers organizations. These are the ways that individuals have traditionally been supported in their decision-making, but they depend on the information being received, understood and not discounted due to a poor experience. In some cases, the sources of information in Quadrant C led to a more limited set of options being considered. For example, in the Upton network, Christine's view was that the Job Centre was the place to go for advice on career choices. Her elder daughter, Jenny, was encouraged to choose what to do through this means, as Jenny describes:

> I think it was September 2003, I just started looking for a job, and went down to the Job Centre in [place name]. I found two jobs and I applied for both of them, and one replied back to me within a couple of weeks, saying I'd got an interview, and that was at the [newspaper name] at the time . . . It was an office junior. So I went to the interview and they gave me the job. So I started there and that didn't really go very well. I wasn't enjoying it. It was in the advertising section, and . . . I didn't really enjoy it very much but the second job that I applied for was a little bit later coming back to me about whether I'd got an interview or anything. And I think it was two weeks into my job at the [newspaper name], they contacted me and said look you've got an interview, so I thought 'Yeah I'll see how that goes'. So I went to the interview and got the job and that was at the Maritime and Coastguard Agency.
>
> *(Jenny Upton, David's daughter)*

In this case the family's strategy for using extra-network sources did not broaden choice, but was used in such a way that it bonded the individual even more tightly to the family norms.

Quadrant D encompasses informal sources that an individual can access beyond their network including through the media and chance social interactions. The internet and the diversification of the media in recent years has meant that such sources of information are freely available to more people, and younger people in particular use them as an early source of information. Such sources will include diverse material of mixed quality, comprehensiveness and accuracy. Individuals need knowledge and skills to help them use these unmediated sources to make 'good decisions'. However, in addition to bridging and linking capital, this quadrant can also provide imagined capital (Thomas and Quinn 2007: 60) which is the 'benefit produced by imagined and symbolic networks which people create to re-imagine themselves and their lives'. In other words, individuals may be able to imagine a different future for themselves away from their family norm. A good example of this is that afforded on social networking sites on the internet where people can be free to develop separate identities.

Adults have particular difficulty in accessing information and guidance about education and career choices. The evidence from the networks suggests that employment can provide a platform for staff development and qualifications, and a driver for participation and progression. In some employment sectors employers have a tradition of providing training and development and encourage their employees to participate in learning. Examples from the networks include the health service and engineering. Participants working in such areas demonstrated more positive attitudes towards progression to HE. The paucity of careers information and advice for adults was recognized as a major problem by the Labour government before its 2010 General Election defeat. At the time of writing, it is not yet clear what the new coalition government's policy will be on adult guidance services.

Conclusions

Evidence from participants in our research suggests that access to good quality CIAG is patchy. Where individuals have poor experiences, attitudes harden and it is then more difficult for perceptions towards skills development and progression to HE to be changed. Current models of CIAG, including at the interface with HE, appear not to provide the linking and imagined capital that would help individuals challenge conservatism in their social networks. For young people, interventions may come too late in secondary schooling, after attitudes and aspirations have already been established.

In our view, there is a case for joining up CIAG services across the HE, FE and employment interface to better serve the people universities hope to attract in the future and that successive governments have hoped will help grow the knowledge economy.

7

THE EXTENT TO WHICH HIGHER EDUCATION IS CONCEIVED AS 'WITHIN THE BOUNDS OF THE POSSIBLE'

Martin Dyke

A major focus of higher education policy in the UK has been to widen participation and diversify the student population. The dominant perspective presents participation as desirable, highly valued and a social good to which individuals should aspire. Our research made no value judgement about people's decisions to participate or not in HE. The project acknowledged that individuals can live happy and worthwhile lives with or without the attainment of a degree. This chapter reinforces the critique in earlier chapters of narrow economic accounts of decision-making. It extends the analysis of social capital to locate decision-making within a framework of power relationships, where circumstances and individual agency combine to provide different capabilities for agency. As noted in Chapter 5, our evidence suggests that social networks produce varying levels and types of resources that create both barriers and enablement to action.

We have drawn upon the work of Giele and Elder (1998) to illustrate how educational opportunities are shaped by specifics of time and place: where and when someone experiences significant life events will profoundly influence their life chances. Similarly, C. Wright Mills (1959) observed that life events reflect both public issues and private troubles. The interaction of personal and public issues provides a landscape of decision-making that shapes the boundaries of what our participants consider possible, particularly in terms of our research participants' engagement with HE.

This chapter focuses on how people come to navigate their way through a differentiated terrain of enablement and barriers to work and education. Connections will be made with theories of power that acknowledge the context in which private concerns connect with public issues. Scholarship that derives from the analysis of power (Mills 1959; Lukes 2005) sheds some light on the processes discussed here. Government initiatives to widen and increase HE participation can easily slide from being a matter of public policy, to one that considers non-participation as some form of shortcoming on the part of the individual rather than a consequence of the structural circumstances and institutional arrangements that influence their thinking and decision-making.

In *The Sociological Imagination*, Mills (1959) ruminated on the fast and worldwide scope of change and the challenge people faced in trying to keep pace with a world where 'the very shaping of history now outpaces the ability of men to orient themselves in accordance with cherished values' (Mills 1959: 10). In a time that predates accounts of globalization, computers and the internet, Mills talked of people being overwhelmed with information that was beyond their capacity to assimilate (1959: 11). He argued that these particular social circumstances required people to possess a sociological imagination:

> What they need, and what they feel they need, is a quality of mind that will help them to use information and to develop reason in order to achieve lucid summations of what is going on in the world and of what may be happening within themselves.
>
> *(Mills 1959: 11)*

This sociological imagination chimes with more recent accounts of reflexivity by Giddens (1990, 1991b) and Archer (2000, 2007). Mills noted that people's actions shape history and that they are influenced by 'contemporary man's self-conscious view of himself' (1959: 14). For Wright Mills, this more reflexive or sociologically imaginative person developed when people's thinking transcended the boundaries of their direct experience. Mills provides an interesting framework for considering why participation becomes an issue at different points in time. He explored the intersection between what he termed 'private troubles and public issues' (1959: 14). Private troubles derive from an individual's character and their relationship with others immediately around them; they 'have to do with the self and with those limited areas of social life of which he is directly and personally aware' (1959: 15). These personal experiences and immediate social relationships provide the milieu that can shape an individual's thinking and actions. For Mills, something becomes a private trouble when an aspect of an individual's way of life that they value becomes threatened.

Public issues concern those structural and contextual issues that may be beyond the scope and inner life experience of the individual. Public issues for Mills include the organization of social institutions, and wider social, political and economic events that transcend the local context and people's private concerns. The financial crash of 2008 is an example of a public issue where the causes and impact transcend local experiences. Consequent unemployment in turn becomes both a public issue and a private trouble. Yet the solution to the problem of economic recession is beyond the actions of any single individual trying to navigate their way through their experience of unemployment. This interplay of the macro- and the micro-structures provides a framework for analysis that is reproduced in the context of educational participation. Chapter 5 considered different forms of social capital (Halpern 2005), with parallels to the perspective adopted here which uses Lukes' (2005) account of the first, second and third face of power as a framework for analysis.

There are a number of levels which influence how people participate, or not, in education. These include the individual's experience and immediate social relationships that produce Mills' private troubles or Archer's similar focus on 'human concerns' (2000). Educational policy presents public issues that can shape material, cultural and political barriers, and enablement to participation. These public and private concerns frame what people come to see as the 'boundaries of the possible' in educational participation. There is a need to understand participation both in terms of the personal situation – people's immediate social relations – as well as in terms of the macro-educational policy and structures that shape the availability of opportunities. Mills' concept of private troubles highlights the importance of personal social relations and here-and-now experience in creating the environment in which people make or choose not to make decisions. This setting of the personal and local is significant for understanding how people make their way through the world, not just in terms of private troubles that derive from a disjuncture between cherished values and changes to life experience, but also in relation to aspects that contribute to their contentment and the wellbeing of their loved ones. Importantly, when people are content with their lives, preservation of the status quo becomes a powerful influence on their thinking about potential participation. Archer (2007) makes a similar point to Mills, separating the public and private in terms of structural factors and individual concerns and predispositions. These may not always present themselves solely as 'troubles', but extend to issues such as personal and social wellbeing, performance and achievement and feelings of self worth (Archer 2007: 199).

Public issues and private troubles also manifest themselves through the exercise of power and Lukes' (2005) framework will be used here as a metaphor for understanding participation. He identified three faces of power. The first face concerns decision-making and looks at the outcomes of decisions, in the context of whether individuals decide to participate or not. The second face of power is concerned with how certain options come to be on the agenda for decision-making. With this face of power, non-decision-making is critical, as power is held by those individuals or groups who set the agenda and can thereby prevent people from being able to consider all the options available to them. For example, governments and employers set the vocational education agenda, even if only by providing support and sponsorship. The third face of power for Lukes (2005) considers how the social-economic context frames decision-making and influences the attitudes, aspirations and capabilities of individuals and groups. These economic and cultural factors may limit the boundaries of what individuals consider possible for themselves in such a way that a decision is never taken, and the agenda need never be set. For many of the participants in our study who were either from working-class backgrounds or older generations, or both, university was simply not within the bounds of possibility, either culturally or economically.

Lukes (2005) makes use of Sen's work on capability to illustrate how social and economic circumstances influence capability. Sen (1999) illustrates two dimensions to the capability approach:

The evaluative focus of this 'capability approach' can be either on the realized functionings (what a person is actually able to do) or the capability set of alternatives she has (her real opportunities). The two give different types of information – the former about the things a person does and the latter about the things a person is substantively free to do.

(Sen 1999: 75)

Sen goes on to give a powerful illustration of the two types of information: 'Fasting is not the same thing as being forced to starve' (1999: 76). Non-participation in HE does not necessarily mean a person does not possess the capability to participate. This chapter will argue that a capability approach can shed more light on our understanding of participation and non-participation than simply focusing on whether individuals elect to participate.

Two of our 16 networks, the Hanley network and the Steers network, will be used to explore the extent to which HE is considered within the bounds of possibility. Both networks centred on working-class men who served craft apprenticeships in the marine industries and had Level 3 qualifications that made them potentially recruitable to HE. They were both aware that they could participate in HE, and they possessed the capability and social capital to do so. Both came from families with limited or no experience of HE.

The Hanley network

The Hanley network centred on John, a 34-year-old section leader and boatbuilder by trade (see Figure 7.1). John was married with two young children and had a close-knit network with limited experience of HE, though his sister had recently entered university as a mature student. He had a good quality of life and did not see a pressing need to engage in further education or training. With strong encouragement from his employer he reluctantly took a management diploma, one with a clear progression route to HE:

> I wasn't looking forward to it to start with because it's the sort of thing, the prospect of doing loads of assignments on a Saturday and Sunday night until three in the morning, you know, racking my brain for ideas . . . But when it actually came to doing them it all came naturally because all I had to do was take what I do in there and just transfer it to paper.
>
> (John)

John did not embark on educational participation in a self-directed way; he did not consider all the programmes available to him. He actively avoided making any decision to participate, but preferred to go with the flow of what was expected of him:

> You go to school, you know, you do your lessons, you get your homework and then you do your exams. It's all a process and I'm one of those people

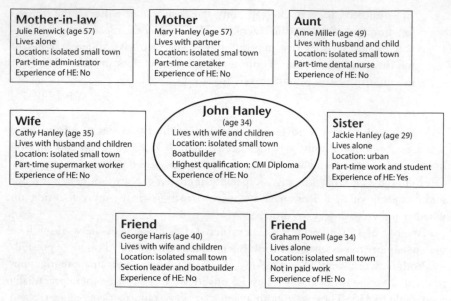

FIGURE 7.1 John Hanley's network

who can quite happily just sit on the bus and go along with it you know. . . . I just basically sat the apprenticeship and it was like a conveyor belt to where I am now really, it all just happened.

(John)

John was adamant he would not progress his management studies into HE unless required to do so. This progression pathway opened up new possibilities, including an opportunity to engage in HE, but this was not something he wanted to do. Through the agenda set by his employer his 'boundary of possibilities', his capacity for HE participation, had been expanded beyond what his employer directly required and beyond what John intended to do. John Hanley was able to make an informed choice not to participate in HE. The opportunity was there; in Sen's (1999) terms he had the capability, but the cultural predisposition to participate was not evident.

The agenda-setting role of his employer and local education providers had been central to his participation in tertiary level programmes. The curriculum organization of these programmes, with a clear progression pathway to HE, had altered John's perception of HE and his relationship to it. In this sense he had been empowered, his capacity increased by educational structures and the demands of his employers; these are aspects of Lukes' (2005) second dimension of power. However, despite the government's pressures to widen participation in HE, John was actively resisting such pressures. He would not jeopardize his quality of life by studying in his spare time unless it became an absolute necessary for him. His boundaries had been redrawn and his capacity increased, but at the time of the research he did not want to enter HE as this might threaten his family's wellbeing and contentment. Perhaps a key issue was that participation represented a considerable opportunity cost to his family's wellbeing; this in itself impacted on his capacity to participate.

John's friend and work colleague, George, had a similar educational profile but had engaged in a wider range of tertiary level vocational qualifications. Only one of these programmes had a clear progression route into HE; his employer-sponsored management diploma. This progression provided George with options he would not have considered before. George, like John, was successful in his diploma though he remained more positively predisposed towards vocational and 'hands on' work. George explicitly recognized that HE had moved within the bounds of his possibilities and might, in the future, become a necessity. It was on his agenda as a possible project, yet George also had a good quality of life and preferred not to engage in further study. For those like John and George, HE is perceived as presenting a threat to their quality of life and family wellbeing. It seemed more likely to be pursued when there was some disjuncture in life, rather than contentment. However, George was much more concerned than John that the nature of his job might change and further study become essential. George had successfully steered his way through a volatile labour market to get to his current position and had not always managed to get satisfactory work. He was much more aware than John of how the economic climate and business imperatives might impact on his quality of life. He had become more aware of the public issues and how global markets impacted on his local labour market. As a consequence, he was more positively disposed to keeping his educational and work-related options open.

George's awareness of how his opportunities and capability had expanded existed alongside a real scepticism about the value of HE and an active resistance to following this pathway. He constantly asserted the value of quality of life over work, learning and status. Work-related HE was perceived as a threat to his quality of life, and non-work-related HE was not considered within his bounds of possibility. If we use Sen's (1999) definition, he could be said to have the capability to enter HE, but did not choose to act upon it. Private troubles for others in this network, however, produced a different response to participation in HE, as illustrated by the experiences of John's sister, Jackie.

Jackie left school after illness had curtailed her A level attainment. She left school determined to work and do no more study. She took the first job she could find and stayed for eight years working for a paternalistic employer who encouraged her to gain vocational qualifications through day release. These she achieved easily. The company changed ownership and became less friendly and satisfying to work for, creating 'private troubles' for Jackie. It was this disjuncture that prompted Jackie to rethink her educational aspirations. There was limited HE experience in her network, and Jackie was the first member of her family to attend university. An Open University advertisement broadcast on television after a documentary programme led her to engage in a short higher level programme. This programme improved her confidence and became a springboard for her entry into full-time HE.

Jackie's options had quickly become very narrowly focused, shaped more by chance than any careful weighing of options. Jackie selected a science degree and did everything in her power to secure a place on it. She telephoned the admissions tutor, who unceremoniously told her that her vocational qualifications and higher level credits were not sufficient to secure a place, and that she should return to college and take science A levels. Jackie would not accept this and approached the admissions tutor again. This time he advised her to take a new science foundation programme at the university. She then visited the university and secured a place on this programme. Jackie was confident; she insisted on an entitlement to HE and she forced the admissions tutor to find a pathway for her when other candidates would have given up. At the time of interview, however, she was uncertain whether she had made the right decision, as the programme of study was not as she had envisaged:

> If someone said shall I go, you know I'm thinking about going back to university at 26 I'd tell them to think about it very seriously because it won't be what they expect. They probably won't fit in very well because of different age groups. I wouldn't say don't do it, I'd just say think about it really hard just because I found it so hard and I'm still finding it hard now.
>
> *(Jackie, John's sister)*

A science degree had also challenged her personal values and beliefs as a vegetarian in a very direct way; she had not anticipated the regular animal dissections that were part of the course. However, she had recently discovered, again by chance, that her degree programme was unexpectedly a sound route for the environmental career she wanted, and future postgraduate study. In the absence of cultural (educational) capital, Jackie's educational pathway had been shaped by chance. It was high risk, based on poor information and difficult interactions with educational bureaucracies. In terms of HE information, guidance and advice she had been poorly served. However, the bonding capital provided by her network of family and friends was instrumental in supporting her through a difficult programme of study. There is an element in Jackie's story of success against the odds. There is also evidence of the mobilization of bridging and linking capital (discussed in Chapter 5) in the forceful and determined approach that enabled her to overcome substantial barriers to both getting on and staying with her programme of study.

Dissatisfaction with work had placed HE on the agenda, but only a limited range of options was considered. Educational provision aimed at widening participation opened up opportunities and provided Jackie with the capacity to participate. It was only in her third year that Jackie had discovered that she had accidentally taken the most appropriate degree for employment in her chosen field. Jackie's boundaries had expanded with new experiences and educational opportunities. The spark for her engagement originated in discontentment with work, yet the drive and determination reflected the work ethos of her social network and the values she shared with both her brother John and their single mother.

Jackie's family initially did not actively encourage participation; indeed, there is a suggestion that her mother was against her leaving the local area to study. Yet once on the programme her family did everything in their power to keep her there. Her immediate family – her mother and John – had been very supportive of her doing whatever she wanted to do. They never really directed her; the emphasis was on Jackie finding her own way, with their support and encouragement always in the background. However, values related to work, independence and perseverance were highly rated and discussed with reference to her immediate family and extended family of uncles and aunts. There was a clear expectation that, having embarked on the degree, she should not quit but finish it. These cultural values, which Halpern (2005) would describe as facets of bonding capital, helped sustain Jackie through the difficult times in her studies. The widening participation agenda and setting up of a foundation programme for access to HE shifted the cultural landscape and enabled Jackie to follow a pathway in to university. These educational interventions extended Jackie's boundaries and set the agenda for her, representing what Lukes (2005) would refer to as the second and third faces of power.

John and Jackie's mother, Mary, was in the top stream at school but left at the age of 15 to work. In these early years of work Mary completed some secretarial training. Since then her experiences of education or training had been limited. Mary had no aspirations to continue her education, and had spent a large part of her working life as a caretaker in a community centre, a job that she enjoyed for its variety and flexibility. Raising her children had been her priority and she continued actively to support them as adults. Mary was keen to stress that she provided unconditional support for her children in whatever decisions they made, but tried to instil a strong work ethic, one that is replicated in both John and Jackie's accounts:

> But I've tried to encourage them to . . . do what, you know what they want in that sense and they've always worked. I've always sort of tried to instil in them that you know you only get where you get by doing it yourself if you know what I mean?
>
> *(Mary, John's mother)*

Educational concerns were very much framed by the needs of family members rather than her own needs. There was a strong element of unconditional love and care that constitutes the micro-level of bonding capital (Halpern 2005: 19–22). Approaches to widening participation tend to focus on enabling the individual to work through rationally what is in their own best interests, yet what emerges from these case studies is that people often act in the interests of others, especially their loved ones. This is particularly evident with Mary, but is also evident with George and John, both of whom put family life first, over and above work or any work-related learning. They reflect an instrumental perspective towards work as a means to an end, not as an end in itself. Both men had sacrificed potential career opportunities such as promotion and transfer to preserve their quality of family life. Amongst this working-class network, then, there is a very strong ethos of being independent, working hard and providing material and emotional support for family members. This overrides any aspirations towards self-advancement in the workplace or educational aspirations. Lukes' revised account of power emphasized that power is a capacity that may not necessarily be applied in terms of self-interest alone (Lukes 2005: 12), but exercised to serve the interests of others. The case studies provide many examples of people prioritizing the interests of others over their own, although examples that provide a critique of rational action or economic approaches are based on the assumption that people seek to exercise power in order to maximize their own self-interest. The trade union examples in the Steers network to which we now turn provide further evidence of such apparent altruism.

The Steers network

The Steers network (see Figure 7.2) had a strong learning ethos. Learning was highly valued and conferred prestige. There existed a cultural predisposition to learning that supported Lukes' (2005) third face of power and clearly placed informal learning high on the agenda for individuals' life decisions. Learning was a capacity that was exercised and respected, though this appetite for learning should not be confused with a desire to participate in formal education; it was a predisposition to *learn*, rather than enthusiasm for formal and institution-based education. For many members of the network who were lifelong learners, there was a certain disdain for formal education, even where opportunities to participate arose.

This network is centred on John Steers, a full-time elected trade union officer who worked in a traditional, unionized, male-dominated heavy industry. John had a working-class background and was clearly passionate about both formal and informal learning. At his secondary modern school, John did so well that he was given a chance to transfer to grammar school at the age of 13–14. This change of

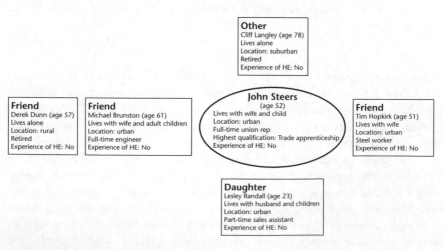

FIGURE 7.2 John Steers' network

school disrupted his education, as he did not thrive in this new school. He spoke of struggling with nerves related to any high stakes examinations. In retrospect, it seems odd to imagine he could simply adjust to and catch up with a new grammar school curriculum, although it is clear that at the time those around him believed it to be in his best interests. Unusually, this poor experience of schooling did not dampen John's enthusiasm for learning:

> I don't think there's a day goes by when you don't learn something if you are a person that's curious . . .

> Well I think all learning, I think all the learning that a person is involved in, no matter what it be in. I enjoy reading. So therefore information that I learn when I am reading can be adapted to the work scenario . . . so I think you couldn't compartmentalise where you would put the learning, I think the learning is, I think the most, how can I put it, I think the most relevant term I've heard in recent years is lifelong learning.
>
> *(John)*

John had engaged in a wide range of both formal and informal learning throughout his life and was self-taught across a range of areas. This was also a feature of those around him, including his work colleagues. It was a predisposition that fitted well with his union role, where he met various technical and legal problems that he had to research himself. His union actively supported learning and training and regularly enabled him to attend courses. Being self-taught would appear to be a feature of this working environment and was something that carried status within his network. It reflected a Labour ethos in many traditional industries, epitomized in the achievements of people like Aneurin Bevan (Foot 1997). Many of the people interviewed across the networks had enormously rich hinterlands of learning, much of which was self-taught and often creative. Examples included designing, producing, building and repairing, tasks that demand highly specialized skills beyond those they needed in the workplace. This lifelong learning was often heavily gendered, with interests in technology, classic cars, house building and dressmaking following predictable demarcations. Informal learning in particular was often seen as an end in itself, not necessarily as part of a progression pathway to higher awards, and John's distinction between formal and informal learning built on this:

> And it's also yeah I do, you know I think anybody would learn from doing a hobby as such, say like photography or you know . . .

> But you know, hobbies. But I always see formal education as being something of a means to an end you know or as a tool.
>
> *(John)*

John was talking here of tools for work, information he could use to support negotiations in the workplace or skills that could help him resolve a problem and get a job done. This included everything from maths and English to law, technical engineering knowledge and craft skills. John had a strong personality with lots of ideas, opinions and confidence. He was comfortable solving problems and navigating through potential conflicts. His standing and respect from his colleagues, who had an opportunity to vote him out of office every year, was built upon his detailed knowledge and learning and his ability to apply this to new situations and solve problems with industrial disputes.

As an apprentice who worked in a manual trade, John appeared more comfortable with the academic elements of his training:

> But also, while I wasn't the best apprentice but a few people did mention that I did show some potential whilst I was an apprentice with them. I always got through my City and Guilds. Always passed with credits and distinctions and that's when they based it on books.
>
> *(John)*

Through his own enthusiasm for learning and the opportunities he had through union-sponsored learning, John's boundaries were expanded and, with this, his capability (Sen 1999). He was positively predisposed towards engaging in HE and was very likely to participate in the future. He recognized that qualification pathways are opening up opportunities and expanding his boundaries.

John had built up a wide range of skills and qualifications throughout his working life. His workplace culture valued learning, and the organization of his working week had the consequence of creating space for outside interests and projects. His informal learning and work experience gave him the confidence to participate. In this sense the working culture supported the extension of his boundaries of possibilities. The union helped set the agenda, together with the existence of qualification pathways with clear progression routes. For both John Steers and John Hanley, work-related learning, within the context of a qualifications framework with clear progression pathways, opened up opportunities and increased their capability to participate in HE. However, this had not (yet) resulted in actual participation for these individuals. In John Steers' network, 'non-participation' reflected neither absence of capability nor lack of enthusiasm for learning.

Many of John Steers' values and orientations were also evident in the life experiences of Cliff, John's father-in-law. Cliff, aged 78, also had a poor experience of schooling, having to change schools after his home was bombed in World War Two. Cliff talked of bombs being dropped and swinging in the trees, and his sister being injured by flying glass; these were considerable distractions from schooling. War provides a most dramatic example of how Mills' (1959) public issues and private troubles can impact on the experiences of particular generations. Cliff also provides a powerful illustration of how generational experience is shaped by the particulars of time and place that alter the life course, a theme explored in more detail in Chapters 3 and 4. For Cliff, school was hard. All the teachers had canes and they used them, especially on him, yet he felt he was quite good at school, especially at maths. The usual path for people like Cliff was to leave school at 14. University was not an option: you 'needed money to be doing that'. Cliff began an apprenticeship as an electrician and was then called up for National Service.

His immediate post-school education was fairly intense until he completed his apprenticeship. It included night classes, intensive theory lessons and examinations, including practical tests of competence. These training opportunities did not go beyond the specific needs of his trade apprenticeship. There was no notion of qualifications pathways and progression. Once a trade was gained, the learning tended to be on the job. In terms of educational participation for Cliff, his agenda was set and framed by a clear set of cultural expectations and by public policy that did not promote educational progression beyond apprenticeship.

Cliff was clearly a powerful figure at work as union convener and was proud of the fact that he got on well both with the 'lads' on the shop floor and with management. He had been a lifelong learner, changing trades with different jobs, learning a wide range of union-related skills, representing people in court and at tribunals, negotiating with managers, representing different occupations and doing union case work. He was self-taught from documents and books he acquired in his union role. In Cliff's day, the trade union did not really engage in training:

> No, no, no, they didn't really, no they didn't really, no you got lots of documents and what have you, but er I picked it up quite well . . . well you used to pick up lots of books . . . No I didn't get any training at all, you just pick it up yourself.
>
> *(Cliff, John's father-in-law)*

Cliff gave many examples where he had worked hard on his research to support and further the interests of others, for example preparing for industrial tribunals. He was proud of the respect he had from both the shop floor and the management. He was clearly engaged in high levels of learning and negotiation, but not within a formal culture of education and training. Archer (2007) notes that working for the benefit of others is not something that is readily accounted for by theories of rational action. This is also acknowledged in Lukes' (2005) revised account of power. It had been a primary motivating factor for both John Steers and Cliff and had driven their engagement with lifelong learning, though for neither of these men had this included HE. Cliff's boundaries of possibilities had not included reference to formal education beyond his apprenticeship. It had not been an aspiration for his employer, his union or himself. This very much reflects the experience of education for men like him across his generation. However, as his biography demonstrates, and in common with his son-in-law, John, he had a rich and lifelong engagement with informal learning.

There were a number of people in the Steers network who were clearly very talented. They had taken the best skilled manual jobs available and represented the labour aristocracy of their time. There was no expectation or aspiration to engage in HE; it simply was not perceived as being for people like them. This applied equally to John's generation, a difference perhaps being that, for John, HE had recently moved onto his agenda. For John and some of his peers there was also an explicit recognition that, if they had been part of more recent cohorts of school leavers, they would have been destined for university rather than the sought-after skilled manual apprenticeships provided by traditional industries in the local area.

John's work colleague, Tim, had attended a secondary modern school where there had been clear expectations that boys would end up doing manual jobs in local industries such as the shipyard. As with others in this network, Tim laid emphasis on learning new things and keeping his brain active. The opportunity to provide examples of things people had produced or taught themselves was highly valued in this network; it was very much learning associated with creativity and products of learning. The agenda for learning was generally self-directed and connected with core interests.

During the interview there was plenty of evidence of self-taught skills and learning, extending to Tim's smallholding, animal husbandry, renovation of cars and work on his house. Tim demonstrated a preference for working with his hands, being practical and working things out in his head. His parallel interest in creative writing emerged right at the end of the interview. This was clearly important to him and was highly valued in his family. Tim walked on local hills where he mulled things over in his head, and often wrote these thoughts down as stories, narratives or poems. These had been kept in folders full of loose paper. He was proud that he could recite them all from memory, which he regularly did on special family occasions.

His daughter studied drama at university and was active in a poetry society. She was convinced that her dad's work was good and that it should be published, and they were currently trying to organize all the papers in some kind of folio for presentation purposes. The influence of the daughter on the father illustrates how cultures shift over time and demonstrates the impact younger generations can have on older generations; in this case his daughter was extending Tim's boundaries of possibilities and potentially enhancing his capability and power to participate in formal education. Yet Tim was content with all his life decisions and career. He had no desire to participate in formal education or training, taking pride in the fact that he was self-taught and could solve most problems himself. He was proud of family members who had been to university, but had absolutely no aspiration to go himself. Indeed, he was quite resistant to the idea and keen to assert the value of the work and skills of those around him. Tim clearly had the capacity to participate in HE, as so many in his network and family already had done. However, it was not seen as within his boundary of possibilities:

> Higher education to me means . . . going to evening classes. And sitting in another classroom. Probably using a computer. Which is something I've avoided all these years. And I will continue to avoid. Not interested.
>
> *(Tim, John's colleague)*

The shipyard operated on the basis of four long working days that enabled employees to take Fridays off and have a long weekend. The working ethos of John and his work colleagues flowed into the weekend, when they actively engaged in a range of projects, many of which involved learning and problem solving. These projects were shared with each other, and the products of these and skills associated with their endeavours were respected by peers and across the network. It was a small network with a strong learning ethos and high levels of bonding capital that supported these extra-curricular activities.

Many of the projects were quite individualized, with people working alone and only seeking advice when they needed to. In this sense it reflected a dimension of work in the shipyard where steel workers work fairly independently of each other on jobs of heroic proportions. Their skills and the products of their work were highly respected in the yard.

The Steers network was a lifelong learning network actively engaged in a diverse range of informal learning. The network had little experience of, or interest in, HE. There was some evidence that the experience of the younger generation was beginning to influence the parents' generation. This, together with the education agenda that had percolated through as work-related learning, had extended the boundaries of what network members regarded as possible. The role of male working-class culture and trade union activity had been central in promoting lifelong learning across generations in ways that predate recent government agendas for lifelong learning and widening of participation. As with the Hanley network, formal education was very much viewed in a utilitarian way, as a means to an end, and there was evidence of some resistance to formal education that sat alongside a very rich and diverse informal engagement with lifelong learning.

Analysis and conclusions

As outlined in Chapter 3, a life course approach needs to acknowledge the power and influence of the specifics of time and place (Giele and Elder 1998). The networks described in this chapter reveal a dynamic relationship between individuals and changing circumstances around private concerns and public issues, including government agendas regarding educational participation. The interviews revealed a range of responses to changing circumstances including scepticism and resistance for some, engagement and openness for others. There was also evidence that people reviewed their perspectives in the light of new experiences, including the experiences of others. The HE experience of younger participants had a particularly powerful impact on altering the perception of older generations, and Heath et al. (2010) have explored this in relation to four other networks involved in our research. We need to theorize such relationships in a way that acknowledges the dynamic and changing situation, rather than providing an account of socio-cultural influences as something static: or, as Archer (2000: 273–6) terms it, we need to theorize for 'morphogenesis' rather than 'morphostatis'. In both of these networks we have traditional working-class cultures evolving and changing in response to personal experiences and, indirectly, to policy interventions that encourage lifelong and work–related learning. There were changing dynamics in these networks and influences flowing both ways across generations.

The above examples demonstrate how variations in predisposition, self–identity, resources, social capital and life chances produce different levels of capability to participate or to elect not to participate. There are parallels here with the account of the Family Learning Centre in Chapter 5, where the boundaries of the possible were shaped by policy interventions that provide institutional resources for building capacity. That capability is further developed where it links to the social capital and interpersonal relations already existing within a community.

Participation in HE cannot simply be explained by theories of rational choice. There are differential levels of capability and inclination to participate. The evidence from our research suggests that people do not make their decisions solely in a perfect market of possibilities and on the basis of individualized judgements about personal economic gain; they are also keenly aware of how their decisions impact on others. This concern for others in their networks is a strong theme in the above accounts. People are constantly aware of how their actions impact on others and frequently put the needs of others before themselves. Participation, therefore, is not simply an issue of socio–economic priorities, but has an ethical dimension, one that chimes with the Kantian ethic celebrated by Bauman (1993) of putting others before oneself. Policies and interventions therefore need to take account of such ethical influences on capability and decision–making.

The above examples resonate with Lukes' (2005) work on power, which provides a useful metaphor for considering the boundaries of possibilities in relation to HE participation. Lukes' earlier work (1974) defined power more in terms of domination of one person or group over another. In his more recent work he acknowledges that this conceptualization is essentially contested (Lukes 2005: 110–24). After 30 years of commentary, Lukes accepts that his original conceptualization of power (Lukes 1974) was inadequate for, like Mills (1959), he confused the exercise of power and the impact of a decision or action with power as a capacity. Lukes now argues, 'Power is a capacity not the exercise of that capacity (it may never be and never need to be exercised); and you can be powerful by satisfying and advancing others' interests' (Lukes 2005: 12). The issue of power as a capacity is significant in discussions of HE participation. There is a need to understand the extent to which individuals see themselves as having the capacity to participate: whether participation is perceived as being materially or culturally within a person's bounds of possibility. Whether or not individuals elect to exercise that capacity and to participate is a different issue. In this respect Lukes' more recent arguments share similarities with Sen's (1999) conceptualization of capability.

As outlined earlier in this chapter, Lukes acknowledges three faces of power. The first concerns the decisions made: in participation terms this would simply be reflected by the number of people who participate. The second face of power concerns agenda setting; how it is that some options appear on the agenda as a possible project under consideration. This approach considers the decision–making process, as well as the non–decision–making process. When a government or employer will only fund certain types of programmes, vocational for instance, it sets an agenda in an obvious and observable way. The analysis presented here has identified the programmes of study which individuals have on their agenda as possible projects. These cover a much more limited range than the entire spectrum of possibilities, but still represent clear, observable considerations. It is useful to consider how such programmes arrive as projects on the individuals' agenda. More subtle forms of agenda setting within a social network of friends and family can influence how particular projects are selected as possibilities. For example, occupational traditions within a family can work both ways, whereby children follow or actively avoid the pathways of their parents. For Lukes, there is also a third dimension to power, influenced by the social and cultural situation of the person. This third dimension is represented here as that which is considered within the 'bounds of the possible' (in terms of educational courses, levels and pathways). This, for Lukes, presents power as 'a dispositional concept, comprising a conjunction of conditional or hypothetical statements specifying what would occur under a range of circumstances if and when power is exercised' (Lukes 2005: 63). Here, dispositions are often bounded by structural and cultural factors that limit what people regard as possible. The third dimension is, for Lukes, focused on 'particular domains of experience and is never, except in fictional dystopias, more than partially effective' (Lukes 2005: 150). While this third dimension provides boundaries to what people consider possible, it is framed by experience and reflexivity. These boundaries are neither fixed nor deterministic, and people revise their positions and make reflexive judgements. Lukes quotes Susan Bordo to illustrate this point:

> People know the routes to success in this culture – they are advertised widely enough – and they are not dopes to pursue them. Often, given the sexism, racism, and narcissism of the culture, their personal happiness and economic security may depend on it.
>
> *(Bordo, 1993: 30, quoted in Lukes 2005: 150–1)*

Predispositions and capabilities are not predetermined, but are shaped by context, and influenced by factors such as class, gender and generation, as well as the education and training environment that the person perceives as being available to them. In terms of participation this third dimension represents the boundaries of a person's thinking about participation. As the individual gains more direct or indirect experience of education and training, these boundaries may shift and new possibilities move into the frame of reference. Such experience may take the form of participation in tertiary level education or 'grapevine' knowledge (Ball and Vincent 1998) about educational opportunities. The boundaries can also be influenced by changes and activities in the field of education and training policy, such as lifelong learning and widening participation initiatives. The cases above have provided examples of ways in which the boundaries of possibilities were extended; these included via employer-sponsored training, trade union education, further education and the experience of younger generations in HE feeding back to older siblings, parents and friends. These case studies illustrate how capability is framed by socio-cultural factors including a person's social network. They also demonstrate how different forms of agency and decision-making influence the agendas, or projects, with which people are engaged.

A consideration of the 'bounds of the possible' does appear to shed some light on the changing patterns of participation. These shifting boundaries are like a flexible membrane, able to expand and contract in different directions as people learn from their own life experience and that of those around them. The boundaries are influenced by structural elements and culture; they set the frame from within which people select their projects reflexively and in active communication with others. From these projects emerge practice, the individual agency of what people actually do: their education and training experiences. This social and situated educational experience in turn shapes new possibilities that frame emergent reflexive projects.

The case study examples also reveal very diverse predispositions towards partici-pation. Circumstances change, for some more than others, but they are not static or simply flowing in one direction; the experience of younger generations influence the thinking of older generations as well as vice versa. Educational interventions may extend a person's boundary of the possible and thereby their capacity to participate. The interviews demonstrate that many people elect not to exercise that capacity; they resist participation in formal education. Yet many of our participants have rich learning biographies and have engaged in a wide range of informal educational activity throughout their lives. Rather than simply focus upon whether or not people participate in HE, perhaps we should pull back the lens a little, consider more carefully whether participation is within a person's power (a real meaningful opportunity, a capacity or capability), and how this capability in turn influences people's concerns and the life projects they consider. Participation considered as a capability, rather than an outcome, helps us to improve our under-standing of how participation in HE is embedded in social practice.

8

POLICY, PRACTICE AND THE 'NEW WIDENING PARTICIPATION': PERSPECTIVES AND IMPLICATIONS

Nick Foskett

The policy context is a critical frame of reference for researching widening participation. As we have noted throughout this book, the concept of widening participation has been an important element of national education rhetoric and policy for much of the last three decades in the UK, and this mirrors what has been going on in the European Union and other national contexts over the same period. This means that the operational decisions of schools, colleges and other parts of the formal education and training system during this time have been made in a policy environment where widening participation has a high profile. At the same time, the decisions of individuals about their education and training futures have been made at a time when participation in further or higher education has been a policy priority. As the intended widening participation outcomes have not been fully achieved, important questions remain about the nature of policy, the policy process and the relationship between policy as text, policy in action and the 'real world' of individuals' decision-making. This chapter explores the recent policy context and its relationship with the decision making of people who are qualified to enter higher education (HE) but have chosen not to do so.

The connection between policy and practice is not simple. Policy intentions do not transfer by a simple, linear process into predictable changes and impacts. Rather, the policy process is an heuristic one that sees political ideals translated into policy documents that are then interpreted through the practice of implementation at every level, from government to grassroots. Hence outcomes cannot be simply 'read off' from policy. Seeking to understand how policy and its implementation have shaped the observable outcomes is essential if future policy is to be designed to achieve more of the intended outcomes.

This chapter focuses on the large-scale components of this process by revisiting the evolution of national policy in relation to widening participation in HE. It will focus on three themes – the origins of widening participation policies in the UK and the issues which have emerged from their implementation; the ways in which those policies appear to have shaped the behaviours and strategies of families and individuals within our study; and the implications of the findings for widening participation policies in the next decade.

Widening participation policies in the UK

UK educational policy has been dominated by three major issues since the late 1980s (Bell and Stevenson 2006). First, the processes of globalization and the pursuit of economic competitiveness have promoted the theme of 'human capital development' that, as Lloyd and Payne (2003: 85) suggest, takes a view of education in which there is 'a paradigm shift . . . towards a post–Fordist, high skill, or knowledge-driven economy whereby investment in human capital . . . constitutes the key to national competitiveness'. Second, there has been a focus on education as a means to reduce social disadvantage in what Bell and Stevenson (2006) describe as 'education policy for citizenship and social justice'. Finally, the emergence of neo-liberal and neo-conservative political contexts has prioritized a third theme in education policy, focused on 'accountability, autonomy and choice' (Bell and Stevenson 2006). This has emphasized the centrality of market accountability for the alignment of national economic and social goals with the high-value concept of individual choice.

The notion that policies relating to HE entry should have some dimension of social justice may be traced back in the UK to the Robbins Report of 1963 (Robbins 1963). Robbins set HE on a pathway of expansion, principally with the aim of making a substantial contribution to the UK economy, but also with a view that growth would make university education accessible to wider groups within society. While the creation of new universities during the 1960s enlarged the sector, of more significance in terms of widening participation was the formation of the polytechnics from 1970 onwards. Thirty polytechnics were established from existing colleges of technology, producing a binary system in which, broadly speaking, universities provided traditional academic programmes while the polytechnics focused on technical and vocational HE. In policy terms, the system was explicit in providing pathways that extended and diversified participation to groups beyond 18-year-olds coming from selective secondary schools with traditional academic A levels. With relatively low participation rates across all sectors of society, however (only 15 per cent of 18-year-olds went into HE in 1985), issues of equity and fair access were not foregrounded by the then government.

The 1990s, however, saw the emergence of widening participation policy in highly significant ways, both in the UK and internationally. The stimulus in the UK lay with the commitment to expand HE substantially and to remove the binary divide. Expansion of HE was predicated on the importance of raising education and skill levels to sustain the UK's economic strength in an increasingly globalized world (DES 1991). The mechanism chosen for stimulating that growth in a financially efficient way was the marketization of the sector, obliging HE institutions to compete for resources and students. To facilitate the market, polytechnics were

given the same autonomy, governance and financial arrangements as univer
under the 1992 Further and Higher Education Act (HMSO 1992), and all chos
become universities in name as well as form.

The 1992 Act was premised on the key assumption that market mechanisms
and competition would meet the desire to increase overall participation. However,
by the middle of the decade it was clear that policy challenges remained. First,
expansion of HE required greater participation from a much wider range of social
groups than had hitherto been the case, both in terms of generating the numbers of
participants and in ensuring that the benefits of such growth spread to all sectors of
society. Second, the removal of the binary divide meant that there needed to be an
explicit consideration of access and diversity in HE participation across the unified
sector.

Widening participation first appeared as a distinctive term and concept in the
political discourse in the UK and Europe in the mid-1990s, for example in the
European Commission 1994 White Paper *Growth, Competitiveness, Employment* and
the 1997 Kennedy Report *Learning Works*. The explicit naming of the concept at
this time suggests that attempts to manipulate patterns of participation had not
previously been made by government. However, in reality it can be better understood as a further development of approaches to widening participation and, as such,
policy from this stage forward could more properly be referred to as the 'new
widening participation'.

As a component of HE policy, widening participation was fundamentally
connected to each of the three broad themes outlined earlier. Thus, while it primarily promoted education as a necessity for a future knowledge economy, it also
had a wider social purpose to 'reduce the correlation between participation and
social or economic disadvantage' (Raffe *et al.* 2001: 174), and to promote autonomy
and choice for individuals from all sectors of society. With such a comprehensive
relationship to key themes, widening participation has remained a plank of policy
for successive governments in the UK and elsewhere in Europe (Foskett 2002). By
2009 the concept was to be found in the policy perspectives of most government
and opposition political parties across Europe in relation both to immediate post-
school and university levels of education (Stoer and Magalhaes 2009). Elsewhere,
McDonough and Fann (2007) have demonstrated that the same patterns of social
inequality that are found in UK are clearly identifiable within HE in the USA,
resulting in an emerging concern to address issues of equity and inclusion within
patterns of participation. Within the less-developed economies, too, such priorities
are recognized. King and McGrath (2002: 10), for example, identify the importance
of both increasing and widening participation in education at all levels for most
African states, in their view that 'the development of the notion of learning-led
competitiveness can help African countries in ensuring that the African Renaissance
has real economic meaning'.

The promotion of widening participation as a central policy tenet in the UK is
linked intimately to the Dearing Report of 1997. The Dearing Report was
commissioned to provide a comprehensive review of HE in the UK (the first since

the Robbins Report) and to make proposals that would equip the sector to meet the country's social and economic needs over the following two decades. Dearing recognized the significance of education as both 'enriching and desirable in its own right . . . [and] . . . fundamental to the achievement of an improved quality of life in the UK' (NCIHE 1997: 4), and sought to shape HE as a key part of a 'society committed to learning throughout life' (NCIHE 1997: 4). The Dearing Report's 72 recommendations touched on all dimensions of the system, but of particular relevance here are Recommendations 1 and 2. Recommendation 1 encouraged a significant growth in student numbers, especially at undergraduate (and sub-degree level), while Recommendation 2 proposed that 'the Government and the Funding Bodies . . . when allocating funds for the expansion of higher education . . . give priority to those institutions which can demonstrate a commitment to widening participation' (NCIHE 1997: 6). This recognized that there 'remain groups . . . who are under-represented in higher education, notably those from socio-economic groups III to V, people with disabilities and specific ethnic minority groups' (NCIHE 1997: 6).

With the adoption of most of the recommendations from Dearing, so began 'the English Experiment' (Parry 2010: 32) – the attempt both to increase participation rates substantially and to break down traditional patterns of participation reflecting socio-economic background. As Parry explains, the Dearing Report provided the starting point from when, 'Under three successive Blair governments and into the Brown administration widening participation emerged as a major policy enterprise and a regular source of political controversy' (Parry 2010: 32).

Parry (2010) identifies four 'phases of activity' in this subsequent development of widening participation policy in England and Wales. The first was the introduction of the funding lever of 'additional student numbers' (ASNs) made available to institutions that could expand their intake through implementing effective widening participation strategies. When this strategy failed to deliver the government's overall goals, a second phase focused on the attainment of national targets for expansion and the introduction of a new targeted qualification, the Foundation Degree.

The third phase was associated with the introduction of variable student fees under the 2005 Higher Education Act. This required universities to commit some of their additional funding from fees to the support of schemes to promote widening participation. Access agreements, negotiated through the new national Office for Fair Access (OFA), included the provision of funds for scholarships and bursaries for low participation groups, and a commitment to engage in outreach activities.

Despite the energies and efforts associated with these three phases of activity, data on participation continued to indicate that the government's widening participation aspirations were not being achieved. As Blanden and Machin (2007) have suggested, the small number of working-class students in leading UK universities has had little effect on the universities themselves, the attitudes and expectations in the communities they come from, or the achievement of meta-level policy goals of government.

Parry's fourth phase of activity relates to the three years to 2009, when the perceived lack of progress stimulated government to seek to understand better some of the key processes that underpin the impact of widening participation activities. This has coincided with the continuing application of existing strategies, but has seen little real innovation in policy. This reflects a) an impasse in understanding what new approaches might enhance impact, and b) the wider financial pressures from 2008 onwards. These pressures have meant that not only has new investment in widening participation not materialized, but that retrenchment on existing funding is a likely policy outcome of the far-reaching review of public funding by the new Conservative–Liberal Democrat coalition government during the summer and autumn of 2010.[1]

Parry describes the evolution of policy between 1997 and 2009 as comprising four phases, yet these simply represent operational changes to a consistent policy goal. These changes have been motivated by the failure to achieve the desired policy impact within acceptable political time frames. Lumby and Foskett (2007), writing in the context of further education policy, have commented on the paradox that rapid policy change may simply be superficial turbulence characterized by action, rather than a fundamental change to policy direction or underpinning principles. The policy environment of widening participation in HE over the last decade is a further example from the UK of turbulence masquerading as change. All the 'changes' represent attempts to achieve a more representative student population, in the light of evidence that the government's key aim for widening participation was not being met.

Three important observations emerge from this account. The first is that it is clear that the social, economic and behavioural context of decision-making on HE participation has been poorly understood (David 2010). Gorard *et al.*'s (2006) review of the research evidence on widening participation demonstrates that there still exists only a patchwork of understanding of how, when and why both young and older potential HE participants make their decisions to go, or not to go, to university. Second, if the evidence on the key underpinning processes is sketchy, the capacity for government to develop policy and strategy that enables their social and economic goals to be achieved in this arena is inevitably lacking. Raffe and Spours have considered at length the policy processes at work in the broad field of 14–19 education and have drawn a number of important conclusions that also provide insight into some of the issues relating to widening participation policy. In particular, they highlight the challenge of 'policy learning', that is 'the ability of governments, or systems of governance, to inform policy development by drawing lessons from available evidence and experience' (Raffe and Spours 2007: 1). In the context of widening participation in the UK, we must conclude that there has been relatively little policy learning even though (and perhaps, in fact, *because*) it has been a high-profile political issue over the last decade.

Third, rapid change in strategy and policy is likely to be in itself a key cause of the failure to achieve the desired policy outcomes. Those least likely to participate are also the least likely to have access to either 'hot' or 'cold' sources of advice and information (Dyke *et al.* 2008), and are the most likely to be unclear about how to use information to engage with HE admissions processes. If the understanding or knowledge they have is fragile and subject to change over short periods, then this will act as a significant impediment to engagement. Similarly, rapid change in the patterns of support, advice and funding for widening participation means that advisors themselves, whether in schools or outside, have difficulty in providing up-to-date and accurate advice and guidance.

In the context of the above analysis of the evolution of policy and the issues surrounding its implementation, it is appropriate now to examine two important aspects of widening participation. The first of these is the evidence of macro-scale changes in participation patterns, and this is addressed in the next section. The second focuses on the experience of potential HE entrants making participation decisions within the contemporary policy environment by drawing on evidence from our own research.

The impact of widening participation policy

The largest group of students in UK universities has traditionally comprised those who choose to enter HE at age 18 or 19. While since the mid-2000s this group has been replaced in its primacy by those aged over 21 (who now make up 54 per cent of all HE undergraduates), traditional age entrants are still a key focus of widening participation policy. HEFCE (2010) has reported that the age-related participation rate amongst such 'young participants' (18- and 19-year-olds) in England has grown from 30 per cent in 1994/95 to 36 per cent of the 2009/10 entry cohort. In absolute terms, the numbers of 18- and 19-year-olds entering HE has grown from 162,000 to 239,000 over this time period, and while a significant part of this increase reflects the 21 per cent increase in the size of the 18 and 19 age cohort over this time, HEFCE (2010: 4) calculates that 'there are 43,000 additional entrants from the 09/10 cohort attributable to the rise in the young participation rate since the mid-1990s'.

The HEFCE study shows that participation rates have increased for young people from both advantaged and disadvantaged neighbourhoods, but with greater percentage growth for those from disadvantaged localities (+50 per cent) than for those from more advantaged areas (+15 per cent) between 1994/95 and 2009/10. Since 'the mid-2000s the majority of additional entrants to higher education have come from disadvantaged areas' (HEFCE 2010: 2). Such changes, however, still leave significant differences in participation rates between advantaged and disadvantaged neighbourhoods, between the lowest socio-economic groups and the highest ones, between young people of different ethnic background, and between young men and young women. Reay *et al.* (2010), for example, report that in 2005 only 24.7 per cent of admissions to university in the UK were from the lowest four socio-economic groups, a figure which shows a disproportionately low representation from such groups in HE. The disparity is exacerbated by higher subsequent non-completion and drop-out rates among students from these backgrounds, because the universities with high widening participation achievements in relation to such groups show the highest drop-out rates.

A second example of remaining disparities is illustrated by the data on gender (HEFCE 2010). Participation rates for young men remained at about 29 per cent for the decade from 1994/95 to 2005/06, before showing an increase to 32 per cent by 2009/10, while participation rates for young women grew steadily over the same period from 30 to 40 per cent. Perhaps even more significant is the observation that, while young women were 23 per cent more likely to enter HE than young men in 2009/10, in the most disadvantaged areas this difference is +35 per cent. This also reflects disparities in achievement of boys and girls at school, where females consistently outperform males.

The patterns described suggest, of course, that policy interventions have contributed to widening participation amongst traditional age entrants in recent years, but it is also clear that significant gaps and discrepancies, while diminished, have not been eliminated. In the section that follows we shall explore how this has been playing out in the lives and decisions of some of our own research participants.

The interaction of policy, behaviours and strategies in networks

Two of the 16 networks in our own study will be used here to illustrate the interaction of widening participation policy and behaviours and decision-making in relation to choosing whether or not to participate in a higher level programme. The analysis points to a number of important conclusions relating to the reality of the impact of widening participation policy in England.

Responses to the widening participation policy context are reflected in all 16 of the networks, and examples in other chapters consider individual and network accounts across a wide range of socio-economic backgrounds. Many networks straddle the middle and working classes, often with a strong tilt toward the working class. In contrast, the two networks discussed in detail in this chapter are solidly middle class. As ever, the networks illustrate how responses to policies, pressures and challenges are mediated at the micro-level and cannot be assumed straightforwardly on the basis of their socio-economic background.

In previous chapters, we have seen how social class background relates to (higher) educational decision-making. These cases illustrate at the micro-level some of the disparity in access to HE according to social class and gender, as described earlier in this book. For members of the post-Second World War generation, university had been largely an elite, middle-class preserve. For several older network members, university might now be viewed as within the bounds of possibility, given the government's policy on encouraging mature learners into HE and their level of qualifications. But evidence from our research suggests that policies encouraging those in mid- and later life to enter HE were, in many cases, unlikely to be successful for a range of reasons. Some had satisfactory careers developed at a time when a university degree was not required for as many jobs as currently, or for career progression. Some had ambiguous feelings about formal education, given unfortunate experiences at school. Others lacked the energy and enthusiasm for HE, and felt it had little relevance to their lives and aspirations. For younger members of the family and the contemporary generation (such as Jamil Masuka, his siblings and his friends; Lorraine Smith's children; and the Gregory children), they had many more choices available to them after leaving school than their parents. Some of this group did choose to participate in HE or anticipate doing so, but even these young people had mixed feelings about the benefits in personal and material terms.

The first network considered in this chapter is that of Helen John. Helen was 21 at the time of our research. She had left full-time education after A levels in a FE college and took up a full-time job in the health sector, where she worked as an education training manager at a local hospital. She lived at home with her mother (Sandra John), who had been widowed when Helen was 14. Sandra was a qualified and experienced nurse, working at a local health centre, while Helen's father had been a medical doctor. Other key members of the network who were interviewed were Helen's older sister (Emma), a teacher who lived with her husband and young child some fifty miles away; Helen's best friend, Becky Cox; Helen's grandmother, Hazel John, who lived nearby; and Jonathan Brown, a retired teacher who was coaching Helen while she was studying part-time for science A levels at the time of the interviews. Network members are represented in Figure 8.1.

The second network is that of Hilary Edwards (see Figure 8.2). Hilary was aged 63 at the time of the interviews, living with her husband Richard. Her working life had been spent in secretarial roles, mostly as a school secretary, and her highest formal educational award was a Level 3 Diploma in secretarial work. The network comprised her brother (Martin Hunter), recently retired from a career in the RAF as a civilian manager, and his wife (Natalie); Hilary's mother, aged 96; Hilary's two sons, Paul (aged 43), a university lecturer and Anthony (aged 42), a middle manager in an engineering company; and two of Hilary's teenage grandchildren, both of

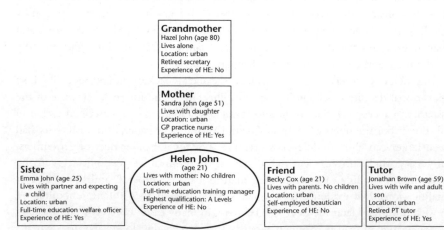

FIGURE 8.1 Helen John's network

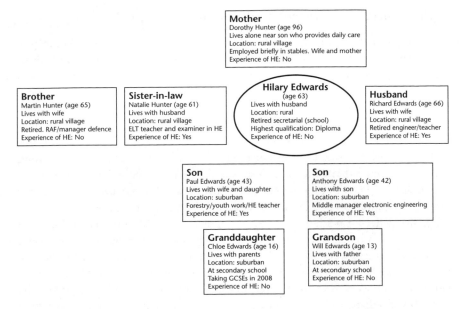

Mother
Dorothy Hunter (age 96)
Lives alone near son who provides daily care
Location: rural village
Employed briefly in stables. Wife and mother
Experience of HE: No

Brother
Martin Hunter (age 65)
Lives with wife
Location: rural village
Retired. RAF/manager defence
Experience of HE: No

Sister-in-law
Natalie Hunter (age 61)
Lives with husband
Location: rural village
ELT teacher and examiner in HE
Experience of HE: Yes

Hilary Edwards
(age 63)
Lives with husband
Location: rural
Retired secretarial (school)
Highest qualification: Diploma
Experience of HE: No

Husband
Richard Edwards (age 66)
Lives with wife
Location: rural village
Retired engineer/teacher
Experience of HE: Yes

Son
Paul Edwards (age 43)
Lives with wife and daughter
Location: suburban
Forestry/youth work/HE teacher
Experience of HE: Yes

Son
Anthony Edwards (age 42)
Lives with son
Location: suburban
Middle manager electronic engineering
Experience of HE: Yes

Granddaughter
Chloe Edwards (age 16)
Lives with parents
Location: suburban
At secondary school
Taking GCSEs in 2008
Experience of HE: No

Grandson
Will Edwards (age 13)
Lives with father
Location: suburban
At secondary school
Experience of HE: No

FIGURE 8.2 Hilary Edwards' network

whom were still at school – Chloe, who is Paul's daughter and severely disabled, and Will, who is Anthony's son.

Both networks comprised families who described themselves as middle class, and who demonstrated family traditions of participation in HE and professional careers. In the case of Helen John, the family had a strong background in the health professions, with the mother a nurse and father a doctor, and Helen's sister a graduate and a qualified teacher. In the case of Hilary Edwards, the family had a tradition of engineering and military-related careers for the male family members, but secretarial careers and a focus on homemaking for the women. In such contexts the policy messages of the value of HE participation might be expected to play through strongly in the educational decision-making of family members, yet the reality of action and choice was more complex. In the Helen John network, both of Helen's parents and her sister had obtained university degrees, and in the Edwards network both of Hilary's sons and her nephew and niece had also participated in HE. Yet, in both networks, the value of HE to achieving longer-term personal goals was still questioned, with a clear recognition that, while it may be a typical progression path for 'middle-class young people', it was neither sufficient nor essential to success in life.

The rhetoric of participation as espoused by policy is not necessarily totally secure, therefore, even in the heartland of the middle classes. This confirms the notion that the interaction of policy intent, policy implementation and the context of choice networks is complex. We can identify four specific insights into the interaction of policy and behaviour that emerge from the analysis of these two networks, and these are discussed in turn below.

Higher education participation doesn't always appeal

A key characteristic of our research was the identification of individuals who, despite possessing the qualifications to enter HE, had chosen not to do so. These individuals represented a wide range of backgrounds, from those from families where HE was a common choice, to those where there was little or no history of participation. Heath *et al.* (2010) have demonstrated how, for four of the entry point individuals, participation by another member of the network had still stimulated neither their participation, nor that of others qualified to participate.

For Helen John, the decision not to enter HE after A levels, despite a strong family expectation that she would do so, was the result of a complex set of personal circumstances. The death of her father when she was 14 destabilized her academic progress, resulting in good but not outstanding GCSE results and progression to A levels that reflected neither her academic interests, nor her original ambition to pursue a career in medicine. The result was a decision not to progress to university, a decision revisited quite frequently but never reversed (at least up to the time of the research). Helen recognized the external expectation (and the family expectation) that she would obtain a degree, but was not yet convinced that, for her, the added benefits that the policy rhetoric indicated would accrue from university would actually emerge.

> I think the family that we have and the friends that we have are obviously all highly educated people doing very well and have all been to Uni. And part of me did feel that in order to you know follow suit I should have been going to university and I should have, but actually it wasn't what I wanted to do . . .

> So for me to go to university and spend thousands of pounds doing something I actually wasn't sure about and wasn't sure if I would be able to commit myself to . . . [I thought it] was a waste of my time and you know our money. So that was kind of why I didn't go.
>
> *(Helen John)*

Similarly, in Hilary Edwards family, 'going to university' has no specific primacy as a choice. In talking about her grandson, Will, Hilary is clear that university is only one possible option:

> I would be happy for Will to do higher education if that is something he wants to do, if he is clear about what he wants to do for a career and it requires a degree then I'm very happy for him to go. But if he isn't, then I would hope that he finds his own way and then eventually finds out what he does want to do and then you've got a reason to go for it.
>
> *(Hilary Edwards)*

Hilary recognizes the potential benefit of university for Will, but is clear that the principal gains are utilitarian and that if these cannot accrue, then HE is not desirable simply for its own sake.

Within Hilary's network there was concern expressed about the limited value or purpose of 'careers advice', both in relation to the older generations but also in relation to Paul and Anthony's, and Will's generations. In Helen's network, both Helen and her friend Becky were scathing about the limited scale of 'information, advice and guidance' (IAG) provision both at secondary school and in further education, and also about its capacity to change the horizons of individuals or to challenge stereotypical presumptions about the likely career directions of particular groups of young people. As Ros Foskett discussed in Chapter 6, these findings about IAG emerged from many of the networks. The capacity of IAG, promoted as a key element of widening participation policy implementation, is thus extremely limited in its existing form and with current levels of resource.

An important insight from our data is that, despite their awareness of policy messages about the putative benefits of HE, entry points such as Helen John and Hilary Edwards are not convinced that participation will contribute to the attainment of either their personal goals or of those in their networks. Hence, it is the veracity of the policy message which is being challenged.

Multi-directional flow of social capital in social networks

The previous section suggested that existing policy messages and processes may stumble because they pay insufficient attention to how decisions are formed in social networks. The established conceptualization of how decisions are shaped is based on the idea that attitudes and values are transmitted downwards from those in relative 'authority' to others (for instance from parents to children, or from teachers to pupils). Strategies for promoting widening participation have traditionally used this notion to underpin a model which sees the message of 'HE benefit' reaching potential students either directly or via formal pathways through teachers and careers advisors. Coleman (1988) describes this transmission in terms of the 'downward' transfer of social capital, which in turn enhances the building of the human capital which is the essence of utilitarian models of decision-making. However, as we have discussed elsewhere (see Chapter 5 and Heath *et al.* 2010), such a model of 'capital transfer' takes no account of the reality of the multi-directional flows of social capital within networks or of other forms of social capital. Recognizing the relevance of bonding, bridging and linking social capital is essential to understanding the process of widening participation, for it relates to the engagement of individuals with new ideas and their access to different kinds of interpersonal and institutional relationships.

The upward flow of influence was illustrated in the case of Helen John. Helen's decision not to progress to university eventually resulted in a change of view for her mother, Sandra, who described how her own unwavering belief that university was 'essential' to career success had changed to a much more measured and ambivalent view. Specifically, her observations of Helen's career accomplishments without HE participation meant that she now advocated in her own social networks the need for young people and parents to be much more positive about non-HE options, post-18.

You would be led to think that you need to have a degree in order to be successful, but I don't think that's actually always right . . . I would say that some of my friends would feel, for instance, that Helen was a failure because she hasn't been to university and there are a selection of friends that think you can't get anywhere unless you've been to university. My response is that I think you can get on without going to university, and people choose to go to university at different times of their life. I don't think university is the be all and end all . . . and I'll get on my high horse about this, if parents are pushing their children to go to university when they're clearly not ready for it, or not able for it.

(Sandra, Helen's mother)

In the Edwards network Hilary's brother, Martin Hunter, demonstrated the impact of an upward flow of social capital. His lifelong resistance to university education had been changed by the positive benefits of HE that had accrued in career and personal terms to both his own children and his nephews, such that he had commenced an Open University undergraduate programme. Martin was still quite strident, though, in his questioning of the validity of the pro-HE message in widening participation policy rhetoric:

When I left school I had no real idea about what I wanted to do with my life and I rather consider the four years I spent at sea as being the university of life. I learnt far more during those four years from the age of 19 to 24 than I would have learnt at a seat of academia or in the rows of academia. I feel that I grew up. I feel I matured.

(Martin, Hilary's brother)

Important within this analysis is the recognition that policy messages through formal cascade approaches may reach their intended target audiences, but may not be sufficiently persuasive to overcome established network norms and attitudes. The influences, both positive and negative, of network members' experiences provide important resources on which others may draw. In considering ways to promote widening participation outcomes, it is clear that policy makers need to recognize the role of such 'non-formal' influences.

Immediate as distinct from long-term goals

One of the key features of widening participation policy is its emphasis on the long-term financial and wider benefits for individuals. However, short-term needs commonly outbid such long-term perspectives in decision-making, and are also typically more readily identifiable and achievable. A common feature of some of our entry points and of others in their networks was their calculation of the risks of engaging in activities, such as HE, that did not have guaranteed and reasonably quick returns.

In Hilary Edwards' network, for example, both Hilary and her brother Martin had engaged throughout their careers in training that could deliver immediate benefit in career terms, by providing skills that enabled a new role to be undertaken. Both recognized the value of the long-term benefits of HE, but emphasized their preference for short-term connections between learning and training and personal outcomes. Evidence from younger generations in the Edwards network illustrates that such views can transcend generations. Hilary's son, Anthony, had both Bachelor's and Master's degrees and was clear about the importance of those qualifications in enabling him to reach his current career position, yet spoke of the greater benefit, from his perspective, of short-term training experiences. Similarly, Hilary's other son Paul had chosen to study at university later in life when a clear pathway to a professional outcome emerged for him. Hilary emphasized the value of this perspective:

> I would hope that [the next generation in the family] would do like our Paul did, make their own way and eventually find out what they do want to do, and then you've got a reason to go for it. I think that's probably as good a way as just assuming that you're going to go, you know, into a normal profession.
>
> *(Hilary Edwards)*

Earlier, Paul had dropped out of a BTEC National Diploma in his late twenties, despite doing very well on the course, because of a combination of rising mortgage rates and having an unsatisfactory placement experience; instead he opted for a job offered by a friend in the building industry. For Helen John, long-term ambitions were often unclear and subverted by events, causing her to change her mind about her future actions. In her first interview, after working in administrative jobs for a few years, she was preparing to take science A levels in order to apply for medical school, but these plans foundered soon afterwards as her college did not enter her correctly for the examinations. She would have had to postpone sitting for her examinations until the following year. By the second interview Helen had a new boyfriend and had decided not to pursue these A levels and a medical career as she thought that the long training involved would leave her in an unsettled position at a time when she would want to be starting a family:

> You don't want to be 30 and in debt . . . And not settled anywhere and moving around for the next five years. You know that kind of destroys any hope of having a decent relationship. And at that age I would like to be fairly settled. Do you know what I mean, or with somebody or you know and I think it's you know, medicine the hours are just horrendous. And you know even my boyfriend now he's, you know he's 31 and he's still doing weeks of nights and you know weeks of on-call where he starts at eight and doesn't get home until midnight.
>
> *(Helen John)*

In some cases, the focus on longer or shorter term educational goals varies over time according to circumstances. In Chapter 4, for example, we saw how Jamil Masuka prioritized leaving school in the middle of his A levels to get a job, but later returned to education through part-time vocational qualifications gained over a number of years. His friend, Jason, who was ambivalent about his experience of HE, became focused on a long-term plan to acquire legal qualifications when he had the specific goal of buying a house with his girlfriend and starting a family.

Each of these examples indicates that the policy emphasis on the long-term benefit of HE participation must overcome the concerns of socially embedded individuals focusing on their immediate situation, if it is to have an impact on their decision-making. It is not that our entry points do not have long-term goals, of course – our evidence shows strongly that they do. However, those are seen to be achievable by mechanisms other than participation in HE. Communication models which presume the primacy of long-term economic goals in the decision-making process, therefore, are fundamentally flawed, especially given that for many the economic returns on HE are uncertain. Roberts (2009) argues that HE involves 'heavy and risky investments' in terms of 'time, money, social and emotional resources'. Many working-class students, in particular, are likely to see modest returns to HE as they are more likely to attend lower-ranked universities, build up more debt than average and achieve poorer quality jobs than their middle-class peers (2009: 365). Roberts therefore argues that these costs will be more easily borne by middle-class families, yet our own evidence suggests that some middle-class families may be equally wary.

The complexity of decision-making in education and training arenas

Our fourth insight relates to the decision-making process itself. An important hypothesis within the research was that educational decision-making is embedded within social networks, and emerges in response to the interplay of complex sets of values, beliefs and behaviours across and within generations. Widening participation policy has traditionally focused only on the 'chooser', and has not sought signifi- cantly to engage with other elements in social networks, hence recognition of the complexity and reality of those networks fundamentally challenges assumptions on how policy may be affected.

In both of the networks considered here, decision-making about participation clearly reflected these long-term 'within network' relations and interactions. Helen John's decision-making, for example, reflected tensions between strong family beliefs in the value of HE, the impact of her father's death; challenging experiences at school and further education college, and the views on HE participation that were evolving in her friendship group:

> When my dad was alive, we spent a lot of time kind of, he always was doing my homework with me and all that kind of thing and even from quite a young age I was quite interested in medicine or veterinary work. So it was one of

the two. And then, actually after my dad passed away I felt I didn't want to do it. Maybe because he was kind of helping me get to that place and I think once, when he'd gone it was kind of well there's no one really to do it with now.

(Helen)

I don't know whether I'd say I'd influenced her, I mean, obviously at the moment where she is re-studying and doing things then like, obviously, I would support her and help her do whatever she needed, you know, her work and that. I suppose we did more when we were at school and college than we do now, but I think more especially at school when you are, you know, when you are deciding whether you're going to go to college and what courses you're gonna take and what you want to do probably. So I guess we did more then than we probably do now.

(Becky, Helen's best friend)

After two previous false starts at study, Hilary Edwards' son, Paul, had chosen to pursue a social policy degree in his early thirties as a result of a complex combination of circumstances. His earlier career in forestry was not working out financially or in terms of career progression. He had decided to work part-time for the local Youth Service, as well as to do a humanities Access course part-time. A helpful learning development manager in the Youth Service had encouraged him to study either social policy or sociology and he went on to do this, very successfully, at a local university. Without the encouragement of his manager and without financial imperatives, he probably would not have embarked on this career route.

In other chapters, we have seen how network members sat amid conflicting push–pull factors, weighing up opportunities, available support and aligning aspirations. The examples in this chapter, as well as others, serve to illustrate an important principle: the gap between conceptualizations of decision-making that underpin policy, and the reality of decision-making as a socially embedded practice. At a theoretical level, the fact that educational decision-making is fiercely complex in detail has been recognized, as researchers have demonstrated the limited explanatory power of traditional choice models (see e.g. Foskett and Hemsley-Brown 2001). That this has not yet connected to the development of and implementation of social policy designed to generate new patterns of behaviour in educational choice is clear, both in the outcomes of our research and in other wider surveys of research evidence in relation to widening participation in HE (e.g. Gorard *et al.* 2006). Such a gap in understanding might be expected to be detrimental to the achievement of policy goals, and it is reasonable to assert that this is one cause of the limited impact and success of government widening participation policy in the UK over the last two decades.

Widening participation – future issues for policy development

The observations reported here, from both an analysis of the trends in participation and the evidence from the case studies, provide a valuable commentary on the potential efficacy of the aims and overall policy of the 'new widening participation in HE'. The broad conclusion is that, if policy formulation and policy implementation processes are based on an inadequate understanding of decision-making in social networks, it is inevitable that the ultimate aims of policy, however well intended and widely supported, are unlikely to be fully achieved.

It is appropriate to draw out a number of observations relating to policies of widening participation in HE, and identify some future directional changes that might support a more realistic set of policies and implementation processes. The emergence of new insights from recent research (David 2010) means that the development of evidence-based policy in the arena of widening participation is now increasingly possible, something which has been singularly lacking in practice to date.

The first observation is that the development of policy and subsequent implementation strategy based on collaboration between key stakeholders (including employers, institutions, students, researchers and those able to represent potential participants) is more likely to generate policies which produce change in the direction desired. Raffe and Spours (2007) identify the policy learning benefits that accrue from such collaborative policy models in contrast to political models. Engaging those stakeholders is an essential first step, together with the need to establish clear pathways for dialogue between government, researchers and the wide range of groups around whom policy is focused. Understanding the motivations of individuals located in their social networks, both those who participate and those who choose not to, is an essential outcome of this process. Our research findings challenge the assumption that it is only through HE participation that the most satisfying life course outcomes can be achieved – most of our participants are content with their education and employment trajectories. Moreover, most are apparently making useful contributions to the national economy.

The second observation is that decisions about participating in HE are embedded in social networks. The importance of developing social capital as part of education decision-making is critical, here, and it is vital to understand both the importance of bonding capital in network maintenance and the necessity of bridging and linking social capitals in extending 'horizons for action' (Hodkinson et al. 1996). This suggests strongly that effecting change towards the achievement of high-level widening participation goals is most likely to be achieved by engaging with processes within and between networks and institutional resources. As discussed in Chapter 5, the role of Family Learning Centres in developing bridging and linking capital in a context where bonding capital is also being reinforced might exemplify how more effective strategies could be constructed.

Linked to the importance of understanding network processes is a third observation, that of considering the role of IAG processes. Despite the valid government rhetoric about the importance of IAG, and the public portrayal of investment in

IAG as a cornerstone of strategy, the reality of face-to-face provision for young people in the first decade of the twenty-first century is that it has deteriorated into a minimalist service, poorly resourced, with declining professional expertise, focused on achieving targets related almost solely to reducing NEET statistics (Foskett *et al.* 2008). In recent years, advice for adults has existed in such online forms as directgov, unionlearn and Learndirect. The first of these is the government website for UK citizens that provides information on employment and adult learning. The second is a union-based website promoting lifelong learning, especially among union members. Learndirect offers routes to online and work-based learning at various levels for adults. However, only one or two of those we interviewed mentioned being aware of and using such services.

Yet IAG is central to education decision-making and is highly relevant to achieving wider participation in HE. A recurring theme within the two networks considered here, as well as other networks, is disappointment with IAG at school and college, underlining the necessity for significant investment in this key resource for building bridging and linking capital. The introduction of the Adult Advancement and Career Service in Autumn 2010 that proposes targeted and individualized guidance using a mix of online, telephone and face-to-face means of communication for those over 19 years of age may go some way to address shortcomings. The new service is planned to address a range of issues that may have an impact on employment and educational decision-making including health, transport, employment rights and finance. It is too early to tell how this will function in practice.

The fourth observation is that the nature of widening participation policy and practice must be sensitive to the changing economic and social environment. An important feature of the economic climate of the next half decade will be constraints on both public spending and employment opportunities. This will challenge the provision of resources for HE, probably leading to a further shift in the responsibility for funding places to the individual and away from the state. At the same time, policy is likely to continue to promote the view that HE strengthens the individual's labour market position. There will be tension, therefore, between the policy priorities that promote widening participation as a way of upskilling the labour force, tackling issues of social exclusion and equity, and policy priorities on reducing public expenditure.

A fifth observation is that work-based HE or advanced training would be viewed favourably in many of the networks discussed in this book. It would not be favoured by everyone, but a significant number of accounts focus on issues of convenience as well as the matter of a clear, work-focused outcome to study.

A cautionary note is that, as mentioned previously in the chapter, rapid changes in the patterns of support, advice and funding for widening participation create particular difficulties for those least likely to participate in the first place. Overall, the research findings suggest the need for both caution and imagination in the future development of policy and strategy at national level, with consideration given to the complexities of motivation, social capital and finance at the micro-level of social networks and their members, as well as to macro-level economic and social imperatives.

Note

1   On 25 November 2010, the Higher Education Funding Council for England (HEFCE) announced that funding for the AimHigher programme would be withdrawn from Summer 2011.

9

CONCLUSION

Alison Fuller, Sue Heath and Brenda Johnston

The effects of the financial crisis that swept across the world during the latter part of 2008 continue to produce headlines. In the UK, recent official statistics report both high levels of unemployment and a steeply growing number of people working beyond the age of 65 (ONS 2010). This situation focuses attention on the challenges faced by adults across the life course, including young people trying to make the transition from education to work, adults in mid-life needing to update or develop new skills, and older people approaching retirement. Given contemporary socio-economic circumstances, we would suggest that interest in the role that higher education (HE) can play in improving people's life chances is only likely to grow. In this context, the empirical and theoretical insights that have been presented in this book make an important contribution to understanding decision-making as an embedded social process.

Our research started from the premise that the debate on widening participation in HE had been too narrowly focused on transitions at 18 and on those who had actually entered or at least applied to HE. In addition, we found that the literature on 'choice' across the social sciences had drawn primarily on data at the individual level. There was, then, considerable scope and potential for exploring decision-making beyond the individual and across the life course through a focus on inter- and intra-generational 'networks of intimacy' and, crucially, in relation to non-participation in HE. Our approach involved collecting data from entry points and network members with diverse social characteristics and representing different generational positions and life stages.

The empirical work that we have undertaken and that underpins this book has produced a highly original dataset comprising case studies of 16 'potentially recruitable' adults and members of their social networks. As Brenda Johnston explains in Chapter 2, analysis of the case studies has enabled us to identify and explore influences on educational and career decision-making and we have tried to make sense of these through adopting a qualitative approach to social network analysis. In Chapter 3, Sue Heath introduced all 16 entry points and classified their routes to, and the contexts within which they achieved their Level 3 qualifications. The following chapters (4 to 8) provided the opportunity to discuss ten of our networks in more detail.

We have written elsewhere (Heath *et al*. 2009) that our analytical approach has not precluded a focus on individual accounts of decision-making, but the particular value of our dataset lies in the opportunity it has afforded to explore *relationship-based* accounts (parent–child interactions, for example, or those between siblings, friends or partners) alongside – most importantly – *network-based* accounts, which may be embedded across the network as a whole or within specific parts of the network. These accounts often reveal shared attitudes and dispositions towards participation in education that have flowed through the generations. For example, in Chapter 4, Felix Maringe and colleagues explored the effects of the Smith family's assessment of themselves as 'ordinary' and 'not clever clogs', which seemed to underpin and sym- bolize their perceptions of the bounds of educational possibility. In Chapters 5 and 6, Alison Fuller and Ros Foskett respectively discussed the Gregory and Upton networks' enduring utilitarian attitudes to participation in post-compulsory education and training. In discussing the Hanley network in Chapter 7, Martin Dyke explored among other things the parent–child account that emerged between the mother, Mary, her son John (the entry point) and her daughter, Jacky. The shared values transmitted across and practiced within generations in this family revolved around expressions of support for (any) education and career decisions contingent on the application of an ethic of hard work, persistence and 'stickability'. Nick Foskett (Chapter 8) introduced the Edwards network, whose members valued participation in HE primarily in terms of its ability to provide access to (graduate) careers requiring professional qualifications. In this final chapter of the book, we take a step back to summarize the key findings, arguments and messages from our study and to link these to the pressing research questions and policy challenges that are relevant to and being debated in the UK, as well as internationally. We do this by identifying and discussing three themes: the importance of life course and life stage perspectives, knowing the potential student, and the influence of social capital/mediating resources.

The importance of the life course and life stage perspectives

The distinctive nature of our approach has allowed us to focus on the importance of social relations as resources that flow into and through social networks. Our empirical findings have also enabled us to explore the extent to which network dispositions and attitudes are reproduced or challenged across and within generations and through the life course. There are lively debates in the sociology of education and youth studies literatures (*inter alia* du Bois-Reymond 1998, 2004; Beck and Beck-Gernsheim 2002; Brooks 2009; Harris and Rainey 2009; Roberts 2010) on the extent to which structural factors such as gender and class continue to shape decisions about participation or whether as argued in the 'detraditionalization' and 'individualization' theses (e.g. Giddens 1990, 1991a, 1994; Beck 1992, 1994), people are more likely to make the sorts of education and employment decisions that break the mould set by previous generations. Although this discussion is already central to understandings of continuity and change in youth transitions (e.g. Brooks 2009), the changing socio-economic conditions under which people live in countries such as the UK and the policy emphasis on lifelong learning suggest an extension of the use of this lens for studying decision-making about transitions across the entire life course (Ecclestone *et al.* 2009; Evans *et al.* 2010). This also needs to be accompanied by a strategy to develop the funding arrangements and institutional resources necessary to support this (Schuller and Watson 2009). The data from our inter-generational networks provide valuable evidence and contributions to this growing area of empirical research and developing theorization.

The evidence presented in this book (see particularly Chapters 3 and 4) confirms that the post-compulsory trajectories of those leaving school in the 1950s, 1960s and, to a large extent, 1970s, were highly shaped by the available opportunity structures, including the selective character of the compulsory education system and the elite nature of HE. Attending school at a time when only a very small minority progressed to university provides a very different context to that which young people currently experience. As an older member of one of our networks observed: 'by "university education" we are actually talking about something now that is very diverse. In my day, university education was Manchester, Cambridge, Leicester . . .' (Jonathan Brown, aged 59, friend, John network).

Jonathan clearly has a point. When he became an undergraduate in the early 1960s, there were only 24 universities in the UK, although another six were being established. By 2010, there were 115 universities and 165 Higher Education Institutions (HEIs) (www.universitiesuk.ac.uk accessed 16 September, 2010) and more than 1.8 million students studying at undergraduate level in all universities and HEIs (HESA 2010). In 1962 (and just prior to the publication of the Robbins Report), there were only around 240,000 students (Scott 1995).

Heath's, and Maringe *et al.*'s chapters (Chapters 3 and 4) illustrate the relevance of the changing availability of opportunities for people's initial post-compulsory education and later participation decisions. Navigating the transition from education to work or career transitions in the contemporary labour market, where entry to many sectors and progression within many careers is dependent on the possession of higher level credentials, is in stark contrast to the wide availability of jobs and the much looser 'job-getting' criteria that were available to school leavers who are now in their fifties and sixties. In line with the extant research, earlier generations were much more likely than the current cohort of young people to leave school at the end of the compulsory phase and to make swifter transitions into the labour market. Nonetheless, as Heath's analysis shows, people such as our entry points who had achieved a reasonable level of educational attainment during their compulsory schooling, were likely to find their way (usually by their early twenties) into some form of initial post-compulsory education and training (e.g. an apprenticeship or course in further education). The key difference is that, in comparison with the contemporary generation of young people achieving similar levels of attainment at 16, very few stayed in full-time education in order to progress to HE, and none progressed to university at the conventional age of 18 or 19. In summary, what were perceived as standardized decisions under previous policy regimes would be perceived as non-standard in the contemporary system.

The network-based accounts provided strong evidence about the gender assumptions that shaped the youth transitions of those now in their fifties and sixties. Perhaps most evocative was the gender narrative discussed in Maringe *et al.*'s chapter (Chapter 4) which illustrated the lasting influence that the Dixon family's expectations have had on Linda's (the entry point) educational and employment trajectory as well as other members of her network. It would be a mistake, though, to underestimate the role that gender still plays in mature students' decisions about whether and when to participate in HE. In particular, social norms about women's primary duties as carers continue to play an important role in shaping expectations about the timing of their potential take-up (see the examples of the Smith network in Chapter 4 and the Armstrong network in Chapter 5, and also Fuller *et al.* in press). Moreover, occupational choice remains highly gendered with males and females throughout the networks following largely gender-stereotypical patterns of participation. For example, one of our younger entry points, Jamil (see Chapter 4) has recently trained as a bricklayer, a very traditional occupation for males.

Evidence from the networks was also illustrative of the relationship between social class and educational progression, where durable societal and family mores around the types of people expected to progress to university imbued many of the network accounts. In addition, as Ros Foskett explained in Chapter 6, there were strong inter-generational occupational traditions passed down through families that continue to influence decision-making about education and training.

The importance of locating decision-making within relevant educational policy regimes and socio-economic contexts has been brought alive through the first-hand accounts of the network members. These provide insights into changes in the experiences and expectations of educational participation between generations. This is most vividly illustrated by the finding that many of our entry points' offspring have either progressed to HE or are likely to do so. There are also instances where trends associated with recent widening participation policies have been resisted. In the Gregory network, for example, Sarah and Robert have followed their parents' example (Andrew, the entry point, and his wife, Mary) and entered apprenticeships at 16, despite both having obtained excellent GCSE results. In another example, Nick Foskett (Chapter 8) discusses the case of the John network, which has considerable experience of HE and professional level employment but where Helen (the 21-year-old entry point) is pursuing an atypical trajectory by not progressing directly into HE following attainment of A levels.

The life course perspective orients us to the different and changing nature of opportunity structures, including the changing availability of educational options to different family and cohort generations. Thereby, it helps contextualize individual trajectories within a wider reality of what is available, when and to whom. The strength of using this approach is that it facilitates the sorts of connections to be made between biography, history and structure that C. Wright Mills (1959) argued is needed to understand the relationship between individual experiences and the pictures of social group behaviour captured in statistical accounts.

In terms of educational transitions, research and policy interest has tended to focus on the key institutional steps taken by young people from school to further and higher education and or to work (*inter alia* Ball *et al.* 2000; Brooks 2005, 2009; Hodkinson *et al.* 1996). Comparatively less attention has been given to contextualizing decision-making in terms of life stage (Pallas 2003) and to understanding decisions about whether to participate in education (including HE) outside the conventional age parameters. Karen Evans and colleagues have noted:

> It is argued that taking a life-course perspective can ensure that educational trajectories are studied in ways that recognize their 'complex intertwining' with social institutions and social roles as experienced at different stages of the life-course. The life-course perspective explores the ways in which individuals' ages, work and family roles influence the dynamics of learning trajectories in and throughout adult life.
>
> *(Evans et al. 2010: 20)*

Our research is innovative in that it has responded seriously to the empirical challenge implied by the life course approach by taking the social network as our unit of analysis and investigating the value this adds to understanding over approaches which focus (only) on the socially positioned individual. The evidence provided in this book has illustrated the collective and historically contextualized nature of decision-making about education.

Knowing the potential student

A key distinctive contribution to the evidence-base on widening participation in HE has been our focus on a group of people who, whilst they possess Level 3 qualifications, have not (yet) engaged in higher level study. In terms of the national population those with Level 3 as their highest qualification constitute a large group (around 5 million people). Recent figures from the Labour Force Survey indicate that approximately 20 per cent of adults have Level 3 as their highest qualification, whilst a larger proportion (nearly a third) has Level 4 or above as highest. We also know that the majority of this Level 3 group have vocational qualifications: Andy Dickerson has found that of those who have Level 3 as their highest qualification, 1.8 million have academic qualifications and a million more, 2.9 million, have vocational equivalents (Dickerson 2008). This is particularly significant given that there are important differences in progression rates amongst students with different types of Level 3 qualifications. A recent report by Joy Carter for the previous Labour government found that, whilst 90 per cent of those with A levels progress to HE, only 45 per cent of those from vocational routes do so (Carter 2009). From the perspective of widening participation, it is also important to note that twice as many young people from lower socio-economic groups choose vocational routes compared with those who have parents in professional occupations (Panel for Fair Access to the Professions 2009).

In terms of age, the current cohort of 18–24-year-olds is the most likely of all age bands to have attained Level 3: about 30 per cent of this group has Level 3 as their highest qualification at this point in their lives. For the over twenty-fives the proportion is lower (approximately 18 per cent), but still means that nearly one in five of those aged 25 to 65 has attained Level 3 as their highest qualification. In terms of gender, older males are more likely than females to have acquired this level, but females have caught up among younger groups. This is symptomatic of girls' performance in educational examinations more generally, where they now out-perform boys. As Sue Heath outlines in Chapter 3, and in similarity with the wider Level 3 population, the vast majority of entry points in our sample had attained Level 3 qualifications via vocational routes and most of the entry points had acquired their Level 3 awards after the age of 18 and some in mid-life.

There is also quantitative survey evidence about the attitudes of adults in England who have not participated in HE. Pollard *et al.* (2008) investigated how respondents' views about HE had changed since they had completed their compulsory education. It is an unusual survey because it focuses specifically on HE, whereas most research on adult learning (e.g. Aldridge and Tuckett 2009) either focuses on learning more generally, or on those who are applying to HE or are already there. The research generated a wealth of interesting findings including, first, that although working adults were generally positive about HE, those from lower socio-economic groups were less so than their more advantaged peers. Second, about three out of ten said they would consider applying to HE in future: younger adults, those from Black and Minority ethnic backgrounds and disabled individuals were more likely to say they would consider it. Third, it was found that the strongest influence on attitudes was family and peer group experiences of HE. Where people had HE experiences in their networks they were more likely to believe that they could go too (see also Connor *et al.* 2001). This finding was reflected in Laura Staetsky's analysis of the HE module of the Youth Cohort Study conducted during our research, which found that the participation of siblings appeared to correlate with younger brothers' and sisters' participation in HE (Staetsky 2007). Finally, a group Pollard and colleagues identified as 'waverers' included those in mid-career who felt less well informed about HE, had family commitments and viewed their participation as contingent on receiving employer support.

The quantitative evidence helps sketch out some of the characteristics of what we might see as a group of people who have recently come under the explicit gaze of widening participation in HE policy, research and practice. We have also seen that there is a big pool of potential recruits and that attracting more participants from this group, particularly those from vocational routes, could have a significant impact on diversifying the student population, particularly in terms of age, life stage and social class. Nonetheless, as our network research has shown, at the time of the interviews the potentially recruitable in our sample were, in the main, located in social networks characterized by relative economic and employment stability, and saw little need to disturb their current employment and domestic circumstances through pursuing higher level qualifications. For many of the older members of this group, the acquisition of Level 3 qualifications had provided them with mostly satisfying career opportunities and trajectories. However, they recognized that, due to credential inflation and contemporary labour market conditions, similar opportunities were now only likely to be open to young people with degrees. For those in mid-career the benefits of participating in HE were often unclear, for example, would there be enough time left in work to reap any salary premium or career returns? From the perspective of policy makers, as well as individuals and their families negotiating their way through the current difficult economic period, it is important that understandings about the attitudes to, perceptions and experiences of HE of people at different ages and life stages is better understood.

In a recent research paper on 'life chances, learning and the dynamics of risk throughout the life course', Karen Evans and colleagues focus on the relationship between risk and participation in lifelong learning. Their review of the evidence indicates that, when adults weigh up the costs and benefits of participation within a short time frame, they are more likely to be reluctant to take the risk of participating in what they perceive as an uncertain and long-term investment. This insight helps contextualize the attitudes of many of our older entry points to HE and the attitudes embedded in their social networks. There were echoes of this view in Nick Foskett's discussion (Chapter 8) of Hilary Edwards' network. Members of this network had, over the course of their careers, benefited from employer-supported training and the more immediate advantages they felt this had conferred on them. There was recognition of the longer-term benefits that could accrue from HE, particularly for some of the network's younger generation who had attained degrees. Nonetheless, there was an inter-generational network preference for job-related training which is lent support by a recent comprehensive review of the returns to training and qualifications. The research found strong evidence in the UK and elsewhere in Europe that job-related training funded by the employer generates good wage returns for the employee. The review concludes: 'Thus, given that employer-provided training bears relatively little or no cost to the worker in terms of foregone earnings or course fees and it is generally much shorter in duration, it represents a very good return' (UKCES 2010: 115–16).

However, in an environment where more people are going to have to remain in paid work for longer, the perception of risk associated with participation may change as people contemplate a longer time frame within which the financial costs of participation may be mitigated. For some, deciding not to participate may come to be perceived as the riskier option. It is important, then, to conceive the relationship between risk and participation as dynamic. The added value of our network approach lies in showing that the negotiation of risk may be identified at the network, as well as the individual, level. How the network's perception or experience of HE reinforces or challenges participation as a risky decision becomes an embedded and collective resource that individuals can draw on as they come to make their participation decisions.

The influence of social capital/mediating resources

The varying degrees of access to forms of social capital are very apparent across our networks or case studies. The network interviews revealed embedded dispositions, attitudes, behaviours and expectations that were affecting participation decisions and perceptions of what was considered possible for people like them. As the empirical evidence presented in the book suggests, we often found that, where views across the network were highly convergent, decisions were better seen as non-choices. It was important then for us to identify resources or experiences within the network that provided different perspectives and potential for 'bottom-up capacity building'. In part this can be illustrated by the example of network members (seven in total) who had experienced HE as mature learners. There was some evidence that, if the network contained at least one person – often a friend – who had experienced or was experiencing HE as a mature student, their example helped to open up possibilities for alternative educational, career or lifestyle trajectories within the network (see the Armstrong case in Chapter 5, for example). Where this occurred there were generally positive responses, indicating the multi-directionality of network influence rather than simply the top-down effect predominantly highlighted in the social capital literature (Fuller and Heath 2009).

Interestingly, the networks in which participation in HE appeared to be more favourably viewed tended to be those that were more friendship-based (Jamil Masuka's network was an exception), rather than those more oriented towards family members. This highlighted the importance of the bridging social capital associated with access to alternative social networks and the resources they contain. One of our entry point individuals, Joanna, a woman in her mid-thirties working in a human resources role in the NHS, noted the positive example of older learners in her own workplace (Fuller *et al.* in press). In this particular network, three of the members (including Joanna's husband and two of her friends) had attained their higher level qualifications in mid-life. This meant that the network itself had a growing reservoir of social capital that could be drawn on as a collective good by those with shared participation goals. These findings illustrate, then, both the nuanced nature of network influence and its multi-directionality. Influences on decision-making can operate between and within generations, both in upward and sideways directions, and not solely from older to younger generations.

The evidence presented in the book on the value and influence of top-down institutional resources on decision-making about educational participation is mixed. In Chapter 6, Ros Foskett provided a highly critical account of the influence of careers guidance and advice services on the decision-making about educational participation. She drew on the experience of careers information, advice and guidance (CIAG) in the Upton network as illustrative of our overall finding that CIAG services had failed to provide a resource that had questioned network expectations about post-compulsory transitions. Rather than challenging taken-for-granted gendered and class-based assumptions, CIAG had tended to provide an adaptive function in steering 'clients' towards decisions typical for their social and educational group (the networks discussed in Chapter 4 provide further examples). One observation was that CIAG interventions (continue to) come too late in secondary schooling, after attitudes and aspirations have already become established. Interestingly, specific widening participation in HE initiatives such as AimHigher have recently been targeted at younger age groups and there is some emerging evidence that this has been having a positive effect on the educational aspirations and participation decisions of the young people involved including those from families with no prior experience of HE (e.g. Hatt *et al.* 2008; Passy and Morris 2010).

In contrast with the evidence on CIAG in schools, evidence from the Armstrong network has been helpful in illustrating how well-targeted institutional resources such as Family Learning Centres (FLC) may have helped transform adult aspirations and foster social mobility by generating 'linking social capital'. The strength of the tie with the FLC lies not only in the nature of the institutional resources it offered but in the way these were bound into and flowed through the interpersonal relations in the community, producing a repository of narratives which helped create a collective good that could be mobilized in the decision-making process (cf Rowson *et al.* 2010).

In drawing attention to the role and potential of mediating resources or linking social capital, it is not our intention to underplay the relevance of structural factors. The costs of participation in terms of fees and the potential foregoing of earnings are relatively straightforward to calculate, but the putative benefits of participation are uncertain. As we know, the ability to weather and negotiate such risks is not evenly distributed across social groups and addressing this is given added urgency by the current economic situation.

Final remarks

In the UK, there has been a political consensus on the merits of widening participation that appears to have survived (at least rhetorically) the transition from the Labour to the Conservative–Liberal Democrat coalition government in May 2010. A key example of this has been the shared focus on lifelong learning and support for pathways to HE from vocational routes, such as apprenticeship (e.g. BIS 2009a, 2009b, 2010). Given the projected decline in the number of 18-year-olds in the coming decade, there appears also to be cross-party policy commitment to widening participation in HE through attracting and enabling older adults to pursue higher level courses, including via part-time and work-based modes. This political aspiration builds on the reality for most past and current mature students, who tend to enrol on part-time courses whilst continuing in (mainly full-time) paid work (Brennan *et al.* 1999; Callender *et al.* 2010). Historically, the part-time HE population has been predominantly made up of those aged over 30, although there are now signs that under contemporary economic and labour market conditions more of the younger generation are turning to this mode of participation. In addition to their age, older students diversify the student population in other ways. They are more likely than their younger peers to come from lower socio-economic backgrounds, have left school earlier and have fewer academic and more vocational qualifications on entry (Fuller 2007c).

Recent survey evidence suggests that more adults in mid-life are engaging, or seeking to participate, in education and training (Tuckett and Aldridge 2010). As we indicated in the book's introduction, HE applications data are also showing strong rises in applicants in the 25–39 and 40 plus age groups (UCAS 2010). At least part of the explanation for adults returning to study relates to individuals' desire to mitigate the risk of unemployment and economic uncertainty by gaining more or different skills and qualifications (Fuller 2007c; Callender et al. 2010). A recent survey by Claire Callender of nearly 4,000 part-time students confirmed that career related goals underpinned their participation: 'for the vast majority of students, both their decision to study (89 per cent) and choice of subject (92 per cent) were firmly linked to these career aims' (Callender et al. 2010: 11). Although, as already mentioned, most students were working while studying, less than a half were receiving financial help from their employers or were allowed time off to study. Moreover, in keeping with successive studies on adult learning, those most advantaged (e.g. in terms of existing qualifications, employment situation and social background) were most likely to be receiving help from their employers. Given the relevance of career benefits to the employment and educational decision-making in the networks we researched, the question of employer demand for higher level skills and qualification as well as the nature of the HE offer (e.g. two-year degrees) are factors that are central to changing patterns of participation amongst older adults.

Recent assessments of and trends in skills and qualification levels in the UK continue to highlight deficiencies in the nation's attempts to become a world leader, defined as being in the top eight Organisation for Economic Co-operation and Development countries, by 2020 (UKCES 2009a). Against this backdrop, the recent rise in individual demand for education and training has been welcomed by policy makers. However, there are concerns about the relatively low level of demand or push for higher level skills from employers (UKCES 2009b) and the effect this may have on participation.

The evidence presented in this book suggests that opportunities in the workplace exert a powerful pull on the construction of career and educational aspirations that takes place in networks. Increasing employer demand for higher level skills and strengthening articulation between the acquisition of professional qualifications and career progression would increase take-up amongst those in mid-life and mid-career. Improving awareness of the currency and value of the vocational qualifications held by the majority of those adults who have Level 3 qualifications as a platform for progression would also be helpful. It would build on the culture of (lifelong) learning that we have identified in many of the networks in this study and which was vividly illustrated through Martin Dyke's discussion of the Steers network in Chapter 7.

We have shown in the empirical chapters that a key strength of the network approach is that it generates broader insights into the values, experiences and aspirations within which decisions are embedded. From the perspective of policy makers and institutions, the importance of knowing the potential student is important. The evidence from the first-hand accounts of our sample is also a critical reminder that many 'non-participants' are often leading comfortable and relatively stable lives and that they do not perceive themselves as in deficit or as missing out on the benefits associated with HE participation. As the extant literature has suggested, there are significant limitations in our understanding about patterns of participation, and knowing more about different groups of potential students is key to achieving further diversification of the student population. In this regard our research has provided an important empirical contribution and addition to the knowledge-base.

A key implication from our findings is that, irrespective of how wide the door to HE is, many people with the potential to benefit from HE will still not go through. A fundamental challenge is that many or probably *most* people do not really know what they are capable of, and this may be especially true for people from backgrounds where there has been no or little experience of HE, even if they have the qualifications that would enable them to participate. In our view, opening up institutional access is only a partial solution which leaves under-explored the characteristics, circumstances and situations of those who have not as yet participated. The evidence from *Rethinking Widening Participation in Higher Education: The Role of Social Networks* suggests that, to increase the likelihood of their participation, we need to think about the social capital resources to which social groups have access, and identify whether there are particular 'mediating resources' and types of HE that might increase the likelihood of their participation in HE. Given the importance many of our entry points and network members placed on the need for HE qualifications to have strong currency in terms of their 'exchange value' for career advancement or access to a ladder of progression in certain professions, the strength of the 'pull' from HE is an important factor. As our research highlights, a key lesson that policy makers can learn from getting to know potential learners better is that widening participation and lifelong learning interventions need to be carefully crafted to build capacity within their specific target groups and their communities, and to be linked to progression opportunities.

This book has indicated the need to rethink institutional structures and interventions designed to provide and support wider participation in HE. They must a) be directed across the life course and attuned to issues associated with life stage as well as age, and b) pay attention to the nature and location of 'top-down resources' *and* 'bottom-up capacity building' such that they mobilize the range of workplace and community contexts and networks in which adults find themselves, and within which social capital resources can be created to help build capacity and facilitate 'non-traditional' transitions. Our research suggests that policy and practice interventions designed to diversify the student population need to recognize the collective as well as personal dimensions of decision-making processes. One size policies and interventions will not fit all!

REFERENCES

Ahier, J. and Moore, R. (1999) 'Post-16 education, semi-dependent youth and the privatisation of the inter-age transfers: re-theorising youth transition', *British Journal of Sociology of Education* 20, 4: 515–30.

Aldridge, F. and Tuckett, A. (2009) *Narrowing Participation, the NIACE Survey on Adult Participation in Learning 2009*, Leicester: National Institute for Adult and Continuing Education.

Antikainen, A., Houtsonen, J., Huotelin, H. and Kauppila, J. (1996) *Living in a Learning Society: Life-histories, Identities and Education*, London: Falmer Press.

Archer, L. and Hutchings, M. (2000) '"Bettering yourself"? Discourses of risk, cost and benefit in ethnically diverse, young working-class non-participants' constructions of higher education', *British Journal of Sociology of Education* 21, 4: 555–74.

Archer, M. (2000) *Being Human: The Problem of Agency*, Cambridge, UK: Cambridge University Press.

Archer, M. (2007) *Making our Way through the World*, Cambridge: Cambridge University Press.

Ball, S. and Vincent, C. (1998) 'I heard it on the grapevine: "hot" knowledge and school choice', *British Journal of Sociology of Education* 19, 3: 377–400.

Ball, S., Maguire, M. and McCrae, S. (2000) *Choice, Pathways and Transitions Post-16: New Youth, New Economies in the Global City*, London: RoutledgeFalmer.

Bauman, Z. (1993) *Post Modern Ethics*, Oxford: Polity Press.

BBC (1999) 'Tony Blair's speech in full', BBC News website, 28 September, http://news.bbc.co.uk/1/hi/uk_politics/460009.stm, accessed 15 September 2010.

Beck, U. (1992) *Risk Society: Towards a New Modernity*, London: Sage.

Beck, U. (1994) 'The reinvention of politics: towards a theory of reflexive modernization', in U. Beck, A. Giddens and S. Lash, *Reflexive Modernization: Politics, Tradition and Aesthetics in the Modern Social Order*, Cambridge: Polity Press.

Beck, U. and Beck-Gernsheim, E. (2002) *Individualization – Individualism and its Social and Political Consequences*, London: Sage.

Becker, G. S. (1975) *Human Capital: A Theoretical and Empirical Analysis with Special Reference to Education*, New York: Columbia University Press.

Becker, G. and Tomes, N. (1986) 'Human capital and the rise and fall of families', *Journal of Labour Economics* 4: S1–39.

Bell, L. and Stevenson, H. (2006) *Education Policy: Process, Themes and Impact*, London: Routledge.

Bernard, J. (1972) *The Future of Marriage*. Harmondsworth: Penguin.

BIS (Department for Business, Innovation and Skills) (2009a) *Skills for Growth*, London: BIS.

BIS (2009b) *Higher Ambitions; The Future of Universities in a Knowledge Economy*, London: BIS.

BIS (2010) *Skills for Sustainable Growth: Consultation on the Future Direction of Skills Policy*, London: Department of Business, Innovation and Skills.

Blanden, J. and Machin, S. (2007) *Recent Changes in Intergenerational Mobility in Britain*, London: London School of Economics and The Sutton Trust.

Bordo, S. (1993) *Unbearable Weight: Feminism, Western Culture and the Body*, Berkeley and Los Angeles, CA: University of California Press.

Bott, E. (1957) *Family and Social Network*, London: Tavistock.

Bourdieu, P. (1986) 'The forms of capital', in J. Richardson (ed.), *Handbook of Theory of Research for the Sociology of Education*, pp. 241–58, New York: Greenwood Press.

Bourdieu, P. (1996) *The State Nobility: Elite Schools and the Field of Power*, trans. Lauretta C. Clough, Cambridge: Polity Press.

Brannen, J. (2003) 'Towards a typology of intergenerational relations: continuities and change in families', *Sociological Research Online* 8 (2), http://www.socresonline.org.uk/8/2/brannen.html, accessed 10 December 2010.

Brennan, J., Mills, J., Shah, T. and Woodley, A. (1999) *Part-time Students and Employment: Report of A Survey of Students, Graduates and Diplomates*, London: QSC, The Open University.

Brooks, R. (2004) '"My mum would be as pleased as punch if I actually went, but my dad seems a bit more particular about it": paternal involvement in young people's higher education choices', *British Educational Research Journal* 30, 4: 495–514.

Brooks, R. (2005) *Friendship and Educational Choice*, Basingstoke: Palgrave Macmillan.

Brooks, R. (ed.) (2009) *Transitions from Education to Work: New Perspectives from Europe and Beyond*, Basingstoke: Palgrave Macmillan.

Bynner, J. and Parsons, S. (1997) 'Getting on with qualifications', in J. Bynner, E. Ferri and P. Shepherd (eds) *Twenty-something in the 1990s: Getting on, Getting by, Getting Nowhere*, Aldershot: Ashgate.

Bynner, J., Ferri, E. and Shepherd, P. (1997) 'Getting somewhere, getting nowhere in the 1990s', in J. Bynner, E. Ferri and P. Shepherd (eds), *Twenty-something in the 1990s: Getting on, Getting by, Getting Nowhere*, 119–28, Aldershot: Ashgate.

Cable, V. (2010) Speech entitled 'Higher education', 15 July, http://www.bis.gov.uk/news/speeches/vince-cable-higher-education, accessed 8 October 2010.

Callender, C., Hopkin, R. and Wilkinson, D. (2010) *Futuretrack: Part-Time Students Career Decision-Making and Career Development of Part-Time Higher Education Students*, A Report to the Higher Education Careers Services Unit (HECSU), June, Manchester: HECSU.

Carter, J. (2009) *Progression from Vocational and Applied Learning to Higher Education in England*, November, Bolton: UVAC.

Carter, M. (1966) *Into Work*, Harmondsworth: Penguin.

Chitty, C. (2009) *Education Policy in Britain*, Basingstoke: Palgrave Macmillan.

Cockburn, C. (1987) *Two-track Training: Sex Inequalities and the YTS*, Basingstoke: Macmillan.

Coleman, J. C. (1988) 'Social capital in the creation of human capital', *American Journal of Sociology* 94: 95–120.

Connidis, I. and McMullen, J. (2002) 'Sociological ambivalence and family ties: a critical perspective', *Journal of Marriage and the Family* 64: 558–67.

Connor, H. and Dewson, S., with Tyers, C., Eccles, J., Regan, J. and Aston, J. (2001) *Social Class and Higher Education: Issues Affecting Decisions on Participation by Lower Social Class Groups,* Research Report no. 267, Norwich: Department for Education and Employment.

Corrigan, P. (1979) *Schooling the Smash Street Kids,* Basingstoke: Macmillan.

Courtney, S. (1992) *Why Adults Learn: Towards a Theory of Participation in Adult Education,* London and New York: Routledge.

Croll, P. (2004) 'Families, social capital and educational outcomes', *British Journal of Educational Studies* 52, 4: 390–416.

Davey, G. (2009) Using Bourdieu's concept of habitus to explore narratives of transition', *European Educational Research Journal* 8, 2: 276–84.

David, M. (2010) 'What are the overall findings and implications for evidence-based policies on fair access and widening participation?', in M. David (ed.), *Improving Learning by Widening Participation in Higher Education,* pp. 147–9, London: Routledge.

de Souza Briggs, X. (1998) 'Doing democracy up close: culture, power and communication in community building', *Journal of Planning Education and Research* 18: 1–13.

Denzin, N. (2001) *Interpretive Interactionism,* 2nd edn, *Applied Social Research Methods Series* vol. 16, London: Sage.

DCSF (Department of Children, Schools and Families) (2010) NEET Statistics, Quarterly Brief, February.

DES (Department of Education and Science) (1987) *Higher Education: Meeting the Challenge,* Cmnd 114, London: HMSO.

DES (1991) *Higher Education: A New Framework,* Cmnd 1541, London: HMSO.

DfEE (Department for Education and Employment) (2001) Statistics of Education: GCSE/GNVQ and GCE A/AS Level & Advanced GNVQ Examination Results 1999/2000, England, Issue No 06/01, London: Office for National Statistics/Department for Education and Employment, available at http://www.dcsf.gov.uk/rsgateway/DB/SBU/b000266/index.shtml.

DfES (Department for Education and Skills) (2003) *The Future of Higher Education,* The Higher Education White Paper, Norwich: The Stationery Office Ltd.

Dickerson, A. (2008) *The Distribution and Returns to Vocational Qualifications across Four Countries of the UK,* SSDA Research Report 21 A, Wath-upon-Dearne: Sector Skills Development Agency.

du Bois-Reymond, M. (1998) '"I don't want to commit myself yet": young people's life concepts', *Journal of Youth Studies* 1, 1: 63–79.

du Bois-Reymond, M. (2004) 'Youth-Learning-Europe. Ménage à trois?', Young 12, 3:187–204.

Duffy, R. D. and Dik, B. J. (2009) 'Beyond the self: external influences in the career development process', *The Career Development Quarterly* 58: 29–33.

Dyke, M., Foskett, N. H. and Maringe, F. (2008) 'Risk and trust; the impact of information and experience in the decision to participate in post-16 education', *Education, Knowledge and Economy* 2, 2: 99–110.

Ecclestone, K., Biesta, G. and Hughes M. (eds) (2009) *Transitions and Learning Through the Lifecourse,* London: Routledge.

Edwards, B. and Foley, M. W. (1998) 'Civil society and social capital beyond Putnam', *American Behavioural Scientist* 42, 1: 124–39.

Edwards, G. (2010) *Mixed-method Approaches to Social Network Analysis,* National Centre for Research Methods Methodological Review, http://eprints.ncrm.ac.uk/842/ accessed 7 October 2010.

Edwards, R., Gillies, V. and Ribbens, J. (1999) 'Shifting boundaries and power in the research process: the example of researching "step-families"', in J. Seymour and P. Bagguley (eds), *Relating Intimacies: Power and Resistance,* Basingstoke: Macmillan, p. 13.

Ertl, H., Hayward, G. and Hoelscher, G. (2010) 'Learners' transition from vocational education and training to higher education' in M. David (ed.), *Improving Learning by Widening Participation in Higher Education*, London: Routledge.

European Commission (1994) *Growth, Competitiveness, Employment*, Luxembourg: European Commission.

Evans, K., Schoon, I. and Weale, M. (2010) *Life Chances, Learning and the Dynamics of Risk Throughout the Life Course*, LLAKES research paper 9, London: Centre for Learning and Life Chances in Knowledge Economies and Societies.

Field, J. (2005) *Social Capital and Lifelong Learning*, Bristol: The Policy Press.

Finch, J. and Mason, J. (1993) *Negotiating Family Responsibilities*, London: Routledge.

Foot, M. (1997) *Aneurin Bevan*, London: Victor Gollanz.

Foskett, N. H. (2002) 'Marketing imperative or cultural challenge? Embedding widening participation in the further education sector', *Research in Post-Compulsory Education* 7, 1: 79–95.

Foskett, N. H. and Hemsley-Brown, J. V. (2001) *Choosing Futures: Young People's Decision-making in Education, Training and Careers Markets*, London: FalmerRoutledge.

Foskett, N. H., Dyke, M. and Maringe, F. (2008) 'The influence of the school in the decision to participate in learning post-16', *British Educational Research Journal* 32, 1: 37–62.

Foskett, R. and Johnston, B. (2010) '"A uniform seemed the obvious thing": experiences of careers guidance amongst potential higher education participants', *Journal of Further and Higher Education* 34, 2, 223–38.

Fuller, A. (2007a) 'Researching adult "non-participation" in higher education', paper at South East AimHigher Annual Conference, 19 April, London.

Fuller, A. (2007b) 'Gender, life stage and educational decision-making: researching adult "non-participation" in higher education', paper at Women in Lifelong Learning Network Conference, May, Birkbeck, University of London.

Fuller, A. (2007c) 'Mid-life "transitions" to higher education: developing a multi-level explanation of increasing participation, *Studies in Education of Adults* 39, 2: 5–23.

Fuller, A. and Heath, S. (2009) 'Educational decision-making, social networks and the new widening participation', in M. David (ed.), *Improving Learning by Widening Participation in Higher Education*, London: Routledge.

Fuller, A. and Paton, K. (2009) 'Widening participation in higher education: mapping and investigating the stakeholder landscape', *Journal of Access Policy and Practice* 6, 1: 4–20.

Fuller, A., Foskett, R., Johnston, B. and Paton, K. (in press), '"Getting by" or "getting ahead"? Gendered educational and career decision-making in networks of intimacy', in S. Jackson, I. Malcolm and K. Thomas (eds), *Gendered Choices and Transitions in Lifelong Learning: Part-time Pathways, Full-time Lives*, London: Springer.

Fuller, A., Paton, K., Foskett, R. and Maringe, F. (2008) '"Barriers" to participation in higher education? Depends who you ask and how', *Widening Participation and Lifelong Learning Journal* 10, 2: 6–17.

Furlong, A. (2009) 'Revisiting transitional metaphors: reproducing social inequalities under the conditions of late modernity', *Journal of Education and Work* 22, 5: 343–53.

Furlong, A. and Cartmel, F. (1997) *Young People and Social Change: Individualisation and Late Modernity*, Buckingham and Philadelphia: Open University Press.

Gambetta, D. (1996) *Were They Pushed or Did They Jump? Individual Decision Mechanisms in Education*, Boulder, CO: Westview Press.

Gayle, V., Lambert, P. and Murray, S. (2009) 'School-to-work in the 1990s: modelling transitions with large-scale datasets', in R. Brooks, *Transitions from Education to Work: New Perspectives from Europe and Beyond*, Basingstoke: Palgrave Macmillan.

Giddens, A. (1990) *The Consequences of Modernity*, Cambridge: Polity Press.

Giddens, A. (1991a) *Modernity and Self-identity,* Cambridge: Polity Press.

Giddens, A. (1991b) 'Living in a post-traditional society', in U. Beck, A. Giddens and S. Lash, *Modernity and Self-identity: Self and Society in the Late Modern Age*, pp. 56–109, Cambridge: Polity Press.

Giddens, A. (1994) *Reflexive Modernisation: Politics, Tradition and Aesthetics in the Modern Social Order*, Cambridge: Polity.

Giele, J. and Elder, G. (eds) (1998) *Methods of Life Course Research: Qualitative and Quantitative Approaches*, London: Sage.

Gorard, S., Smith, S. E., May, H., Thomas, L., Adnett, N. and Slack, K. (2006) *Review of Widening Participation Research: Addressing the Barriers to Participation in Higher Education'*, A Report to HEFCE by the University of York, the Higher Education Academy, and the Institute for Access Studies, Bristol: HEFCE.

Granovetter, M. (1973) 'The strength of weak ties', *American Journal of Sociology* 78, 4: 1350–80.

Granovetter, M. (1983) 'The strength of weak ties: a network theory revisited', *Sociological Theory* 1, 201–33.

Griffin, C. (1985) *Typical Girls: Young Women from School to the Full-Time Job Market*, London: Routledge.

Guba, E. G. and Lincoln, Y. S. (1994) 'Competing paradigms in qualitative research', in N. K. Denzin and Y. S. Lincoln (eds), *Handbook of Qualitative Research,* pp. 105–17, Thousand Oaks: Sage.

Guba, E. G. and Lincoln, Y. S. (2005) 'Paradigmatic controversies, contradictions, and emerging confluences', in N. K. Denzin and Y. S. Lincoln (eds), *Handbook of Qualitative Research,* pp. 191–215, Thousand Oaks: Sage.

Halpern, D. (2005) *Social Capital*, Cambridge: Polity Press.

Harris, B. and Rainey, L. (2009) 'Interrogating the notion of transition: learner experiences of multiple transitions between the vocational- and higher-education sectors', in R. Brooks (ed.), *Transitions from Education to Work: New Perspectives from Europe and Beyond*, Basingstoke: Palgrave Macmillan.

Harrison, N. (2006) 'The impact of negative experiences, dissatisfaction and attachment on first year undergraduate withdrawal', *Journal of Further and Higher Education* 30, 4: 377–91.

Hatt, S., Baxter, A. and Tate, J. (2008) '"The best government initiative in years". Teachers' perceptions of the Aimhigher programme in the South West of England', *Journal of Further and Higher Education* 32, 2: 129–38.

Heath, S. and Cleaver, E. (2003) *Young, Free and Single? Twenty-somethings and Household Change*, Basingstoke: Palgrave.

Heath, S. and Johnston, B. (2006) 'Decision-making about employment and education pathways as an embedded social practice: methodological challenges', Working Paper no. 1 for the NPinHE project, initially a conference paper at the Annual Conference of the Society for Research in Higher Education, 12–14 December, Brighton.

Heath, S., Fuller, A. and Johnston, B. (2009) 'Chasing shadows: defining network boundaries in qualitative social network analysis', *Qualitative Research* 9, 5: 1–17.

Heath, S., Fuller, A. and Johnston, B. (2010) 'Young people, social capital and network-based educational decision-making', *British Journal of Sociology of Education* 31, 4: 395–411.

Heath, S., Fuller, A. and Paton, K. (2008) 'Network-based ambivalence and educational decision-making: a case study of "non-participation" in higher education', *Research Papers in Education* 23, 2: 219–29.

HEFCE (Higher Education Funding Council for England) (2010) *Trends in Young Participation in Higher Education: Core Results for England*, Bristol: HEFCE.

Hemsley-Brown, J. (1999) 'College choice: perceptions and priorities', *Educational Management and Administration* 27, 1: 85–98.

HESA (Higher Education Statistics Agency) (2010) *Students in Higher Education 2008/09*, Cheltenham: HESA.

HMSO (1992) *Further and Higher Education Act 1992*, Norwich: The Stationery Office.

HM Treasury (Leitch Review) (2006) 'Prosperity for all in the global economy – world class skills', *The Leitch Review of Skills*, London: HM Treasury.

Hockey, J., Robinson, V. and Meah, A. (2002) '"For better or worse": heterosexuality reinvented', *Sociological Research Online*, 7, 2, at http://www.socresonline.org.uk/7/2/hockey.html.

Hodkinson, P. and Bloomer, M. (2002) 'Learning careers: conceptualising lifelong work-based learning', in K. Evans, P. Hodkinson and L. Unwin (eds), *Working to Learn: Transforming Learning in the Workplace*, pp. 29–43, London: Kogan Page.

Hodkinson, P. with Hodkinson, H. (2008) *Learning through Life, Learning Lives*, Summative Working Paper no. 1, April, University of Leeds.

Hodkinson, P. and Macleod, F. (2010) 'Contrasting concepts of learning and contrasting research methodologies: affinities and bias', *British Educational Research Journal* 36, 2: 173–89.

Hodkinson, P., Sparkes, A. C. and Hodkinson, H. (1996) *Triumphs and Tears: Young People, Markets and the Transition from School to Work*, London: David Fulton.

Hollands, R. (1990) *The Long Transition: Class, Culture and Youth Training*, Basingstoke: Macmillan.

Jackson, B. and Marsden, D. (1962) *Education and the Working Class*, London: Routledge and Kegan Paul.

Janis, I. and Mann, L. (1977) *Decision-Making: A Psychological Analysis of Conflict, Choice and Commitment*, New York: Macmillan.

Jarvis, L., Exley, S., Park, A., Phillips, M., Johnson, M. and Robinson, C. (2006) *Youth Cohort Study of England and Wales, 2002-2005; Cohort Eleven, Sweep One to Four* [computer file]. Colchester, Essex: UK Data Archive [distributor], September. SN: 5452.

Johnston, B. (2007) 'Methodological review: mapping the literature in relation to the challenges for the non-participation project', Working Paper no. 4, NPinHE project, School of Education, University of Southampton, http://www.education.soton.ac.uk/nphe, accessed 10 December 2010.

Johnston, B. and Heath, S. (2007) 'Educational decision-making as an embedded social practice: methodological challenges and ways forward', Working Paper no. 7, NPinHE project, initially a conference paper at the Annual Conference of the British Educational Research Association, 5–8 September, London.

Johnston, B. and Heath, S. (2008) 'Reflections on the methodological challenges of investigating social network influence in educational decision-making: data collection', paper at ESRC National Centre for Research Methods event, University of Southampton, 17 December.

Johnston, B., Fuller, A., Heath, S. and Paton, K. (2008) 'The influence of family and friends on educational and employment decision-making: report to project participants', Working Paper, NPinHE project, School of Education, University of Southampton.

Kelly, K. and Cook, S. (2007) 'Full-time young participation by socio-economic class: a new widening participation measure in higher education', *Research Report No. 806, Department for Education and Skills*, London: DfES.

Kennedy Report (1997) *Learning Works*, Coventry: FEFC.

King, K. and McGrath, S. (2002) *Globalisation, Enterprise and Knowledge: Education, Training and Development in Africa*, London: Symposium Books.

Lacey, C. (1970) *Hightown Grammar*, Manchester: Manchester University Press.

Law, B. A. and Watts, A. G. (1977) *Schools, Careers and Community*, London: Church Information Office.

Lazarick, D. L., Fishbein, S. S. and Loiello, M. A. (1988) 'Practical investigations of volition', *Journal of Counselling Psychology* 35: 15–26.

Levin, B. (2003) 'Educational policy: commonalities and differences', in B. Davies and J. West-Burnham (eds), *Handbook of Educational Leadership and Management*, pp. 165–77, London: Pearson.

Lloyd, C. and Payne, J. (2003) 'The political economy of skill and the limits of educational policy', *Journal of Educational Policy* 18, 1: 85–107.

Lukes, S. (1974) *Power: A Radical View*, Basingstoke: Palgrave Macmillan.

Lukes, S. (2005) *Power: A Radical View*, 2nd edn, Basingstoke and New York: Palgrave Macmillan.

Lumby, J. and Foskett, N. H. (2005) *14–19 Education: Policy, Leadership and Learning*, London: Sage.

Lumby, J. and Foskett, N. H. (2007) 'Turbulence masquerading as change: exploring 14–19 policy', in D. Raffe and K. Spours (eds), *Policy-making and Policy Learning in 14–19 Education*, Ch. 4, London: Institute of Education, Bedford Way Papers no. 26.

Luscher, K. (1999) 'Ambivalence: a key concept for the study of intergenerational relations', in S. Trnka (ed.), *Family Issues Between Gender and Generations. Seminar Report*, pp. 11–25, Brussels: European Observatory on Family Matters. European Commission: Directorate-General for Employment and Social Affairs Unit E/1.

Luscher, K. (2005) 'Looking at ambivalences: the contribution of a "new–old" view of intergenerational relations to the study of the life course', *Advances in Life Course Research* 10: 95–131.

Manski, C. (2000) 'Economic analysis of social interactions', *Journal of Economic Perspectives* 14, 3: 115–36.

Maringe, F. and Fuller, A. (2006) 'Widening participation in UK higher education: policy perspectives', Working Paper, NPinHE project, School of Education, University of Southampton, http://www.education.soton.ac.uk/nphe, accessed 10 December 2010.

McDonough, P. and Fann, A. (2007) 'The study of inequality', in P. Gumport (ed.), *Sociology of Higher Education,* pp. 53–93, Baltimore, MD: Johns Hopkins University Press.

Merton, R. K. (1984) 'Socially expected durations: a case study of concept formation in sociology', in W. W. Powell and R. Robbins (eds), *Conflict and Consensus: A Festschrift in Honor of Lewis A. Coser*, pp. 262–83, New York: Free Press.

Miles, M. B. and Huberman, A. M. (1994) *An Expanded Sourcebook: Qualitative Data Analysis*, 2nd edn, London: Sage.

Miller, H. (1967) *Participation of Adults in Education. A Force-field Analysis*, Boston: Center for the Study of Liberal Education for Adults.

Miller, R. L. (2000) *Researching Life Stories and Family Histories*, London: Sage.

Mills, C. W. (1959) *The Sociological Imagination*, Harmondsworth: Pelican Books.

Ministry of Education (1963) *Half Our Future* (The Newsom Report), London: HMSO.

Morrow, V. (1999) 'Conceptualising social capital in relation to the well-being of children and young people: a critical review', *Sociological Review* 47, 4: 744–65.

NCIHE (National Committee of Inquiry into Higher Education) (1997) *Higher Education in the Learning Society, Main Report (Dearing Report)*, London: NCIHE.

Nuffield Review of 14–19 Education and Training (2008) *Issue Paper 5: Guidance and Careers Education*, Oxford: Nuffield Review.

OECD (Organization for Economic Co-operation and Development) (2004) *Career Guidance: A Handbook for Policy Makers*, Paris: OECD.

ONS (Office for National Statistics) (2006), *Labour Force Survey Five-Quarter Longitudinal Dataset, March 2005 – May 2006*, Social and Vital Statistics Division, and Northern Ireland Statistics and Research Agency Central Survey Unit, [computer file], Colchester, Essex: UK Data Archive [distributor], September. SN: 5469.

ONS (2010) *Statistical Bulletin, Labour Market Statistics November 2010*, http://www.statistics.gov.uk/pdfdir/lmsuk1110.pdf accessed 7 December 2010.

Oxford English Dictionary online (2009) http://www.askoxford.com/concise_oed/career?view=uk accessed 22 December 2009.

Pallas, A. M. (2003) 'Educational transitions, trajectories, and pathways', in J. Mortimore and M. Shanahan (eds), *Handbook of the Life Course*, New York: Kluwer Academic Publishers.

Panel for Fair Access to the Professions (2009) *Unleashing Aspiration: The Final Report of the Panel on Fair Access to the Professions*, London: The Cabinet Office.

Parry, G. (2010) 'Policy contexts, differentiation, competition and policies for widening participation', in M. David (ed.), *Improving Learning by Widening Participation in Higher Education*, pp. 29–31, London: Routledge.

Passy, R. and Morris, M. (August 2010) *Evaluation of AimHigher: learner attainment and progression: final report*, Bristol: HEFCE.

Pedley, R. (1978) *The Comprehensive School*, Harmondsworth: Penguin.

Perlesz, A. and Lindsay, J. (2003) 'Methodological triangulation in researching families: making sense of dissonant data', *International Journal of Social Research Methodology* 6: 25–40.

Pollard, E., Bates, P., Hunt, W. and Bellis, A. (2008) *University is Not Just for Young People. Working Adults' Perceptions of and Orientation to Higher Education*, DIUS Research Report 08 06, London: Department for Innovation, Universities and Skills.

Pratt, J., Bloomfield, J. and Seale, C. (1984) *Option Choice: A Question of Equal Opportunity*, Slough: National Foundation for Educational Research.

Prince's Trust (2010) *Britain's Lost Talent?* London: The Prince's Trust.

Pugsley, L. (1998) 'Throwing your brains at it: higher education, markets and choice', *International Studies in Sociology of Education* 8: 71–92.

Putnam, R. (2000) *Bowling Alone: The Collapse and Revival of American Community*, New York: Simon & Schuster.

Quinn, J. (2005) 'Belonging in a learning community: the re-imagined university and imagined social capital', *Studies in the Education of Adults* 37, 1: 4–18.

Raffe, D. and Spours, K. (2007) 'Three models of policy learning and policy making in 14–19 education', in D. Raffe and K. Spours (eds), *Policy-Making and Policy Learning in 14–19 Education*, Ch. 1, London: Institute of Education, Bedford Way Papers no. 26.

Raffe, D., Brannen, K., Fairgreve, J. and Martin, C. (2001) 'Participation, inclusiveness, academic drift and party of esteem: a comparison of post-compulsory education and training in England, Wales, Scotland and Northern Ireland', *Oxford Review of Education* 27, 1: 173–204.

Raggatt, P. and Williams, S. (1999) *Government, Markets and Vocational Qualifications: An Anatomy of Policy*, London and New York: Falmer Press.

Reay, D., Crozier, G., and Clayton, J. (2010) '"Fitting in"or "standing out": working class students in UK higher education', *British Educational Research Journal* 36, 1: 107–24.

Reay, D., David, M. and Ball, S. (2001) 'Making a difference?: Institutional habituses and higher education choice', *Sociological Research Online* 5 (4), http://www.socresonline.org.uk/5/4/reay.html, accessed 10 December 2010.

Reay, D., David, M. and Ball, S. (2005) *Degree of Choice: Social Class, Race and Gender in Higher Education*, Stoke on Trent: Trentham Books.

Ribbens McCarthy, J., Holland, J. and Gillies, V. (2003) 'Multiple perspectives on the "family" lives of young people: methodological and theoretical issues in each case study research', *International Journal of Social Research Methodology* 6: 1–23.

Robbins (1963) *Higher Education,* Cmnd 2154, London: HMSO.

Roberts, B. (2002) *Biographical Research,* Buckingham: Open University Press.

Roberts, K. (1993) 'Career trajectories and the mirage of increased social mobility', in I. Bates and G. Riseborough, *Youth and Inequality,* Buckingham: Open University Press.

Roberts, K. (2009) 'Opportunity structures then and now', *Journal of Education and Work* 22: 5: 355–68.

Roberts, S. (2010) 'Misrepresenting "choice biographies"?: a reply to Woodman', *Journal of Youth Studies* 13, 1: 137–49.

Rosenthal, G. (1998) *The Holocaust in Three Generations: Families of the Victims and Perpetrators of the Nazi Regime.* London: Cassell.

Rowson, J., Broome, S. and Jones, A. (2010) *Connected Communities: How Social Networks Power and Sustain the Big Society,* London: RSA.

Schoon, I., McCulloch, A., Joshi, H. E., Wiggins, R. D. and Bynner, J. (2001) 'Transitions from school to work in a changing social context', *Young* 9, 4: 4–22.

Schuller, T. and Watson, D. (2009) *Learning through Life: Inquiry into the Future for Lifelong Learning,* Leicester: National Institute for Adult and Continuing Education (NIACE).

Schuller, T., Baron, S. and Field, J. (eds) (2000) *Social Capital: Critical Perspectives,* Oxford: Oxford University Press.

Scott, P. (1995) *The Meanings of Mass Higher Education,* Buckingham: SRHE and Open University Press.

Sen, A. (1999) *Development as Freedom,* Oxford: Oxford University Press.

Sharpe, S. (1976) *Just Like A Girl, How Girls Learn to be Women,* London: Penguin.

Shopes, L. (1996) 'Using oral history for a family history project', in D. Dunaway and W. Baum (eds), *Oral History: An Interdisciplinary Anthology* (2nd edn), pp. 231–40, London: Altamira.

Song, M. (1998) 'Hearing competing voices: sibling research', in J. Ribbens and R. Edwards (eds), *Feminist Dilemmas in Qualitative Research: Public Knowledge and Private Lives,* pp. 103–12, London: Sage.

Staetsky, L. (2007) *Investigation into the Characteristics of the Higher Education Module of the Youth Cohort Study (Cohorts 10 and 11).* Unpublished analysis for the Non-participation in Higher Education project, School of Education, University of Southampton.

Staetsky, L. (2008) 'Review of the quantitative literature', Working Paper no. 10, NPinHE project, School of Education, University of Southampton, http://www.education.soton. ac.uk/nphe, accessed 10 December 2010.

Staetsky, L. and Rice, P. (2010) 'Analysis of the Labour Force Survey: gender, generation, occupation, the pursuit of further credentials and highest level of qualification in the United Kingdom', Working Paper no. 13, NPinHE project, School of Education, University of Southampton.

Stanbury, D. (2005) *Careers Education Benchmark Statement,* Association of Graduate Careers Advisory Services (AGCAS) Careers Education Task Group.

Stoer, S. and Magalhaes, A. (2009) 'Education, knowledge and the network society', in R. Dale and S. Robertson (eds), *Globalisation and Europeanisation in Education,* pp. 45–63, London: Symposium Books.

Sukhnandan, L. and Lee, B. (1998) *Streaming, Setting and Grouping by Ability: A Review of the Literature,* Slough: National Foundation for Educational Research.

Thomas, L. and Quinn, J. (2007) *First Generation Entry into Higher Education: An International Study,* Maidenhead, Berkshire: SRHE and Open University Press.

Thompson, P. (1996) 'The development of oral history in Britain', in David Dunaway and Willa Baum (eds), *Oral History: An Interdisciplinary Anthology,* 2nd edn, pp. 351–62, London: Altamira.

Tomlinson, S. (2005) *Education in a Post-welfare Society* (2nd edn), Maidenhead: Open University Press/McGraw-Hill.

Trotter, R. (1999) 'Friends, relatives and relevant others: conducting ethnographic network studies', in J. Schensul, M. LeCompte, R. Trotter, E. Cromley and M. Singer (eds), *Mapping Social Networks, Spatial Data, and Hidden Populations, Ethnographers Toolkit* vol. 4, Walnut Creek: Altamira Press.

Tuckett, A. and Aldridge, F. (2010) *A Change for the Better: The NIACE Survey on Adult Participation in Learning 2010*, Leicester: NIACE

UCAS (2010) 'Variety of factors behind 11.6% rise in applications to UK higher education', Press release, 16 July, http://www.ucas.ac.uk/about_us/ media_enquiries/media_releases/2010/160710.

UKCES (UK Commission for Employment and Skills) (2009a) *Ambition 2020: World Class Skills and Jobs for the UK, The 2009 Report*, Wath-upon-Dearn: The UK Commission for Employment and Skills.

UKCES (2009b) *Working Futures 2007–2017*, Wath-upon-Dearn: The UK Commission for Employment and Skills.

UKCES (2010) 'Ambition 2020: world class skills and jobs for the UK', *UKCES 2010 Report*, London: UKCES.

Veness, T. (1962) *School Leavers: Their Aspirations and Expectations*, London: Methuen.

Vignoles M. and Crawford, C. (2010) 'The importance of prior educational experiences', in M. David (ed), *Improving Learning by Widening Participation in Higher Education*, London: Routledge.

Warin, J., Solomon, Y. and Lewis, C. (2007) 'Swapping stories: comparing plots: triangulating individual narratives within families', *International Journal of Social Research Methodology* 10, 2: 121–34.

Watts, M. and Bridges, D. (2006) 'The value of non-participation in higher education', *Journal of Education Policy* 21: 267–90.

Weeks, J., Heaphy, B. and Donovan, C. (2001) *Same Sex Intimacies: Families of Choice and Other Life Experiment*, London: Routledge.

Wengraf, T. (2001) *Qualitative Research Interviewing: Biographic Narrative and Semi-structured Methods*, London: Sage.

Weston, Kath. (1991) *Families We Choose: Lesbians, Gays and Kinship*, New York: Colombia University Press.

Woolcock, M. (1998) 'Social capital and economic development: toward a theoretical synthesis and policy framework', *Theory and Society* 27, 1: 151–208.

Young, M. and Wilmott, P. (1957) *Family and Kinship in East London*, London: Routledge.

INDEX